African Soccerscapes

Africa in World History

SERIES EDITORS: DAVID ROBINSON AND JOSEPH C. MILLER

James C. McCann
Stirring the Pot: A History of African Cuisine

Peter Alegi
African Soccerscapes: How a Continent Changed the World's Game

Forthcoming:

John M. Mugane
The Story of Swahili

Charles Ambler
Mass Media and Popular Culture in Modern Africa

African Soccerscapes

How a Continent Changed the World's Game

Peter Alegi

OHIO UNIVERSITY PRESS

in association with the

OHIO UNIVERSITY CENTER FOR INTERNATIONAL STUDIES

Athens

Ohio University Press, Athens, Ohio 45701
www.ohioswallow.com
© 2010 by Ohio University Center for International Studies
All rights reserved

Printed in the United States of America
Ohio University Press books are printed on acid-free paper ⊗™

18 17 16 15 14 13 12 11 10   5 4 3 2 1

Library of Congress Cataloging-in-Publication Data
Alegi, Peter.
  African soccerscapes : how a continent changed the world's game / Peter Alegi.
      p. cm. — (Africa in world history) ("The white man's burden" : football and empire,
  1860s–1919 — The Africanization of football, 1920s–1940s — Making nations in late colonial
  Africa, 1940s–1964 — Nationhood, Pan-Africanism, and football after independence —
  Football migration to Europe since the 1930s — The privatization of football, 1980s to
  recent times — South Africa 2010 : the World Cup comes to Africa)
    Includes bibliographical references and index.
    ISBN 978-0-89680-278-0 (pb : alk. paper) — ISBN 978-0-89680-472-2 (electronic)
    1. Soccer—Africa—History. I. Title.
  GV944.A4A45 2010
  796.334096—dc22

                           2009049198

To Africa's footballers, past, present, and future

CONTENTS

ILLUSTRATIONS

Figures

Maps

Tables

PROLOGUE

On May 15, 2004, Nelson Mandela wept tears of joy as the Fédération Internationale de Football Association (FIFA) awarded South Africa the right to host the 2010 World Cup finals—the first on African soil. "I feel like a boy of fifteen," he told the audience in Zurich. In South Africa, people of all races erupted in simultaneous, raucous celebration of the much-anticipated announcement. "To some extent this outburst of euphoria surpassed 1994," the year of the first democratic elections in South Africa, writes Ahmed Kathrada, a former political prisoner incarcerated with Mandela for twenty-six years. "The scenes of jubilation, the spontaneous outpouring of celebration following FIFA's decision, the solidarity of pride and unity evoked by a sporting event should serve as a shining example to black and white alike."[1] Winnie Madikizela-Mandela later explained South Africa's intention to use the planet's preeminent sporting event as political theater: "The 2010 World Cup is about nation-building, putting us on the global map and making us a nation to be reckoned with. The event is going to make us proud. We are going to show the world wonders come 2010."[2] How did an African country come to host the World Cup?

This book tries to answer this question by telling the little-known story of football in Africa and how the continent changed the world's game. Played almost everywhere, in the center of huge modern cities and in isolated rural villages, football (or soccer) is the most popular sport in Africa and possibly the most popular cultural activity on our planet.[3] According to a survey conducted in 2006 on behalf of FIFA, the game's governing body, 46 million of the world's 265 million registered players—more than one in six—are African.[4] This simple, fun, and accessible game captures the attention of ordinary Africans, men and women, children and adults, workers and students, political leaders and apolitical masses, the business elite and the unemployed. Not many other African social practices are so tightly bound up with local, national, continental, and global dynamics.

African Soccerscapes is one of the first academic studies to connect Africans' intense passion for the game to their experiences with European domination; the growth of cities and towns; the struggle for independence and nationhood; migration; and globalization.[5] Drawing primarily on published sources in English and French, the book looks at the ways in which Africans appropriated football from European colonizers and transformed it into a professional industry shaped by transnational capital and mass media. Firmly situating teams, players, and associations in the international framework in which Africans have to compete, I focus on how the game influenced, and was influenced by, racial, ethnic, and national identities, cultural values, economic interests, and power struggles. Selected case studies from around the continent highlight differences and similarities and bring out connections between sport and society. My central argument is that African players, coaches, officials, and fans have written crucial chapters in the history of football and therefore any interpretation of the game's global past must address the interaction of African practitioners and fans with this exciting and nearly universal expression of human culture.

The book is divided into six narrative chapters arranged thematically and chronologically. Chapter 1 opens with the arrival of football with European imperial expansion in the late nineteenth century and traces the game's spread beyond port cities by means of railroads, colonial military forces, and mission schools. Chapter 2 examines how Africans from Algeria to Zululand wrested control of football from the hands of the colonizers during the interwar period, turning it into a distinctively African activity featuring magicians and healers, innovative playing styles, and an indigenous fan culture. The three case studies presented in chapter 3 demonstrate how football contests and organizations fueled Africa's broader quest for political and cultural liberation in the mid- and late twentieth century and helped to construct a sense of nationhood among diverse populations.

Chapter 4 begins with an examination of the ways in which stadiums and national leagues bolstered a sense of nationhood after independence. It then goes on to probe how the Confédération Africaine de Football (CAF) fostered pan-African solidarity and democratized world football through antiapartheid activities and its campaign to expand the number of African teams in the World Cup finals. Chapter 5 looks into the causes and consequences of African player migration overseas—a historical process that has disproportionately rewarded Europe at Africa's expense. Chapter 6 analyzes the increasingly commercialized and globalized African football of the 1990s and 2000s, as seen in privatized clubs and competitions, as well as in the launch of youth football academies and the growth of the women's game. The book's epilogue is devoted to the run-up to the 2010 World Cup in South Africa. A discussion of the significance of this sporting megaevent illustrates how race and racism, nationhood, and capitalism continue to play an important role in African football today.

ACKNOWLEDGMENTS

I must first thank David Robinson and Joseph C. Miller, editors of the Africa in World History series at Ohio University Press, for giving me the opportunity to write *African Soccerscapes*. The final manuscript was vastly improved by detailed and constructive comments of two anonymous reviewers. Gill Berchowitz, Nancy Basmajian, and the production staff at Ohio University Press deserve special recognition for their professionalism and enthusiasm in bringing this book to fruition.

Generous funding from the Department of History, the Center for Integrative Studies in the Arts and Humanities, and the Internal Research Grant Program at Michigan State University enabled me to complete this project ahead of the 2010 World Cup in South Africa. I am massively indebted to Peter Limb for discovering an incredible number of sources on African football and building a superlative library collection on the topic. History chairperson Mark Kornbluh gave me release time and, with David Bailey, taught me the art of writing effective grant proposals. Leslie Hadfield and Jill Kelly were indefatigable research assistants, and many colleagues in the Department of History and the African Studies Center gave their friendship and backing, including Nwando Achebe, Ibro Chekaraou, Pero Dagbovie, Laura Fair, Walter Hawthorne, Deo Ngonyani, James Pritchett, and David Wiley.

Many individuals expanded my understanding of African sport and society through conversation, e-mail, manuscripts, and comments made at seminars and conferences in North America, Europe, and Africa. I would like to thank Gerard Akindes, Simon Akindes, Charles Ambler, Susann Baller, Wiebe Boer, Chris Bolsmann, Ben Carton, Herbert Chipande, David Coplan, Paul Darby, Ashwin Desai, Laurent Dubois, Bob Edgar, Marc Fletcher, Sarah Forde, Solomon Getahun, Mark Gleeson, Albert Grundlingh, Verne Harris, Sean Jacobs, Anthea Josias, Matthew Kirwin, Chuck Korr, Pelle Kvalsund, Richard Maguire, Christopher Merrett, Wapu Mulwafu, Sifiso Ndlovu, Derek Peterson, André Odendaal, Folu Ogundimu, Rodney

Reiners, Martha Saavedra, Solomon Waliaula, Ibrahima Thioub, Goolam Vahed, Robert Vinson, David Wallace, and Justin Willis.

Writing about football was made easier by the camaraderie I enjoyed with my teammates in the Mid-Michigan Men's Soccer League and Michigan State University's intramural leagues, as well as by coaching East Lansing youth teams. As one of my daughters told me recently: "Papà, you really are a twelve-year-old boy inside." I am also thankful for the encouragement and support received from my parents, family, and friends. But most of all, I thank Catherine, Anna, and Sophie for their humor, tolerance, and love.

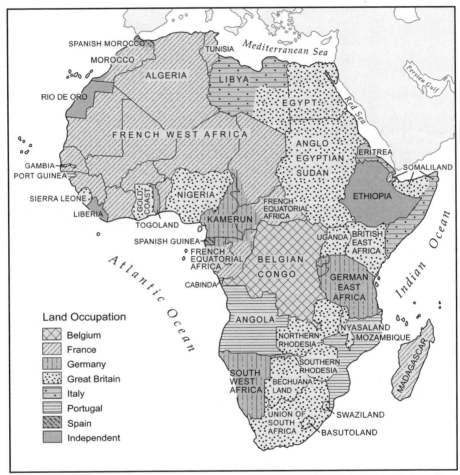

MAP 1   Colonial Africa, 1914. *Map by Claudia K. Walters. Source: http://exploringafrica.*
matrix.msu.edu/images/colonialism1914.jpg.

MAP 2 Contemporary Africa and major cities. *Map by Claudia K. Walters. Source: http://exploringafrica.matrix.msu.edu/images/capitals.jpg.*

CHAPTER ONE

"The White Man's Burden"

Football and Empire, 1860s–1919

MODERN SPORTS start with European imperial expansion in the last two centuries. The agents of that imperialism played sports among themselves, but also saw sport as a tool of civilization. For example, British soldiers, sailors, traders, and government employees enjoyed football for their own entertainment, but they also saw it as pivotal in the European "civilizing mission" in Africa. Building on their experiences with youth and urban workers in industrial Britain, teachers and missionaries used this inexpensive, easy-to-learn fun to satisfy "the white man's burden." This expression, taken from Rudyard Kipling's famous formulation, meant teaching African converts and colonial subjects about the virtues of Christianity, capitalist commerce, and Western civilization. In this opening chapter, I intend to show how the game of football arrived in Africa in the late nineteenth century through the major port cities and then began to spread into the interior by the 1920s by means of newly laid railway lines, Western-style schools run mainly by missionaries, and the colonial armed forces.

Africans, of course, had their own sports, but these activities were little esteemed by their new imperial masters. Sports such as wrestling, martial arts, footraces, canoe racing, and competitive dancing offer compelling evidence of how agrarian African societies embraced *Sportgeist*—the spirit of sport.[1] As the historians William Baker and Tony Mangan explain: "Throughout pre-colonial Africa . . . dances and games were long performed with a seriousness akin to sport in modern industrial societies, and for purposes not altogether different: the striving for status, the assertion of identity, the maintenance of power in one form or another, and the indoctrination of youth into the culture of their elders."[2] Indigenous sports were spectacles of fitness and physical prowess, technical and tactical expertise. Major competitions were community festivals with their rituals of spectatorship, including oral literary performances of bards (griots) and praise singers in honor of the athletes. Clearly, precolonial athletic traditions had much in common with Western sport. As such, they provided the "soil into which the seeds of [European] sport would be later planted."[3]

Not surprisingly, the first recorded football matches come from South Africa, where Europeans began settling nearly four centuries ago. The games involved whites in the Cape and Natal colonies. The record of this European sport seems to begin in 1862, when games between teams of soldiers and civil servants, between "home-born" (i.e., British) and "colonial-born" (i.e., South African) whites, were played at Donkin Reserve in Port Elizabeth and on the Green Point racecourse in Cape Town.[4] In 1866, "city" and "garrison" sides played in the Market Square in Pietermaritzburg, the capital of Natal colony. These early rough-and-tumble games featured elements of both rugby and soccer, which was not unusual because different forms of the game existed before the rules of association football were codified on October 26, 1863, in London. Devotees of the kicking game were soon referred to as "soccers" (an abbreviation of "assoc"), as opposed to "ruggers," who played the handling game of rugby, the rules of which were devised in 1871.[5]

The influx of working-class British soldiers into southern Africa during colonial military campaigns against the Zulu state and the Afrikaners (mainly descendants of the Dutch and also known as Boers) inspired the founding of the first official football organizations in Africa. Pietermaritzburg County Football Club and Natal Wasps FC were formed around 1880 and the Natal Football Association in 1882. The whites-only South African Football Association (SAFA), founded in 1892, was the first national governing body on the continent. SAFA became the first member of FIFA on the continent in 1910.[6] Despite its colonial origins, soccer in South Africa by the 1920s would be increasingly perceived as a blue collar, black sport, while rugby, cricket, and other middle-class sports such as tennis and golf became intimately linked to white power and identities.

Looking around the Continent

In other parts of the continent, football's early history was also connected to expatriate European colonizers. Between 1894 and 1897, for example,

FIGURE 1   "Dakar—a Football Match," c. 1919 *(Alegi collection)*

French settlers in Oran (Algeria) channeled their sporting passion into the formal creation of a football club.[7] In Tunis there was enough interest in the game by 1906 to warrant the formation of Racing Club. The following year in Cairo saw the formation of Al Ahly, which initially included some Europeans but would become an all-Egyptian club in 1924—and a venue for anticolonial protest, as we will see. By 1913, French and other Europeans were playing regular matches in Dakar and Brazzaville, the capitals of French West Africa and French Equatorial Africa, respectively.[8]

The game was on an even firmer footing in the Belgian Congo, where a whites-only Ligue de Football du Katanga began in May 1911 in the copper-mining town of Élisabethville (today Lubumbashi).[9] Since only four teams competed in the 1925 B. Smith Cup—the Katanga championship—white football was limited in scope. In Léopoldville (Kinshasa), the capital, matches were taking place around 1912. By 1919–20, a formal association existed that later assumed the name Fédération de Football Association du Pool and affiliated with the Belgian football association in 1927. Much like colonists in other parts of Africa, the French, Flemish, Portuguese, and British in the Congo organized teams along the lines of European nationality. In the 1920s, a new championship against Brazzaville teams energized local football, which by this time had started to attract small sponsorships from private firms.

Africans Take Hold of the Ball

The shared patriarchal assumptions of European and African cultures curtailed sporting opportunities for African women. Colonial racism also underpinned practices of domination and exclusion in African football and society. In the Congo, for instance, white teams enjoyed access to adequate playing facilities built with African taxes, a privilege not afforded to colonial subjects. Furthermore, racial segregation reigned at the grounds. Europeans occupied the more expensive and comfortable grandstand seats, while ordinary Congolese paid to stand around the pitch. Passions ran high in white football, with reports of violent incidents on and off the pitch appearing quite frequently in the records. Despite these trying conditions, African fans enjoyed watching different styles of play on display. They even assigned top white players nicknames, tangible proof of Africans' passion and active involvement in the sport through spectatorship.

The evidence from Francophone Africa was less unified. While the British rapidly introduced modern sport to sub-Saharan Africa after conquest, the French, along with the Belgians, Portuguese, and Italians, were considerably slower.[10] Two factors are relevant here. First, during the scramble for Africa and immediately after conquest, most European countries lacked a sporting culture comparable to that of Britain. A second consideration is that many Europeans "were less certain than their British rivals that modern sports created moral fiber along with muscle mass."[11]

These factors partly explain why in Francophone Africa few provisions were made for team sports before the Second World War. The focus, particularly in French territories, was more on expanding physical education programs in the schools, a policy made compulsory in 1923 in French West Africa.[12] Students at elite institutions like the École Normale William Ponty in Dakar, Senegal, which opened in 1918, played football and other games, but it was only in the 1930s and 1940s that French colonial administrators began to connect sport more explicitly to their self-ascribed *mission civilisatrice*.[13] Similar changes occurred in the Belgian Congo in the 1930s and 1940s, although the influence of the Catholic Church was stronger than in French-ruled territories due to the less rigid division between church and state. The Catholic rendition of muscular Christianity, encapsulated by the Latin phrase *mens sana in corpore sano* (a healthy mind in a healthy body), found a receptive audience among the Belgian authorities. As a result, in Léopoldville and Élisabethville, sports like football would gain favor as a way "to provide civilized black youth with healthy distractions and to complete their physical and moral education at the school of discipline and endurance that the practice of sport entails."[14]

In general, the arrival of football in Africa paralleled the global pattern of the game's diffusion. It precisely followed the assertion of British commercial and imperial power. It was, of course, no accident that expatriates and local men played football in the major port cities of Barcelona, Genoa, Buenos Aires, Rio de Janeiro, Cape Town, and Calcutta. These ports were important nodes in an increasingly connected world economy based on Western extraction of cheaply produced African, Asian, and American crops and precious metals and their conversion into manufactured goods for sale in international markets.

The importance of African coastal trading towns extended beyond the earliest areas of settlement such as South Africa and Algeria. In West Africa, for instance, British sailors are credited with making Cape Coast the birthplace of the game in the Gold Coast (the colonial name for what would become Ghana). At the turn of the twentieth century, Cape Coast was the colonial capital and thus "was home to a large number of British nationals and other European civil servants and company officials," many of whom liked to play football in their free time.[15]

In Nigeria as well, the game arrived first in the port towns of Calabar in the east and Lagos in the west. Historian Wiebe Boer discovered that the first documented match in Nigeria was played on June 15, 1904, at the Hope Waddell Training Institution in Calabar, an elite school described in more detail below.[16] Hope Waddell students and staff members took the field against sailors from the HMS *Thistle*, which was docked in the harbor. Thanks in large part to Hope Waddell, the popularity of football grew rapidly in Calabar. The Beverley Cup, possibly the first organized soccer tournament in West Africa, was held there in 1906. In Lagos, Frederick Mulford, a British commercial agent, was instrumental in the game's initial diffusion. He organized matches on the racecourse between teams of European traders, soldiers, and civil servants. But Mulford also invited Nigerian teams to play, and he even coached local school teams. Nigerian football enthusiasts referred to him as "Baba Eko," meaning "Our Father" in the Yoruba language. Nnamdi Azikiwe, Nigeria's first president (see chapter 3), provided a glimpse into how the British game was finding its way into the everyday lives of Africans around the time of the First World War. "We played football there with mango seeds, limes or oranges or old tennis balls," Azikiwe wrote in his autobiography. "Any collection of boys would be divided into two sides and a spirited game would ensure. We made and altered our rules to suit each game and so we emerged to become self-made soccerists."[17]

A similar pattern unfolded in eastern Africa. In the late 1870s, football first came to Zanzibar island. European and Asian employees of the Eastern Telegraph Company, a huge British firm laying the submarine cable from Aden that would eventually reach South Africa, spent their evenings playing team sports.[18] Ordinary Zanzibari men of different ethnic and class backgrounds learned the game by watching and occasionally playing with the workers from overseas, as well as with students from St. Andrew's College of the Universities' Mission to Central Africa. By the 1910s, according to Khamis Fereji, the game had become a popular urban pastime.

> Football started in *uzunguni* [Europe] but everyone here learned how to play. For a football we would buy a tennis ball; they were cheap in those days—for a few cents we could buy a ball. And then we would run off and play anywhere there was a little space. We played with each other in the narrow streets (*vichochoroni*) . . . or we would go over near the port. Before they had built the Public Works it was a big football ground. In the evening the men would come down and rest, enjoy the breeze, or fish and we kids would play football. This was the very beginnings of football, us kids playing in the narrow streets with our tennis balls.[19]

Into the Interior: Railroads and the Armed Forces

Once football had filtered through Africa's ports, it closely followed the path of railroads into the interior. Railroad lines were central to the development of colonial capitalism, as they connected the coast to the interior for the purpose of evacuating crops and minerals and transporting military forces to suppress anticolonial rebellions. Railway towns became important nodes of cultural transmission and exchange where football featured prominently. In the town of Atbara, headquarters of the Sudan Railways, the sport developed rapidly in the 1920s. According to historian Ahmed Sikainga, the British attempted to use sport to promote team spirit; football was "considered an essential ingredient for molding railway employees and helping them internalize the norms and values of the industry."[20]

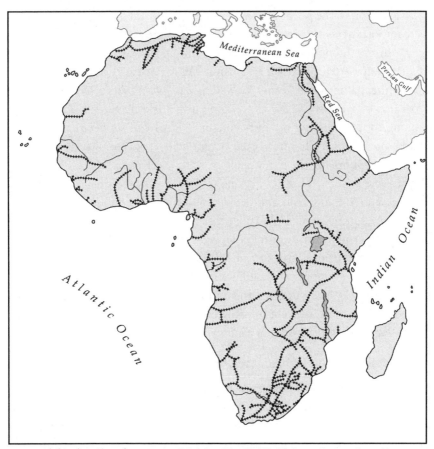

MAP 3   Africa's railroads, c. 1995. *Map by Claudia K. Walters. Source: http://exploringafrica.matrix.msu.edu/images/map23.gif.*

One of the first documented examples of football in Yaoundé, the main city in central Cameroon, is illustrative of the importance of colonial railways in the history of football in Africa. In March 1927, as part of the festivities celebrating the arrival of the first locomotive from Douala, football matches were staged before large crowds. Representative sides from Douala and Yaoundé played in two racially segregated contests. First, Africans from Yaoundé defeated their counterparts from Douala; then the European teams played to a draw.[21] Many more examples could be made, but in the interest of brevity I will just point out that the development of railways in southern, central, and eastern Africa from the 1890s to the 1920s propelled the formation of numerous football clubs and associations in Southern and Northern Rhodesia (today Zimbabwe and Zambia), Congo, and Uganda.

In addition to the ports and railways, colonial militaries and police forces were important vectors for the spread of football in Africa.[22] At first, British army officers did not encourage football among the rank-and-file members of the Kenya African Rifles and Royal West African Frontier Force. For some time, games were "either viewed as part of soldiers' physical training programs or were so *ad hoc* as to amount to little more than knockabout evening football among off-duty soldiers."[23] African servicemen generally played soccer informally, often barefoot and "with mixed results." In the 1930s, however, support for the game grew in both the Kenya African Rifles and Royal West African Frontier Force. As British officers warmed to football (as well as track-and-field and boxing) as a means to enhance troops' self-discipline, aggressive masculinity, and camaraderie, African soldiers enthusiastically participated in army championships and (in West Africa) even national competitions. By 1946, a British Army Physical Training Corps instructor was so impressed that he noted how, in the Gold Coast, "football creates great interest among the population and all matches are well attended. The spectators are sensibly critical and always show a knowledge of the game."[24]

Schools, Sport, and "Muscular Christianity"

The knowledge and practice of football owed much to the establishment of Western-style schools across the continent. British public schools (privately funded boarding institutions) provided a model for the educational training of an indigenous elite with the clerical and leadership skills needed for jobs in colonial administration. In nineteenth-century Britain, elite schools spawned a movement devoted to using sport for academic education and moral training. For middle- and upper-class reformers of the Victorian age, sport became a highly valued component of a broader program of rational recreation, and "muscular Christianity" aimed at producing disciplined, healthy, and moral citizens.[25] "Through sport, boys acquire virtues which no books can give them," pontificated Charles Kingsley, a leading proponent; "not merely daring and endurance, but, better still, temper, self-restraint, fairness, honour, unenvious approbation of another's success, and all that 'give-and-take' of life which stand a man in good stead when he goes forth into the world, and without which, indeed, his success is always maimed and partial."[26]

Legions of colonial administrators and missionaries graduated from public schools and universities in Britain. These individuals brought with them to

Africa a deep commitment to the "games ethic," the belief that sport forged physically strong, well-rounded men of sound moral character for imperial service.[27] Reverend J. E. C. Welldon, headmaster at Harrow (1881–95), stressed the significance of the sporting cult for British power abroad: "The pluck, the perseverance, the good temper, the self-control, the discipline, the co-operation, the esprit de corps, which merit success in cricket or football, are the very qualities which win the day in peace or war. . . . In the history of the British Empire it is written that England has owed her sovereignty to her sports."[28]

Mission schools and government schools made sport into an important meeting ground for Western and indigenous cultures. Before 1930 less than 1 percent of the African population received secondary education. Nevertheless, students organized many of the first teams and competitions. In South Africa, for example, *kholwa* (Christian Africans) made up a significant portion of the membership of the earliest clubs.[29] Sport was a mainstay of the academic curriculum and the student experience at elite mission schools such as Adams College near Durban. Known as Amanzimtoti Training Institute before 1914, Adams was founded in 1849 by Congregationalist missionaries of the American Board of Commissioners for Foreign Missions, based in Boston, Massachusetts. It had a reputation as one of the best schools in southern and central Africa. The Adams College football team, the Shooting Stars, was among the oldest and most prestigious African sides in Durban, having competed against outside opponents since the 1890s.[30] American Board missions had produced many of the earliest African clubs in Durban, such as Ocean Swallows of Umbumbulu (established in the 1880s), Natal Cannons of Inanda (1890s), and Bush Bucks of Ifafa (1902). Other mission schools, such as Healdtown, Lovedale, and St. Matthews in the Cape, also fielded football teams, though these schools were better known for their excellence in rugby and cricket.[31]

Similarly, the Hope Waddell Training Institution in Calabar, a prestigious Presbyterian mission school for Nigerian boys and girls founded in 1895, gave birth to soccer in that colony. Rev. James Luke reportedly introduced the game in 1902, two years before the aforementioned documented match between the school and British sailors.[32] Best known for its large campus and strong programs in physical sciences and physical education, Hope Waddell produced about a third of Nigeria's teachers through the 1930s and "provided early incubation for budding nationalist politicians," including Nnamdi Azikiwe.[33] In Lagos, sport and physical education was part of the curriculum at the Church Missionary Society Grammar School (founded in 1859) and at the Wesleyan High School (1878), much as it was later at King's College (1909) and Yaba Higher College (1934).

By the interwar years, the British authorities in Nigeria had incorporated sport as a core component of colonial education. This policy had gained further legitimacy with the publication in 1922 of Lord Lugard's treatise on indirect rule, *The Dual Mandate in British Tropical Africa,* in which the former governor-general of Nigeria endorsed sport and physical education in schools for the training of an African elite. "It is, of course, essential that playgrounds and gymnasia should be provided," Lugard wrote. "In Nigeria we have found that polo was a specially good game for the sons of chiefs and others who could afford it, while for other boys cricket, football, and 'athletics' bring the staff and pupils into close touch, and have the best effect in training character."[34] Nigerian students complied. "You had to play games, it was compulsory," remembered Raphael Shonekan, a former King's College student. "The games that used to draw a crowd was this inter-secondary school football match . . . between King's College and St. Gregory . . . and so games played a dominant part in the upbringing of Kings College boys. In fact one of the mottos of the school says, 'always play the game' which means you are always fair, honest and a good sportsman when you play."[35]

In 1903 in colonial Gold Coast, the Government Boys School at Cape Coast inspired the creation of the first local team. In a town with a small but growing football culture among the Europeans, it was not surprising that African students would prove to be among the first practitioners of the sport. Having already launched cricket and tennis, Mr. Briton, a Jamaican headmaster, organized a football side for the students. According to one source, soon thereafter "the urge for the game spread beyond the confines of the school. A few boys from the Cape Coast township showed interest and soon it was decided to bring all of them together to form a club which Mr. Briton named *Excelsior.*"[36] A quarter of a century later, "even academically weak students could be saved, nay, thrust into the limelight, by agility in sports and games" at the new Achimota College established in 1927 outside Accra.[37] Elsewhere in British West Africa, Fourah Bay College and the Church Missionary Society Grammar School in Freetown, Sierra Leone, also boasted sports programs. At the latter, "games were compulsory . . . we played cricket in the dry season, and football in the rainy season . . . there were competitions for the house shields in cricket, football, and athletics, including cross-country training."[38]

In Northeast Africa, Gordon Memorial College was singularly responsible for popularizing football in Sudan. Known among the British as the "Eton of the Sudan" and "Winchester by the Nile," this institution, like Fourah Bay, Achimota, and Makerere College in Uganda, emphasized vocational and technical training with a view to preparing students for government jobs. At Gordon, "character-building activities—sports first, and literary and social activities second—took up almost as much of the daily schedule as did classes."[39] Historian Heather Sharkey has shown that students played regular afternoon football matches while college staff organized intramural competitions that promoted team spirit and rewarded individual achievement with trophies and prizes. As we shall see in later chapters, Gordon alumni went on to form government departmental teams and, in the 1950s, took control of the Sudan Football Association—an example of both the role of Western schooling as a crucible for African nationalism and the resonance of football in the popular struggle against colonialism (see chapters 3–4).

In British-controlled eastern Africa in the 1880s, local students learned football in the schools in Zanzibar of Universities' Mission to Central Africa (UMCA), run by young "muscular" Christians like Henry Goodyear, whom a sports newspaper editor praised as a "splendid football player and so genial a man."[40] In 1887, the UMCA's jubilee celebrations closed with a "game of football played by the Kiungani boys in smart blue and white caps . . . with many thousands looking on."[41] By 1891, the school's daily routine regularly featured football and other sports. On the mainland, the Anglican G. L. Pilkington was another missionary who actively promoted soccer in the 1890s at a school in Mengo, Uganda. A few weeks before his death, Pilkington wrote: "We have started football lately. I play most afternoons. It is great fun and good for the boys." A visitor observed that Pilkington was "diligently coaching the boys . . . he enters with great earnestness into it. . . . I, with my boys and about ten others, stood Pilkington and another lot. We got two goals each. We play on a large grass field between Kampala and Rubaga."[42] Not all "muscular Christians" were men. For example, Marion Stevenson, a Scottish teacher at Tumutumu mission school in Kenya, embraced football to such an extent that, her biographer noted, "one might wax lyrical over the part that football has taken in attracting and educating the lads, and giving them an outlet for their energies, in place of fighting and bad dances."[43] At notable secondary schools like King's School in Budo, Uganda, Alliance in Kenya, and Tabora ("the Eton of Tanganyika"), one contemporary observed, "Christianity and games were only a part of the life of the school but were indeed its most important elements."[44]

A vignette from Kenya captures the extent to which British and other European colonizers believed football to represent the "stylized epitome of a moral order and the metaphoric essence of a cultured civilization."[45] In Central Province, missionaries taught Kikuyu and other local youths the game and in 1909 organized the first interschool cup. Teams from the Church of Scotland mission in Thogoto and the Church Missionary Society school in Kabete contested the trophy. John Arthur, a newly arrived missionary doctor, reported on this match in the *Kikuyu News* (without mentioning the final score). His evocative column, entitled "A Great Football Match," is worth quoting in full.

> There was a goodly gathering of spectators, amongst whom were seen quite a number of highly painted warriors, relics of a day fast giving place to a new, in which the battlefields of spear and knife will give place to the playing fields of sport, in which manliness, courage, and unselfishness shall add their quota to the formation of true character. . . . It is our hope in these our games to stiffen the backbone of these our boys by teaching them manliness, good temper, and unselfishness—qualities amongst many others which have done so much to make many a Britisher, and which we hope to instill into our boys in such a way as to make them strong men indeed. Our belief is that our games may be, when properly controlled, a mighty channel through which God can work for the uplifting of this race. They need to be strengthened in the realm of their physical nature, where Satan so strongly reigns, and how better than by the substitution of their own evil dances by such a game as football, inherent in which are magnificent uplifting qualities.[46]

For Europeans like Arthur who were dutifully carrying out the "white man's burden," football was potent enough to keep the devil at bay and to provide a healthy and moral outlet for Africans' supposedly savage instincts. As the consolidation of colonial rule took root in the first two decades of the twentieth century, football gained a central place in African education and in the development of a new culture that bridged "traditional" and modern, rural and urban, and indigenous and Western worldviews and experiences.

Needless to say, Africans were not simply duped into adopting Western sport: they enjoyed the game for their own reasons and on their own terms. As the next chapter shows, football was an attractive aspect of Western culture that Africans appropriated and deployed in different ways—and often for different purposes than those originally intended by European colonizers and capitalists.

CHAPTER TWO

The Africanization of Football, 1920s–1940s

DURING THE interwar years, as African towns and cities grew in size and importance, football expanded in scope and popularity. Town dwellers formed football clubs and organized competitions from Accra and Algiers to Zanzibar and Zululand. From the point of view of colonial officials and white residents, football might have seemed like a characteristically British or French or Portuguese pastime; but African players and fans made football distinctively Nigerian or South African or Senegalese. When employers and colonial officials organized the first teams, those Africans drafted into participation initially saw games as another kind of work. But a passion for the game among these workers—and then among youth—soon turned an obligation into pleasure.

In every city and town, and then spreading out into the countryside, football players and ex-players joined in school and work teams or scrambled to form their own. These voluntary associations often became the focus of social life for new urbanites, and the teams they sponsored attracted the support of urban communities—and in turn defined those communities. "In those days [Orlando Pirates] players used to weep if they lost. They had the commitment of a soldier fighting for his country. This patriotism was because he is from Orlando and his family and friends are watching," remembered Skumbuzo Mthembu, a longtime supporter of one of the South Africa's oldest and most popular clubs.[1]

Participation in football was exciting and fun, but it also was a way to make connections and build networks in the rapidly growing towns of that era. In the larger contest between residents and rulers for control of urban areas, football could sometimes be a tool in the hands of players and fans to find some leisure activities they could call their own and in the process build a local culture beyond the reach of colonial rulers, missionaries, and employers. And as Africans wrested control of football from the hands of those European officials who had first seen the game as a means to inculcate the values of colonial capitalism and empire, they also turned the game into an activity that was distinctively African. The game may have been played according to international rules, but the incorporation of magicians and healers, the rise of different playing styles, and the performance of various rituals of spectatorship revealed that football was taking on distinctive indigenous characteristics.

Making Men: Gender, Class, and Generational Dimensions

Until the 1970s, the world's game was predominantly male. African soccerscapes were no different. Public culture in colonial Africa was initially dominated by men, but that did not mean that women were absent from football. Through their work inside and outside the home and their moral support, many mothers, sisters, and wives made it possible for boys and men to play the game. Younger, unmarried women also went to the games to have fun and socialize with men, while other women earned money by selling liquor, food, drinks, and other goods to fans. In the 1960s in South Africa, black women assumed leadership roles in fan clubs, but far too little is known about women's involvement in men's sports elsewhere in colonial Africa.[2] What we do know is that African women, like Western women, became increasingly involved as players in the 1970s and 1980s (see chapter 6).

Recent scholarship in African studies has looked at how sport influenced, and was influenced by, changing relationships between men and women and the elaboration of different kinds of masculinities.[3] The strength, skill, courage, and tenacity required of footballers enabled precolonial martial and athletic masculinities to be reborn, albeit in different forms, in the colonial setting. Rowdy fans sometimes turned to hooliganism as a way to prove their manhood and acquire fame and social honor, while other fans and supporters transformed football into a public stage for the display of an educated, middle-class masculinity.

As we saw in chapter 1, male students at government and mission schools played a pivotal role in the early years of the game. Another key constituency was made up of wage-earning urban workers with some Western education—men with discretionary income and leisure time. The development of formal football organizations owed much to African civil servants, clerks, interpreters, soldiers, policemen, port and railway workers, and traders. Dressed in jackets and trousers, the pioneers of organized football in Africa were secretarial workers engaged in a struggle for self-advancement in racist colonial societies. They were situated in what African historian Andreas Eckert describes as "a position of intermediary ambivalence. They acted as cultural commuters or brokers, as mediators between different worlds."[4] Having excelled in sport and physical education in mission schools, many clerks embraced an aspect of colonial culture that enabled some to acquire social honor through individual sporting skills rather than wealth and family pedigree.[5]

Graduates of elite schools were crucial to organized football in Africa. In Sudan, for example, graduates of Gordon Memorial College absorbed the lessons of the British game ethic and later went on to play for government department teams in cities and towns, where they taught in schools or worked as accountants or in other relatively well-paid professions.[6] Gordon College graduates would go on to assume the mantle of leadership in the Sudan Football Association in the 1950s. A similar process unfolded in Nigeria involving alumni of the Hope Waddell Training Institute in Calabar, as we saw in chapter 1. In the first two decades of the twentieth century, Hope Waddell graduates popularized the game in Lagos—capital of the new Protectorate of Southern Nigeria after 1906—where they eagerly took white-collar government jobs.[7] The prestigious École Supérieure in Cameroon was a reliable supplier of players and administrators to African clubs in both Douala and Yaoundé. In Tanganyika in the 1920s, former students of the Universities' Mission to Central Africa school in Kiungani, Zanzibar, fostered the growth of football both on the island and in Dar es Salaam. In South Africa, the *kholwa* (Christian Africans) learned the game at institutions such as Adams College and Ohlange Institute and then became instrumental in the rise of an indigenous football culture in Natal and in Johannesburg.

African intermediaries planted the seeds of the game in the interior of the continent. For example, in Bobo Dioulasso, a military, administrative, and commercial center in what is today Burkina Faso, the presence of many African soldiers, functionaries, and employees of large French firms underpinned the gradual growth and expansion of local football. One year after the railway reached Bobo in 1934, the director of the Compagnie française de la Côte d'Ivoire recruited Gold Coast, Togolese, and Beninois employees into his company team. That team later took the name Union Sportive Bobolaise, and in 1949 would merge with Union Soudanaise (comprised of workers from Mali) to become Racing Club de Bobo, which remains active today.[8] The involvement of Malians in Burkina Faso illustrates the significance of expatriate African functionaries of the colonial administration in the early history of the game in French Africa. West Africans and Gabonese formed the first black teams in Porto Novo, Benin; in Douala, Cameroon; and also in Brazzaville, then the capital of French Equatorial Africa (and now of the Republic of the Congo).[9]

Hyder Kindy, a Swahili civil servant and influential political leader in Mombasa, Kenya, devotes a full chapter of his autobiography to his favorite sport: football. He describes growing up Muslim and learning the game like most African boys: by kicking a tennis ball with friends and participating in rough-and-tumble street matches against other neighborhood teams. Then, in 1922, Kindy enrolled at the elite Government Arab School, where he was immediately picked to play for the school team. At club level, he played for Britannia FC, a team comprising young men living in the Kuze and Mkanyageni areas of the city.

Mombasa resembled most colonial African cities in that the first organized football teams identified closely with particular neighborhoods. Territorial affiliations and club fealties were taken seriously. According to Kindy, "Any player from one locality who joined another team was considered as having committed high treason. He would be isolated and no one would talk to him."[10] Initially, teams played informally, but in 1926 an official Mombasa league began under the control of a newly established Coast Province Athletic Association, a local affiliate of the white-run African and Arab Sport Association in Kenya (formed the previous year). Kindy reports that despite his club's poor performances, his scoring prowess was good enough to earn him a spot in the starting eleven of the Mombasa representative side in the Remington Cup, Kenya's intertown tournament. In 1932, Kindy's playing career, like that of many African footballers of the period, ended with fatherhood. With age, gender identities, norms, and expectations changed as youthful athletic masculinity gave way to patriarchal notions of masculinity. Kindy continued to be involved in the game but in an administrative capacity. He managed the Mombasa team in the Remington Cup in the 1940s and also served on the executive committee of Coast FC, Oxford Sports Club, and the Mombasa league.

Beginning in the 1910s, football became a distinguishing feature of life in the dramatically growing colonial African cities (see table 1).[11] It is no accident that several of contemporary Africa's most important and oldest football clubs trace their origins to this pioneering era, including Accra Hearts of Oak (1911), Espérance of Tunis (1919), Jeanne d'Arc of Dakar (1921), Canon and Tonnerre Yaoundé (1930 and 1934), Young Africans and Simba of Dar es Salaam (1930s), Diables Noirs and Renaissance of Brazzaville (1930s), AS Vita Kinshasa and TP Englebert Lubumbashi (1930s), and Orlando Pirates from outside Johannesburg (1937).

European influence was visible in the names of African teams. Aston Villa and Wolverhampton Wanderers in Accra, Sunderland in Dar es Salaam, and Blackpool in Johannesburg mimicked the names of elite English clubs. Black clubs like Devonshire Rovers in Cape Town and Highlanders in both Johannesburg and Bulawayo reflected the influence of the military. The active role of European missionaries surfaced in the adoption of religious names such as Jeanne d'Arc in Dakar and Saint-Éloi in Élisabethville.

Moonlighters Football Club in Johannesburg illustrated the strong connections between football, family, and neighborhood identity.[12] Founded in 1892, when Johannesburg was just six years old, this working-class Indian club was based in the Doornfontein area of the city. It was taken for granted that sons would join Moonlighters and continue the tradition, following in the footsteps of their fathers before them. From the 1930s through the 1950s, Moonlighters represented a particular group of families, including Asvat, Moodley, Moosa, Naidoo, Padayachee, Thomas, and Vassen. Club elders spent considerable time and energy fostering this tradition of continuity and family ties, coaxing, cajoling, and coercing youths into membership. Movement from the second team to the first team was almost a rite of passage from boyhood into manhood.[13] Those youngsters who rebelled and attempted to break away from Moonlighters to join a different club faced disciplinary action or, in extreme cases, social exclusion. Like traditional family heads, football's patriarchs oversaw the everyday business of organized sport festivals, settled disputes, and assigned playing fields. Players frequently called club and league officials "elders."

Referees represented another form of patriarchal authority. Despite the elders' efforts to enforce obedience, hooligans sometimes disrupted matches. Fans often saw referees as biased and set about settling scores on the pitch. A local colonial officer in Cameroon reported that the vigorous nature of football rivalries led to teams "protesting almost every decision of the

**TABLE 1   POPULATION OF SOME MAJOR AFRICAN CITIES
IN THE COLONIAL ERA (IN THOUSANDS)**

Date	c. 1900	c. 1939	c. 1960
Cairo, Egypt	910 (1897)	1,312 (1937)	2,852 (1959)
Lagos, Nigeria	74 (1910)	127 (1931)	364 (1960)
Accra, Ghana	18 (1901)	61 (1931)	491 (1960)
Dakar, Senegal	18 (1904)	92 (1936)	383 (1960)
Kinshasa, DRC	5 (1908)	27 (1935)	420 (1961)
Nairobi, Kenya	12 (1906)	119 (1948)	267 (1962)
Dar es Salaam, Tanganyika	25 (1906)	69 (1948)	140 (1962)
Johannesburg, South Africa	102 (1896)	283 (1931)	1.097 (1959)

Source: Bill Freund, *The African City: A History* (Cambridge: Cambridge University Press, 2007), 66.

referee and to matches ending in general chaos."[14] African football's patriarchal elite clearly had trouble keeping control over younger, independent men eager to assert their manhood during competitive spectacles. In the late 1940s in Johannesburg, South Africa, Orlando Pirates Football Club, an ethnically mixed black team that stood as a symbol of civic pride and social responsibility, temporarily stopped competing due to an ongoing conflict with the white authorities over playing grounds. The young men fully understood the reasons for the decisions by the club's older officials, but the players resented missing games and the small sums of cash they were sometimes paid, as well as the notoriety that came with being well-known athletes in the community. Tensions eventually subsided after Pirates joined the Johannesburg African Football Association.

While Pirates was a cosmopolitan and multilingual team, ethnic sides were common elsewhere in Africa during this period, mainly because club membership was linked to residential patterns. By the 1930s, many of these clubs started to recruit top players from outside their immediate community, sometimes offering them material compensation and employment. But club administration usually remained in the hands of individuals who identified as members of a particular ethnic group. Ethnic football was also common in the mining compounds of southern and central Africa.

European mine managers encouraged African employees to form ethnic football teams as a way to boost production and as an inexpensive means of social control (i.e., by dividing workers along ethnic lines). As a supervisor on a Rhodesian gold mine in the 1920s put it: "The native is intensely imitative, often vain, and always clannish, and all these are qualities which would further 'sport'—a parochial spirit of sport if you like—but one which would forge ties of interest and *esprit de corps* between the laborer and his work-place. A patch of ground, a set of goal-posts and a football would not figure largely in the expenditure of a big mine."[15] On the Zambian and Belgian Copperbelt, football and ethnicity were closely connected. On the Zambian mines in the late 1920s and early 1930s, according to historian Hikabwa Chipande, Lions were linked to Lozi workers; Elephants to Bemba; and Tigers to Ngoni and Chewa people.[16] On the Belgian side of the Copperbelt, the mining giant Union minière du Haute Katanga (UMHK) provided crucial assistance to the colonial government and the Catholic Church in establishing in 1925 the Union des fédérations et associations sportives indigènes, which ran an immensely popular football league aimed at fostering an obedient, efficient, and healthy African working class.[17] On the gold mines of the Witwatersrand in South Africa, black workers formed a league in 1917 in accordance with a major segregationist aim: that football should be separated by race and ethnicity. But after the mine league collapsed in 1929, Zulu clerks resurrected it in 1931 without ethnic sections. A new propensity had developed among some mine clerks to think of themselves as African, as well as Zulu, and ethnically defined sport lost some of its appeal. The cosmopolitan character of urban Africa and the spirit of competition led some ethnically homogenous teams to recruit players from outside their cultural group.

Teams representing urban workplaces were critical to the Africanization of football. Nigeria was a typical case. Historian Wiebe Boer highlights the extent to which Nigerian football culture in the pre-1960 period was shaped by teams from government agencies and departments such as Nigeria Police Force, Nigeria Regiment, Public Works Department (PWD), Nigerian Railway, Marine (i.e., Ports and Harbors), and Posts and Telegraphs.[18] As we have seen, policemen and soldiers were traditionally strong sportsmen. According to former Nigerian international footballer Justin Onwudiwe, "they have all the facilities. They are given the wherewithal, the money to buy equipments [*sic*]. They had time and they are physically fit."[19] PWD opened its first sports club for both white and black employees in 1927 in Lagos. Subsequently, other PWD sports clubs were developed across the colony, which contributed to the growth of football and other sports as well. In 1929, PWD Lagos organized a football team under the stewardship of H. A. Porter, an English architect in the department. Porter ultimately became the first president of the Lagos League and the founding president of the Nigerian FA (see chapter 3). Nigeria Railways was another government agency that built leisure clubs for its workers in railway towns across Nigeria. Unlike the PWD clubs, however, they were segregated into Railway Institutes for whites and Railway Recreational Clubs for Africans. Football's prominence in railway workers' leisure underpinned the success of African railway teams in Nigeria from the mid-1940s to the late 1950s.[20]

The dominant role of government departmental clubs was by no means unique to Nigeria. In Dar es Salaam's top league in 1942, historian Tadasu Tsuruta identifies Government School, Post Office, Railways, Kings' African Rifles, Police, and Medical Department as the main competitors for Young Africans and Old Boys (later known as Sunderland and Simba)— the most popular clubs in Tanzania today.[21] Government agencies, like the mine companies, believed in football's capacity to engender team spirit among employees as well as loyalty to the colonial state. According to Kindy, Mombasa's medical officer of health built the Nianda team by securing government employment for skilled players and by obtaining the use of an enclosed football ground (with a small stand)—a rare and highly prized possession for any African club.[22] In Zanzibar, colonial agencies also gave talented players jobs so as to strengthen teams like Public Works Department, Police, and Medical Department. As a soccer-playing tailor employed by the police explained: "I had no choice. If you worked for a department they could take any player they wanted. The department teams took all the best players! Really they did! They even gave people jobs because they were good footballers."[23] In South Africa, too, enterprising clubs in the 1930s recruited players with promises of a wage-earning job. "With soccer skills a player could get a job, easily too!" Peter Sitsila, a player and manager at the time, told me: "Even the association, not just his own team, the association would join forces with his team and try to look for a job for him because the association would be making use of that good player" and benefiting from his performances.[24] Moreover, top-notch black players in South Africa could circumvent racist laws by securing passes (identity documents designed to control the movement of Africans) at a time when the government was tightening restrictions on black people's freedom of movement through legislation such as the 1923 Natives (Urban Areas) Act, which sharply limited African migration into towns and laid the foundations for urban residential segregation.

Football also bred familiarity, thereby encouraging the creation of mixed teams. Recalling the rise of "pan-ethnic" teams in Zanzibar in the 1940s, a former player noted how the game reduced racial and ethnic tensions: "It helped a lot. Because now you would find a Comorian playing with an Arab together with an African in one club. . . . You can't hate me while I'm playing with you in the same club. You love me because I'm playing with you. You learn to appreciate me like a brother."[25]

Football and Resistance

This evidence underscores that while European colonizers intended for sport to prop up their self-proclaimed "civilizing mission" in Africa, they unwittingly created new opportunities for various forms of African resistance, not only against colonialism but also against social inequalities within African communities. Local football clubs occasionally expressed opposition to colonial power and authority. The "political" character of a club could be overt, as in the case of Al Ahly of Cairo, the most successful club in Africa and the Middle East. Its name means "National" in Arabic, and its red insignia came to symbolize patriotic resistance to British rule in the late 1920s when Europeans were excluded from the club.[26] But most times, players found more subtle ways to express their opposition to colonial authorities. In the railway town of Atbara in Sudan, Sudanese railway workers gave their football side the name the "Forty Team"; according to historian Ahmed Sikainga, "the number forty [w]as a rejection of the European football rule, which limited the number of players on each team to eleven."[27] In Namibia, Tigers FC, a team of clerks and government employees based in Windhoek's Old Location, and one of the earliest black sides, was forced to change its name in the 1920s because the authorities associated it with the name of a local resistance movement. The Tigers responded by simply rearranging the letters and renaming themselves Rigets.[28]

In Brazzaville in the 1930s, French authorities imposed a rule requiring Africans to play football in bare feet. Even though most players could not afford football boots anyway, they resented colonial domination, the lack of proper equipment, and shoddy playing facilities.[29] Older players quit the game, while many younger ones moved over to the mission league. Challenges to colonialism and white power occurred in eastern and southern Africa. In Zanzibar, local footballers protested against the perceived bias of referees appointed by the British-run Sports Control Board.[30] In South Africa in 1932, the Durban association dropped the term "Native," which by then had acquired a derogative connotation, and adopted the new, more racially affirmative name of Durban and District *African* Football

Association.[31] At the time, Africa's first Nobel Peace laureate, Chief Albert Luthuli, later president of the African National Congress, was actively involved in the Durban association. Similarly, in Bulawayo in the mid-1940s, protests erupted against white oversight of African football. Among the leaders of the protest were activists like Benjamin Burombo, founder of the British African National Voice Association and a member of Mashonaland FC, and Sipambaniso Manyoba, a trade unionist and captain of Matabele Highlanders and the Bulawayo representative team, or "Red Army."[32] Involvement in football and formal resistance politics went hand in hand for many urban, Western-educated, Christian Africans.

But the forms of resistance more commonly associated with the game between the wars were less overtly oppositional. African clubs exhibited an ethos of self-reliance and solidarity that highlighted their partial autonomy from white interests—the government, missionaries, and private companies. In colonial Africa, it was not uncommon for teams to function like mutual aid societies that provided a social safety net for members in the form of money for a variety of purposes, including lost wages, educational scholarships, weddings, and funerals. Clubs like Orlando Pirates and Durban Bush Bucks in South Africa, Sunderland/Simba in Dar es Salaam, and Botafogo in Angola built a sense of *communitas* (oneness).[33]

Regional variations meant that challenging colonial control of football was virtually impossible in areas like the Belgian Congo, where the game spread quickly among urban Africans.[34] Catholic missionary Raphael de la Kethulle (1890–1956) was a key figure in Léopoldville, where there were 815 registered players in 53 teams by 1939. A passionate football fan and former player, he launched a league for Africans in 1919 and then convinced the colonial authorities to build the first sports facilities for blacks, an effort that would culminate in the opening of the fifty-thousand-seat King Badouin Stadium in 1952. "Tata Raphael's" counterpart in Élisabethville was Father Gregoire Coussement, who organized a league in 1925 with the assistance of other elite Congolese men. By 1937, the African Football Association featured eleven teams and two major football grounds: the fifty-thousand-seat Leopold II stadium and the smaller St. Jean stadium at the mission. While organized on a smaller scale than in Léopoldville, football was by far the most popular sport in Katanga. Team names reflected multiple local identities, including religious (Vaticano), government (Union Sportive Militaire Saio), ethnic (Empire Lunda), and urban (Lubumbashi Sports).

An Urban Culture of Competition

The indigenization of soccer in Africa had much to do with the rise of prominent city leagues and intertown contests. These institutionalized the game and entrenched it in urban popular culture.[35] One of the first colonial cities in sub-Saharan Africa to host a formal league was Accra in the Gold Coast. After a false start in 1915, the league kicked off in 1922 with Hearts of Oak taking the coveted Guggisberg Shield, named for the progressive British governor of that period.[36] In Senegal, the Union sportive indigène was formally constituted in 1929 in Dakar, the capital of French West Africa. In Nigeria, the Lagos league began play in 1930, one year before the formation of the Lagos and District Amateur Football Association. In 1937, the Ibadan District Amateur Football Association supervised that city's league.[37]

In Léopoldville, the Association sportive congolaise, formed in 1919, started an annual league for Africans in 1924.[38] The following year, the FASI emerged as the controlling body for African sport, including football, in the southern copper-mining center of Élisabethville.[39] In Brazzaville, the Native Sports Federation was set up in 1929 to organize local African football.[40] In French Cameroon, the Union sportive indigène de Douala and the Union sportive indigène de la région de Yaoundé were both founded in 1934, and in 1935 these two bodies organized a "national" tournament between the champions of the two cities.[41]

In East Africa, the Dar es Salaam Association Football League was underway by 1928–29, although the precise founding date is not known.[42] On the nearby island of Zanzibar, the Zanzibar Cup was inaugurated in 1926, with the only European team in the competition, Mnazi Moja, defeating New Kings 1–0 in front of four thousand spectators. Two years later, when the Sports Association of Zanzibar came into existence, the size of the crowd at the final match swelled to ten thousand spectators.[43] In South Africa, mission-educated, Zulu-speaking clerks from Natal, known as the *umabhalana,* were pioneers in the institutionalization of black football. These men formed the Durban and District Native Football Association in 1916 and also helped to establish the Witwatersrand and District Native Football Association in 1917. "Attending football competitions along with thousands of other fans was one of the defining characteristics of urban living during the 1920s," explains historian Laura Fair, "and one of the highlights of a trip to town for visitors from the countryside."[44] But the segregated nature of colonial society also fostered separate spheres of black and white leisure, including sport. Racism and segregation plagued settler colonies like South Africa, Algeria, Kenya, and Rhodesia, but was by no means unusual in non–settler colonies as well. It was only in places where there were too few Europeans to form their own "national" teams that racially mixed games took place.[45]

In South Africa, the game continued to grow but in a racially balkanized form typical of colonial societies. By the 1930s, "national" tournaments for different racial groups held sway. These included the Currie Cup for whites (established in 1892), the Sam China Cup for Indians (1903), the Moroka-Baloyi Cup for Africans (1932, but known as the Bakers Cup prior to 1938), and the Stuttaford Cup for Coloureds (sponsored by a department store, 1933). North of the Limpopo River, "by the end of the 1920s soccer pitches had sprung up in remote villages and towns across Zimbabwe . . . and by the end of 1930s soccer was flourishing in colonial Zimbabwe's main urban centres."[46] As of 1937, the Osborn Cup determined the "African" champions of Southern Rhodesia, which often came from Bulawayo, the economic center of the colony and a hotbed of African football.

Segregated football was also the norm in colonial Zambia.[47] In 1922, a British mine employee named William Nelson Watson formed the whites-only Broken Hill (Kabwe) Amateur Football Association, and in 1929, Africans were excluded from the new Northern Rhodesia FA. With the assistance of some European officials, African players and organizers in the 1930s responded by founding the Rhodesia Congo Border African FA, which would be renamed the Copperbelt African FA in 1950. Teams from the Copperbelt came to dominate Zambian football, winning the prestigious Inter-District championship (established in 1930) twenty of twenty-three times. Also, Copperbelt clubs claimed the Northern Rhodesia Challenge Cup (first played in 1938) eleven times in fifteen editions. Farther south, in Mozambique in the 1930s, racially separate leagues prevailed in Lourenço Marques (Maputo), Beira, and Inhambane. In the colonial capital, Portuguese and English whites competed in the Associação de futebol de Lourenço Marques, while most blacks played in the Associação africana de futebol. A small number of mixed-race players were allowed to participate in the white-run league, a reflection of how local football followed the Portuguese colonial logic of reserving "assimilation" rights for a carefully chosen few.[48]

The North African Champions Cup, beginning in 1920, initiated inter-territorial competitions on the continent, building popular excitement for the game. Over a period of twenty years, this knockout (single elimination) tournament involved the winners of regional leagues in Algeria, Tunisia, and Morocco (Morocco first entered a team in 1928–29). The same colonial territories also fielded teams in the North African Cup, which began in 1930–31. This tournament initially featured eight teams also playing in a knockout format. After World War II it expanded to sixteen teams, a format it kept until its demise in 1955 on the eve of Tunisian and Moroccan independence. Elsewhere in francophone Africa, in 1923 teams of Europeans in Brazzaville and Léopoldville competed in the maiden Stanley Pool Championship, which honored the broad expanse of the Congo River separating the two cities. In 1931, thousands of supporters from both sides of the river watched Étoile of Brazzaville defeat visiting Union of Kinshasa 5–1 in the African version of the Pool championship.[49]

The British in East Africa matched French enthusiasm for interterritorial contests. In 1926, for example, representative sides from Uganda and Kenya contested the William Gossage Cup for the first time. In one of the earliest examples of business sponsorship of African sport, a soap manufacturer donated the trophy. This annual single match contest, which alternated between Nairobi and Kampala through 1945, attracted enormous popular and media interest in East Africa. During that period, Uganda won the Gossage Cup twelve times (including six times in a row in 1935–40) and Kenya five. Tanganyika entered the tournament in 1945, followed by Zanzibar in 1949.

The Role of Magic

As African enthusiasm for football grew, players, teams, and fans "Africanized" the game. While it was played according to international rules and standards, the use of magic and religious specialists infused the game with distinctive African traits. Anthropologist Christian Bromberger has noted how occult practices in football are part of a global pattern of "domesticating luck."[50] As a way to cope with uncertainty and unpredictability, players and fans are known to practice rituals without necessarily "believing." As a former player in South Africa confided to me: "I didn't believe in that stuff. It was mostly people who come from the rural areas who believed in witchcraft. People born here [in the city] don't believe in those things." That may indeed have been the case, but it also undeniable that many African players from a wide range of social and cultural backgrounds, from rural traditionalists to urban, Western-educated Christians, seemed to accept—either by choice or peer pressure—the use of magic. The ritual use of magic had strong psychological and team-building qualities.

Almost from the very beginning of the game in South Africa's major cities, African clubs, to swing results in their favor, employed healers, diviners, and sorcerers to ritually prepare their squads before important matches.[51] Ritual preparations included pregame consultations with a diviner who threw the bones to predict the outcomes of the match. *Izinyanga* (healers) also tried to strengthen athletes by rubbing players' legs with *umuthi* (traditional medicine) or making them inhale "some smoke from herbs so that they bring fear and weakness on the opponents."[52] The discovery of a small bottle filled with umuthi in one of the goals during a championship game in the early 1920s in Durban led to accusations of witchcraft, which exploded into a major controversy. Some African officials of the Durban association, as well as its English president, Douglas Evans, attacked the use of magic in football, labeling it an example of "uncivilized" behavior. But the practice continued. An elderly Cape Town–born former player told me in an interview that in the 1940s and 1950s, before important matches, "a witch doctor or whatever will come and smear some Vaseline on our shoes and whatever it was. When I ask him what it is all about he says: 'this is going to make you run faster, kick great' and so on. [Laughs]." During the first decade of apartheid, these practices had become so widespread that it was common for black South African clubs to pay large amounts of money to acquire the services of an *inyanga*. Naturally, fierce competition for the best magicians developed.

The making of locally distinctive football cultures also drew in propitiatory rituals associated with precolonial military campaigns. In South Africa, a symbolic regeneration of nineteenth-century Zulu military prowess in the name of sport displayed virtuous cultural identities while fostering team spirit. Match preparations often commenced with team officials consulting a diviner who threw bones to predict the outcome of a game. Before a key contest, clubs went on a retreat to reenact purification ceremonies similar to those performed by nineteenth-century Zulu *amabutho* (age-regiments) before major military encounters. This tradition of prematch seclusion is common elsewhere in Africa, as well as in Europe and Latin America. What was distinctive in the case of KwaZulu-Natal, as the area is now known, is that the players drank an emetic and vomited, thus emulating the *ukuhlanza* (cleansing) practice of nineteenth-century Zulu soldiers on the eve of war. Moreover, the sprinkling of umuthi on the football and on boots recalled the doctoring of warriors' weapons, as did the burning of special roots.

The infusion of agrarian spiritual beliefs and ritual practices into modern football was evident also in French Africa. According to Martin, "in the early days of Brazzaville football, the potency of rituals and medicines controlled by West African marabouts [Muslim holy men] were [*sic*] particularly sought after by leading clubs."[53] One particularly successful man who worked for several local teams earned the nickname "Merci beaucoup" (Thank you very much). Many believed that a "skilled magician could turn the opponent's ball into stone or make the ball invisible until it was in the back of the other team's net." In West Africa, it was reported that in May 1950 pregame pleasantries between teams from Guinea and Senegal were upset when the Senegalese captain refused to touch the pennant offered by his Guinean counterpart, for fear that it had been "doctored" with polluting magic.[54] In 1936, the Cameroonian newspaper *Gazette du Cameroun* reported that "superstition" in football was commonplace: "One consults a sorcerer to obtain from him herbs whose immediate effect is to paralyze opposing players, or drugs that give diarrhea to the enemy, etc."[55] "On the Middle Congo," Martin writes, "where resources were seen as finite, a match started with a preordained number of goals. The role of team magicians in this zero-sum game was to steal points from their opponents while protecting their own goals. African sport is 'bathed in the occult,' wrote a [Congolese] referee."[56]

Magicians produced charms, talismans, and amulets that African players wore as bracelets, chains, and rings to defend themselves from the spiritual onslaught of opposing religious specialists.[57] Individual match preparations usually included rubbing specially treated ointments on skin, shoes, jerseys, and other equipment. These magical practices aimed to enhance a striker's shooting accuracy, ward off opposing wizards' curses on a midfielder (a ferociously contested area in football), or assist a goalkeeper in keeping the ball out of his net. Anthropologist Arnold Pannenborg observed similar traditions in contemporary Cameroon:

> The team manager received instructions as to how to prepare the jerseys himself. "I had to put all the jerseys on the table," Kalla says. "I lit five candles around it, a red one, yellow, black, blue and green. I was merely following orders. He [the spiritual adviser] wanted me to fill a glass of water and say some prayers. The water turned green. This means that the spirits were present and helping. The water started to give out a very strong

scent. I poured the water over the jerseys. The next day I gave the players their jerseys. Any evil spirits that may have been among them would disappear. . . . It brought unity to the team. One spirit.[58]

Teams did not always shy away from deploying "negative" magic, or sorcery either. In one common practice, a charm was buried below the playing surface to adversely affect opponents' performance. Sorcerers also unleashed "sympathetic magic," as shown by Royer in Burkina Faso: "In order to paralyze a football team, eleven pieces of a broom, one for each player, are cut and tied together, or to paralyze a goalkeeper, the legs of a frog are tied on its back."[59] Sorcerers cast spells and curses to disable the opposition. Strikers and goalkeepers—key players on the field—were preferred targets, although referees were also targeted to elicit favorable calls or prevent adverse decisions. In this spiritually loaded context, the duties and responsibilities of religious specialists included protecting playing grounds and stadiums, as well as hotels, eating facilities, buses, and other spaces used by the players, coaches, and staff. Political scientist Michael Schatzberg has interpreted sorcery as an African way to "level the playing field" between unevenly matched teams and also as a means to gain individual success and financial returns.[60] Despite repeated attempts by regulatory bodies to stamp out magic and sorcery, this "game within a game" between magicians, sorcerers, and spiritual advisors continues to shape African soccerscapes. A famous incident took place on the pitch in Bamako in 2002, when the Malian police beat up and arrested Cameroonian goalkeeping coach Thomas Nkono before an African Nations Cup semifinal between Cameroon and host Mali. He was accused of "doing magic" and suspended for one year by CAF. Ultimately, it is important to recognize that many Africans regard football and magic as complementary, not mutually exclusive. Among practitioners, physical, technical, and tactical training are generally understood as necessary for any coach and team to achieve success, but so are religious specialists.[61]

Rituals of Spectatorship

Fan rituals and traditions also increasingly gave a distinctive African character to soccer games. Home teams attracted devoted fans, such as those who attended the annual matches between Dar es Salaam and Zanzibar that began in 1926. These events were imbued with a festival atmosphere.

Traveling fans took advantage of the August bank holiday and half-price fares to board steamers to accompany their teams. "Work in the town came to a virtual standstill when the ships returned," Laura Fair was told by elderly Zanzibari men, "as 'everyone' converged on the port to greet the teams as they come off the boat. . . . The streets again were filled with the sounds of revelers and *ngoma* and *beni* bands as thousands of spectators proudly escorted the teams back to their clubhouses."[62] Seven hundred Zanzibaris made the trip to the mainland for the 1939 competition, when "*Ngoma* festivities went on for three days and nights, involving even Indians and Europeans. Social clubs such as the Jamil El Manzil Club and Japani Club enthusiastically supported the event, staging *masegese* and *lelemama* dances to entertain their guests. Meanwhile, the Sudanese Sports club arranged *dansi* (Western style dancing) events over two days."[63] In Angola, football and music would come to be similarly intertwined in black working-class neighborhoods of 1950s Luanda.[64]

In the days before concrete stadiums and admission charges, anybody could go to football grounds. As the previous examples from East Africa suggest, the games were spectacles, feasts, and popular entertainment all wrapped into one. Typically, music and dance filled the air. Fans dressed in club colors chanted in support of their team and favorite players. Drums and other percussion instruments provided the soundtrack to matches. Fans cheered and chanted in support of their team, jeered the opposition, sang and danced, and some strummed ukuleles and guitars.

In South Africa, migrants carried the tradition of praising and praise names (*izibongo*[65]) from their homesteads to cities and towns, where the practice was then incorporated into African rituals of spectatorship. "It is the same with the Zulu warrior . . . a recitation," the late Sam Shabangu, a founding member of Orlando Pirates, told Richard Maguire. "I know your story, you did this, you killed like this . . . that's exactly what these names are for. It's through your actions, your bravery, that you get your name. The fans are saying these players are their great warriors."[66] A footballer's physical attributes or technical abilities often inspired fans' nicknames for him. Sometimes players could also be compelled to deliver a particular style of play in accordance with their nicknames. Peter Sitsila told me how his trademark dribbling move, the half-moon, earned him the Xhosa name "Jikeletshobeni" (he who controls the reins). This difficult but highly entertaining move entails sliding the ball past one side of the defender while sprinting around the other side, disorienting the opponent for a moment, then regaining control of the ball and moving forward. The cue for Sitsila to perform the half-moon came from fans chanting "Jikele! Jikele!"[67]

Praise names also revealed interesting aspects of the everyday experiences and consciousness of urban Africans. In South Africa between the wars, Sitsila's older brother earned the nickname "British Empire" after working on the diamond mines. In the Johannesburg area, match reports were filled with nicknames evoking colonial ties, such as "Cape to Cairo" and "Prince of Wales"; educational achievements or aspirations, such as "Junior Certificate"; and appreciation for American automobiles, such as "Buick" and "V8." Other nicknames were more mundane, but no less telling, as with "Waqafa Waqafa" (heavy drinker, delinquent, in Zulu) and "Scotch Whiskey," the latter name reportedly given because the player's performance "drives the sorrows away and brings enjoyment" to the crowd. Similar naming practices were observed elsewhere in colonial Africa, often inspired by Hollywood movies and African American cultural styles. Overall, players' nicknames demonstrated the continuities and changes of agrarian cultures in an urban milieu as well as the meritocratic possibilities of sport. As an expression of fan culture, nicknames bestowed social honor on students, manual laborers, clerks, and teachers, and in the process soldered the bonds of affection and loyalty between supporters and their sporting heroes.

The emotional dimension of the game also sparked rivalries between teams that could be fierce and lead to fan violence. Episodes of crowd disorder, often fueled by consumption of alcoholic drinks, sometimes spilled onto the pitch. In Johannesburg in 1933, ethnic gangs of migrant youths (*amalaita*) "attacked those who were playing football and a dangerous situation arose. Women and children fled before a shower of stones. Many people were injured including the referee."[68] In Brazzaville in the 1940s and 1950s, commentators noted the "'unsportsmanlinke' conduct of spectators and players" and the warlike character of certain matches.[69] Tragically, in Johannesburg in 1940, a referee was murdered by an angry mob. Africa was not unique in this respect, for violent crowd disorders and stadium disasters occurred in Europe and Latin America as well. And for the most part, African rituals of spectatorship were peaceful and celebratory; what people came to see was the fine football on display.

Distinctive Playing Styles

African players, like Latin Americans and continental Europeans, did not simply mimic British ways of playing. They developed their own playing styles, providing an example of how "one of the pleasures of football's internationalism was that different countries played it differently."[70] This outcome frustrated colonial officers who believed that teaching Africans how to play the game was as important as getting them to accept football in the first place. As historian Terence Ranger explains, "The precise *form* of each European game was crucially necessary to convey, for it was the peg on which to hang 'attitudes, rules, leadership, team-work, community feeling, self-imposed discipline and organizational and emotional associations.'"[71] Predictably, these paternalistic efforts generally failed.

While many contemporary international football commentators make references to an "African" style of play, history shows that many different ways of playing existed within the continent, and that these were hybrid styles that changed constantly. Beginning in the 1920s and 1930s, Africans adapted English "kick-and-rush," the Scottish short-passing game, and other European modes of play to suit local sensibilities and conditions. Some tentative observations can be made about African football styles based on scraps of written documents, oral history interviews, and educated guesswork.

Local circumstances fundamentally shaped how Africans played the game. Streets, sandlots, and open spaces honed boys' ball control, toughness, and improvisational skills. Street games had neither referees nor time limits and involved any number of players. They produced a grassroots aesthetic that placed a premium on "spectacular display of individual talent . . . often more memorable, more enjoyable, and ultimately, even more desirable than the final score."[72] As Conrad Stuurman recalled about growing up in black Cape Town, "We played with tennis balls. When we played in the streets we maybe played three or four or five 'cause in the streets it's very narrow, you can't take a big team." Like most young footballers in Africa, Stuurman had fond memories of time spent sharpening his crafty style. "When I've got the ball and I wanted to beat somebody, I played the ball against the pavement, on the other side I'd get the ball back again. That's how we came to know the wall pass. I didn't even know there was a name like wall pass! [Laughs.]"[73]

Material poverty, lack of equipment (only the most privileged boys could afford football cleats, for example), and inadequate facilities influenced vernacular styles of play. Yet many players overcame this inconvenience. According to a typical comment on playing barefoot in the 1930s, "We knew what the disadvantage [was] if we played barefooted and how to avoid somebody with boots . . . you don't have to collide with him. Let him chase the ball; before he gets close . . . I dish my ball off. That's what taught us good football!"[74] Salif Keita of Mali, voted "African Footballer of the Year" by *France Football* in 1970 (see chapter 5), remembered what football was like growing up in colonial Bamako:

> For me, playing for fun, being together joined by the same love for the ball, for the full well-being of body and mind, was amply sufficient to make me happy. One goal, one smart dribbling move gave me sheer enchantment. Also the pleasure of juggling the ball and letting my instinct take the lead. Because in Mali especially, all over Africa actually, technical moves are spontaneous, improvised, not learned through regular training as it is the case in Europe. I must say that at the time I was madly keen on dribbling. Juggling, dribbling, faking, a successful nutmeg [putting the ball through the opponent's legs], there is nothing more natural for the African soccer player! What I achieved in those neighborhood matches my young partners were also capable of. It was only a question of daring.[75]

Despite such resilience and creativity, lack of formal coaching and fitness training made it painfully difficult to acquire the full range of technical and tactical fundamentals. Contemporary match reports in local newspapers rarely described goals scored from headers, combination passing, and set plays (e.g., corners and free kicks)—the kinds of plays that tend to succeed only with formal instruction and extensive practice on adequate pitches. As a result of playing on grounds that were either hard and dusty or impossibly muddy, individual ball control and dexterity trumped more systematic play. "They are ball controllers [i.e., dribblers], but that is not football," wrote a French observer in Cameroon in 1941. "However, I noticed some players who, in the hands of a good coach, would be able to improve."[76] Thus, contrary to racialist explanations that view sporting accomplishments as the outcome of "innate" attributes of a particular racial group, African football skills were developed through extensive training, sporting artistry, and tough urban masculinity.

Top clubs in city leagues exhibited the most refined approaches to playing. As the number of teams expanded in the late 1930s and into the 1940s, competition increased and experience and physical force alone could not guarantee success. Some players began practicing once a week, either playing on their own or organizing a late afternoon intrasquad scrimmage. Even so, before 1940 it was almost unheard of for teams to have trained, full-time coaches. But from time to time, touring European professional and amateur teams gave players and fans tutorials on European play. In South Africa, for example, visits by the Scottish professional side Motherwell in 1931 and 1934 triggered a shift in black football away from kick-and-rush and *laissez-faire* marking toward the more intricate short-passing game and a more guarded defensive approach. "Playing a fine Motherwell" became a symbol of urban sophistication and success for Highlanders Football Club in Johannesburg.[77] Hybrid modes of playing drew on the pace, power, endurance, and directness of the English and the improvisational showmanship and rowdiness of street soccer.

The importance of vernacular modes of play to the growing popularity of the game in colonial Africa was reflected in many player nicknames. In Brazzaville, Martin noted how crowds "showed their appreciation for team-work such as passing and solid defence, but their affection for individual stars was marked."[78] Congolese fans christened players according to technical qualities and styles, as in the case of a goalkeeper named "Elastic" and other stars named "Dancer," "Phantom," "Magician," "Steamboat," and "the Law." In Léopoldville, African players occasionally attended coaching clinics conducted by Belgian instructors who operated on the racist assumption that European "scientific knowledge" could be combined with "the natural flexibility" and "real athletic qualities" of Africans.[79] However, local footballers refused to play the European way. According to a European observer writing in 1938, their performance was so extraordinary that he wondered whether he was watching "a football match or an acrobatic exercise." In interwar Zanzibar, audiences also reportedly "held a definite preference for the beauty of fast, bold, and unconventional moves by individual players, an emphasis that remains a defining feature of the island style to this day."[80] In short, African players and fans self-consciously enjoyed the cleverness, beauty, and excitement of feinting and dribbling, delightful moves that elated fans but also captured the cultural importance of creativity, deception, and skill in getting around difficulties and dangerous situations in colonial societies.

On the eve of the Second World War, the game in Africa was organized into formal clubs and competitions and was being politically, socially, and culturally Africanized. The continent's engagement with the latest trends in international football was summed up by Egypt's participation in the 1934 World Cup in Italy, the first time an African country played in the tournament. But football had also grown in popularity outside its strong-holds of the Maghreb and South Africa. The game spilled out of the main cities and towns and was being played by young boys in rural areas. By the 1940s, "the game was universal" even in remote areas, where "herd-boys spent any spare moments kicking a tennis-ball around," learning how to juggle, pass, and trap by "kicking a tennis-ball up against the wall of one of the typical round-huts. This was excellent practice since it demanded absolute accuracy."[81] By this time, the relationship between football and politics was becoming increasingly close.

CHAPTER THREE

Making Nations in Late Colonial Africa, 1940s–1964

AS ANTICOLONIAL militancy intensified in the 1940s and 1950s, African nationalist movements forged connections with popular football teams, players, and fans. Stadiums and clubhouses became arenas in which workers, intellectuals, business owners, and the unemployed challenged colonial power and expressed a shared commitment to racial equality and self-determination. Football constructed a fragile sense of nationhood in political entities arbitrarily created by colonial powers and fueled Africa's broader quest for political liberation. Until now, however, academic historians have overlooked the role of sport in African independence movements.[1]

To demonstrate this, I will build around three dramatic cases. The first is Nigeria, the most populous nation in Africa. I chronicle how "Zik," the nationalist politician and journalist Nnamdi Azikiwe, who was Nigeria's first president, founded black-controlled sporting clubs to counter colonial racism and foster a sense of nationhood among Nigerians. The second example is Algeria. During the war of independence against France, the National Liberation Front (FLN) formed a "national" football team in exile. Featuring top Algerian professionals based in France, this sporting symbol of the emerging nation legitimized the leadership of the FLN and raised global awareness of the Algerian cause. The final example comes from South Africa. In the aftermath of the rise of apartheid, black football leagues and organizations began to challenge racial segregation as well as the white minority's claim to represent "South Africa" in international sport. In one of the first major indictments of the Pretoria regime, the antiapartheid

South African Soccer Federation actually secured the country's suspension from FIFA in 1961.

Football, Anticolonial Movements, and "Nigerian-ness"

Football in Nigeria began under British colonial rule at the turn of the twentieth century, and by the 1950s it was the national game.[2] During the Second World War, the center of gravity shifted from its birthplace at the Hope Waddell Training Institution in the southeastern town of Calabar (see chapter 1) to the booming city of Lagos in the southwest, where the population increased from 126,000 in 1931 to 267,000 in 1953 to 364,000 by 1961.[3]

Nigeria's postwar economic expansion, the result of high commodity prices and imperial developmental policies, was a crucial factor in driving the growth of Lagos football. Between 1946 and 1960, the wage labor force increased by 80 percent while wages for manual laborers increased by 70 percent.[4] As a government and business center, Lagos developed an ethnically and religiously diverse population with many civil servants, railway men, merchants, artisans, elite professionals, ex-servicemen, and laborers. The city's wage-earning men wanted modern entertainment in their leisure time and had the means to pay for it.[5] Lagos also boasted the highest concentration of schools per resident in Nigeria, so legions of young players and fans in the city grew up loving this fun, inexpensive, and accessible game. Thousands of Lagosian men, and some women, chose to spend their limited free time and disposable income on football.

The clubs in Lagos, as in many African cities, were often based in government departments. Colonial employers aggressively recruited talented African players by offering them relatively secure and good-paying jobs while treating them like second-class citizens. The racial prejudice embedded in this widespread practice was satirized in a political cartoon in a Lagos newspaper (see figure 2).

As the game gained a predominantly Nigerian constituency, especially among Western-educated men, Nnamdi Azikiwe emerged as a key figure connecting sport and politics in the late colonial period. Like many leaders of anti-imperialist movements in colonial Africa and Asia, Zik cleverly turned the values and principles embedded in the "civilizing mission" of the West, including sport, against the colonizers. In the 1930s and 1940s, white civil servants maintained a tight grip on football administration, which maintained racially segregated leagues for Europeans and Africans. Zik's commitment to the meritocratic ideals of the British "game

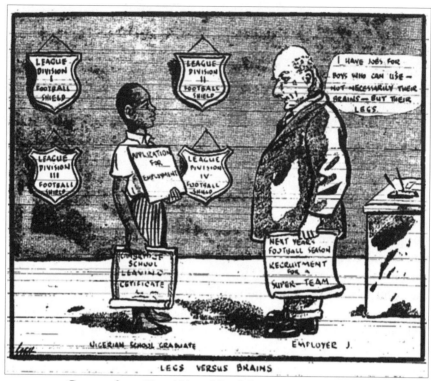

FIGURE 2   Cartoon from *West African Pilot*, July 23, 1949

ethic"—fair play, courage, physical strength, and self-reliance—inspired his belief in football as a populist medium for the promotion of racial equality and self-determination.[6]

Azikwe had himself been a gifted athlete. Like most African boys of his age, he had learned football in the streets of Lagos. Zik then played for Wesleyan Boys' High School and then Hope Waddell Training Institution in Calabar, the birthplace of football in Nigeria. In Lagos, he joined the Diamond Football Club, winning the city championship in 1923. Two years later, he transported his passion for sport to the United States, where he participated in numerous sports and captained the 1929–30 Lincoln University (Pennsylvania) soccer team. His sporting experience at Lincoln enriches our understanding of how historically black colleges and universities in the United States opened new vistas on the black diaspora and exposed early African nationalist leaders to the international dimensions of race and anticolonialism. Once back in West Africa Zik was spurred to action by the persistence of racial segregation and racism in sports.

Two specific incidents of discrimination assaulted his dignity and spurred him to action. While working in Accra as editor of the *African Morning Post,* he was denied the opportunity to compete in a track-and-field event at the 1934 Empire Games (now Commonwealth Games) because Nigeria was not allowed to participate. Then the Yoruba Tennis Club in Lagos rejected his application for membership due to his Igbo background. "I decided to establish an athletic club," he wrote in his autobiography, "which would open the doors of its membership to sportsmen and women of all races, nationalities, tribes and classes residing in Nigeria."[7] Zik's Athletic Club (ZAC) was inaugurated in Lagos in April 1938.

On the eve of the Second World War, ZAC was the only major African-controlled sports club, as opposed to the white clubs for administrators and other Europeans and the teams controlled by colonial officials and British men employed in the private sector in Nigeria. The club symbolized African self-organization and modernity. Its ethnic diversity and urban cosmopolitanism embodied its founder's brand of pan-ethnic African nationalism. Thanks to funds from Azikiwe's press empire, which provided income as well as publicity, ZAC had facilities for football, athletics, swimming, boxing, tennis, and cricket. In 1940, the club built a small stadium in the Lagos suburb of Yaba, and then in 1942 it went on to win both the Lagos League and the War Memorial Cup. This remarkable success inspired Azikiwe to open ZAC branches throughout Nigeria, from Abekouta in the west and Port Harcourt in the south to Kano in the north.

The rise of ZAC in Nigeria mirrored trends elsewhere in British Africa. Football teams on the East African island of Zanzibar enabled Swahili-speaking Muslim men to sharpen their nationalist consciousness and challenge colonial authority.[8] In Sudan's railway town of Atbara in the 1940s and 1950s, football clubs and the sociability they encouraged enabled trade unionists, nationalists, communists, intellectuals, and other men to challenge colonialism.[9] Dr. Abdel Halim Mohamed, a former president of the Confederation of African Football, put it this way:

> We had our social clubs and we were talking about independence. The British had accused us of being *afendeya* (elitist and bourgeois)—that we were not with the masses of the people, that we do not represent them. As a counter to this we started football clubs as social clubs where we would talk the principles of civics to the masses—that this is their country and that they

have the right to independence. This helped to show that while it was we, the intelligentsia, who were the architects of the independence movement, we were backed by the people.[10]

During the war years Azikiwe took the Lagos ZAC football club on "goodwill tours" throughout Nigeria. These tours permitted Azikiwe and other educated nationalists to openly challenge colonial authority at the same time that they were supporting the Allied effort in the war, though this was done through "thinly veiled anti-colonial rhetoric in the guise of pro-war support."[11] The 1941–42 tour drew record crowds in every town. The touring team usually followed the same pattern: it played (and usually won) against a local ZAC side in front of two thousand to five thousand spectators. The match was followed by a speech criticizing colonial rule, in which Azikiwe regularly pointed out the hypocrisy of Britain in waging a war for "freedom and democracy" while oppressing Africans and denying them the right to self-determination enshrined in the Atlantic Charter. In this way, the tour showed how a "framework of sporting values that stressed playing the game for the game's sake . . . had been formulated, propagated and held up as a symbol of cultural superiority by the colonialists was now used by Zik and his press as a gauge of imperial decadence and unfitness to rule."[12]

Each stop on the tour closed with an evening fund-raising dance where local grievances were also aired. The 1941–42 football tour helped popularize the game nationwide and strengthened the national political networks of Azikiwe and the educated elite. While this kind of anticolonial rhetoric was already part of Nigerian politics, what was new about Azikiwe's approach was the extension of the geographical reach of these ideas (through the spread of football) and his creation of a political machine.

The second goodwill tour of 1942–43 aimed to raise money for the Nigerian Prisoners of War Fund. Wartime construction of new roads and communication infrastructure enabled the team to travel longer distances in a shorter time. After traveling to Ibadan in the west, the ZAC tourists journeyed to the northern cities of Kaduna, Kano, Zaria, Jos, and Makurdi, before heading south into the Niger Delta. As in the previous year, huge crowds gathered in every town, eager to take in a match between ZAC Lagos, rechristened "Bombers" (and a second team named "Spitfires"—both commemorating the aircraft of the Battle of Britain), and the local ZAC branch team. The improving standard of play in Nigeria made the tour more competitive and entertaining. On rare occasions, antagonism on the pitch degenerated into chaos. Toward the end of the tour, ZAC actually had to abandon a match in Port Harcourt because of a hotly disputed refereeing decision. Despite this unpleasant incident, the two tours of 1941–43 soldered the connections between distant places and diverse people through an increasingly popular leisure activity. In doing so, football fueled the construction of a frail sense of nationhood, one that was resisted in Northern Nigeria and eventually reduced Zik's support to a largely regional base in the southeast.

The launch of the Governor's Cup in 1945 bolstered this emerging idea of nationhood. The competition followed the format of the Football Association (FA) Cup in England. Initially, it fell under the control of the Lagos and District Amateur Football Association. But in 1948 the Nigerian Football Association (NFA) took over responsibility, boosting the game far beyond the old strongholds of Lagos and Calabar. The number of teams entering the Cup grew from thirteen in 1945 to eighty-seven in 1959. As the competition expanded, the size of the crowds swelled. For example, forty thousand spectators attended the 1951 Cup semifinal between Plateau and Benin! In 1955, the NFA renamed the trophy the Nigeria Challenge Cup (a name it retains to this day), signaling the impending demise of British rule and the emergence of an independent nation-state. While every major region supplied at least one Challenge Cup champion by 1960, the dominant side of this era was the Lagos-based Railway club. Backed by a powerful government department and a seemingly endless supply of talent, such as Titus Okere and Tesilimi "Thunder" Balogun, Railway won six Governor's Cup titles between 1946 and 1957 and nine Lagos league championships between 1943 and 1956.[13]

The process of constructing "Nigerian-ness" in football gathered pace thanks to an enterprising black press. The race-conscious and internationalist *West African Pilot* newspaper introduced popular journalism to Nigeria. It was Azikiwe's flagship daily, with an estimated circulation of about twenty-five thousand (and many more readers). The *Pilot* made football discourse an integral part of indigenous print media. The cumulative effect of the *Pilot*'s diligent coverage of Cup and league competitions asserted the humanity of black workers in a colonial political economy and, in the process, afforded African men new opportunities to acquire social honor. The *Pilot*'s open contempt for the myth of the separation of politics and sport absorbed football into the Nigerian anticolonial struggle. The game became part of the vernacular language of nationalism and provided a venue for the representation of a "Nigerian" identity.

The June 16, 1953, issue of the *Pilot* showed how football was used as a political metaphor with an article entitled "Nigeria Wins Freedom Cup in Thrilling Political Soccer." It recounted a fictional match in which "Britain and Reactionaries United lost considerable ground when Nigeria beat them by a score of 10 goals to nil," thanks to Azikiwe's goalscoring feats. The story went on to describe how this "woeful defeat of imperialism" sparked a raucous stadium celebration with six million [*sic*] spectators singing freedom songs! Clearly, Azikiwe's newspapers contained much that was self-serving and self-important. Yet the *Pilot* also demonstrated some of the ways in which football and the media in Nigeria "created the possibility of a new form of imagined community . . . [and] set the stage for the modern nation."[14]

A football tour of England in 1949 brought the definition of a "Nigerian nation" into sharper focus.[15] Colonial authorities organized the tour to showcase British political, economic, and cultural power at a time of growing anticolonial and labor protests in Nigeria and in Africa as a whole. The selection committee included Zik but was supervised by Captain D. H. Holley, the white chairman of the Nigerian Football Association, demonstrating how the British were trying to extend African representation while retaining ultimate power and authority. While the captain was from the Marine club, Railway and ZAC contributed seven and five players, respectively, to a team of eighteen. The men were mainly civil servants and colonial government employees. Nine of them had attended the Hope Waddell Training Institution. The group disembarked on August 29 in the port of Liverpool. These "ambassadors of friendship," as Holley dubbed the team, played nine matches against amateur and lower-tier professional clubs. Playing barefoot in all but one match, the Nigerians won two, drew two, and lost five.

The African side impressed many English observers. "[Titus] Okere is worth £15,000 and a row of houses. Their artistry is superb, their deportment and their behaviour exemplary," noted a *Daily Graphic* reporter.[16] Astonishing performances by Railway's Okere and "Thunder" Balogun made them the first Nigerians to sign professional contracts in Europe. Okere went to Swindon Town in 1952, while Balogun signed with Queen's Park Rangers in 1956, part of a trend examined in chapter 5.[17] The team also made an impact on Nigerian fans in the stands. "I was very proud to see them play," Raphael Shonekan recalled. "People were thrilled. They couldn't believe it you know, it was the first team to come and play in England from Africa."[18] The pride in a Nigerian-ness that extended beyond territorial and political boundaries—an imagined community imbued with pan-African sentiments—was evident.

On the way back from England, the tourists stopped in Freetown, Sierra Leone, where Nigeria defeated the locals by two goals to nil. More than a decade before independence, this match marked the birth of Nigeria's national team. On an administrative level, the game became more "national" in the 1950s thanks to a "northernization" program that brought significant numbers of Northern Nigerian (especially Hausa) functionaries into the Nigerian FA, which had been perceived by some as overly represented by southerners and especially Igbo people originally from the southeast. In 1959, the last British official left the NFA, and on August 22, 1960, a few weeks prior to its formal independence, Nigeria joined the world football body FIFA.

Nigeria's international experience was not unique. Representative teams from Accra had played against Lagos several times before the creation in 1951 of the Jalco Cup (named after a local auto dealer). This new intercolonial trophy crystallized national identities in the 1950s by pitting Gold Coast (now Ghana) against Nigeria in Accra and Lagos. Nigeria won the Jalco Cup four times and the Gold Coast three, including a 7–0 victory in 1955. In 1957, the teams drew 2–2 in Accra, the only time the home side failed to win. The similarities between Gold Coast and Nigeria did not end here. In 1951, a Gold Coast team also toured England.[19] Kwame Nkrumah and his Convention People's Party used football and popular culture in 1950s to increase their popularity among urban constituencies and young men in particular.

Intercolonial contests, as the previous chapter noted, had their origins in French Africa. The Coupe d'Afrique Occidentale Française (French West Africa Cup), inaugurated in 1947, was a new competition that featured popular clubs like Union Sportive Indigène, Jeanne d'Arc, and Union Sportive Gorée from Dakar; Jeanne d'Arc and Foyer de Soudan from Bamako; Racing Club from Conakry; Jeunesse Club and ASEC from Abidjan; and Étoile Filante from Lomé.[20] As in Nigeria, the media popularized the game, but in French West Africa radio played a key role. The Senegalese radio announcer "Allou" merged traditional oral performance with modern technology to become a kind of football griot (bard). He is remembered for memorable broadcasts like a 1951 match in which Diop Iba Mar scored a last-minute game-winning penalty only to collapse and die of a heart attack on the pitch moments later.[21] By listening to Allou on the radio, new fans were drawn into football.

The French West Africa Cup expanded from 16 clubs participating in 1947 to 302 in 1958–59. In order to accommodate this enormous pool of teams, regional qualifiers were introduced in the early 1950s. In Dakar, Cotonou, Abidjan, Lome, and Bamako, thousands of spectators filled the local stadiums for marquee matches.

If French officials had imagined that the French West Africa Cup would distract Africans from political engagement and provide an example of the supposed "benefits" of membership in the French Empire, they must have been disappointed with the result.[22] On the pitch, competition encouraged the creation of embryonic national identities in the different territories of the federation: Senegal, Mauritania, Guinea, Ivory Coast, Benin, Mali, Burkina Faso, and Niger. Antagonism sparked rivalries that occasionally degenerated into violence and tended to undermine pan-African unity. The French "territorialization" policy of 1956, which granted each entity within the colonial federations control over domestic affairs while leaving foreign policy and defense matters under French control, further encouraged the emergence of distinct territorial, and therefore "national," identities.[23] In the end, the French attempt to use sport as an example of more benevolent postwar colonial policies failed to pacify African politicians and their supporters.

Football and identity formation were also closely linked in the French and Belgian Congo. In Brazzaville and Léopoldville, the game "allowed fans to forget their differences and to forge a broader sense of identity when regional or international matches were staged. When a Brazzaville select team played against a Léopoldville team, Bacongo and Poto-Poto fans buried their differences and became Brazzavillois."[24] Beating European teams at their own game sparked widespread street celebrations. "And as independence approached, Brazzaville players joined their national team to play matches against other colonies in AEF [French Equatorial Africa]. Sport contributed to a growing sense of nationalism, as it has done all over the world."[25] In the city of Élisabethville in the southern Katanga-Shaba region, the Belgians staged a sub-Saharan African championship in 1950. Much to the delight of the local population, Katanga defeated Northern Rhodesian and South African teams to take the title.[26] In many ways, then, intercolonial matches, national competitions, and domestic and international tours after 1945 were avenues of African cultural resistance that fuelled anticolonial nationalism. Everywhere on the continent, football teams and spectators contributed to the emerging consciousness of national identity and popular resistance to colonial rule.

Footballers of the Revolution: The Algerian FLN Team

One of the most dramatic examples of the linkage of African football to anticolonial resistance was the formation of the Algerian National Liberation Front's "national" team during the war of independence against France.[27] On April 13, 1958, ten Algerian professional players based in France surreptitiously left the country through Switzerland and Italy and made their way to Tunis, home of the Provisional Government of the Republic of Algeria (GPRA). The only setback was the arrest at the Franco-Swiss border of Mohamed Maouche of Stade Reims.[28] In a communiqué issued on April 15, the FLN explained the team's objectives: (1) to deny France the service of key players; (2) to heighten international awareness of the Algerian fight for independence; and (3) to demonstrate that the FLN's war enjoyed the broad support of Algerians, at home and abroad.[29]

The departure of the Algerian footballers from France made news all around the world. Even in the United States, the mainstream media covered the event. "Soccer got into French-Algerian politics," reported the *New York Times* in an article about a group of "Algerian Moslems" based in French professional teams who left "to join the nationalist cause against France."[30] *Time* magazine dubbed it "The Disappearing Act." Contextualizing the significance of the players' flight for an American audience, *Time* explained: "It was as if, overnight, the best Latin American baseball players in the major leagues—men like Chico Carrasquel, Bobby Avila, Minnie Minoso, Ruben Gomez—had fled the U.S. and challenged the Yankees and Braves for the world championship."[31] The American press reluctantly acknowledged the FLN's success: "The flight may not have been pure patriotism, but was far from kidnapping," noted *Time*. "The exodus, with its complicated movements of wives and children, luggage and refrigerators and washing machines, was elaborately planned over a long period of time to avert suspicion, and not a single player appealed to the police." At a press conference in Tunis, the Algerian players declined making grandiose political statements. Instead, the athletes relied on familiar sporting clichés, saying simply that "they were glad to be here."[32]

Algeria was France's oldest colony in Africa, beginning with the conquest of the capital city of Algiers in 1830. Football developed rather early, initially among the numerous European settlers but soon among the indigenous population, particularly students and urban elites. The idea for a national team in exile had its origins in the politicization of football before the Second

World War. As early as 1926, the sporting club of the Étoile Nord-Africaine was already a center of anticolonial sentiment. Occasional matches between Europeans (French settlers or *colons,* as well as Italians, Spaniards, and others) and Arab and Berber Muslims had political overtones, "characterized by their hard physical confrontations, not only between players on the pitch but also between spectators on the terraces, and, afterwards, outside the stadium."[33] Violence peaked during the war of independence. In 1955, a riot broke out in Algiers during a match between Moulodia, an Algerian club, and AS Saint-Eugène, a white team. The FLN immediately ordered the withdrawal of all Muslim teams from the local league. The FLN's turn to urban terrorism in 1956–57 led to a series of guerrilla attacks in stadiums, none more spectacular than the assassination of an Algerian collaborator at the French Cup Final in Paris in May 1957.[34]

That year the politicization of football deepened. An Algerian amateur team participated in a tournament held at the World Youth Festival in Moscow. In a public display of emerging nationhood, the Algerian delegation marched in front of Soviet premier Nikita Khrushchev during the opening ceremony waving a new national flag.

The manager of the Algerian team in Moscow was Mohamed Boumezrag (1912–1969), soon to become the FLN team's mastermind and technical director. Like many African footballers, Boumezrag had played professionally in France (1936–46). After the Second World War, he had embarked on a twelve-year coaching career and then joined the FLN underground in France. Boumezrag's political consciousness was unusual in sporting circles. It was inspired by the experience of his grandfather, a prominent imam in the inland city of El-Asnam, who had spent thirty-three years in a colonial prison (1871–1904) for participating in local anticolonial resistance activities.[35] Soon after Boumezrag's return from Moscow, the National Liberation Army (ALN) sent an amateur football team on a four-month fundraising tour through Libya, Egypt, Syria, Iraq, Kuwait, Saudi Arabia, Jordan, and Palestine (Jerusalem). This team of guerrillas enjoyed the full backing of the Comité de coordination et d'exécution, the executive cabinet of Algeria's first sovereign parliament, the Conseil national de la révolution algérienne.[36]

Key leaders of the Algerian struggle appreciated football's value as a symbol of national identity and as a legitimizing tool for the FLN itself. Ferhat Abbas, the moderate chief of the provisional government in the late 1950s, played the game in his youth. He had served as president of the Union Sportive Musulmane de Sétif (founded in 1933, now USFMS), a leading Algerian club that supplied a steady stream of professional players to France.[37] For Abbas, the game was a vehicle for the assertion of Algerians' self-reliance and equality vis-à-vis their French colonial masters. As he put it, "On a man to man basis, on the field of football, we can show them who is really superior."[38] Ben Bella, Algeria's first president, shared Abbas's understanding of the interconnected nature of football and politics. Describing the racism and segregation that characterized high school sport in colonial Algeria, Bella recalled that Muslim students were permitted to play against the whites only once a year. "When I maneuvered at speed against the enemy [*sic*]," Bella pointed out, "nobody asked me whether I was European or Algerian—I either scored a goal or I didn't, and that was that. I was responsible only to myself for success and failure alike."[39] The metaphor of sport as an arena of meritocracy and fair play was taken seriously in the colonies, and it came to express African people's desire for equality and freedom. Like other anticolonial movements in Africa and Asia, Algerian nationalists interpreted Western sport as "a phenomenon of appropriation. That which was not freely offered by the colonizer was seized from him."[40] The FLN shrewdly concluded that football's capacity to symbolize Algerian national identity could make a unique contribution to the diplomatic and political struggle that defined the second phase of Algeria's war of independence.

It was Mohamed Boumezrag who set in motion the stunning strategy of 1958. The experience of Algerian amateur teams in Moscow and the Middle East in 1957 inspired the FLN leadership in exile to give Boumezrag the task of forming an Algerian "national" team in exile. Boumezrag immediately accepted. He set about meeting with Algerians in the French First and Second divisions. Avignon manager Mokhtar Arribi agreed to serve as manager/coach. The consensus among the Algerians seemed to be that if AS Monaco centerback Moustapha Zitouni agreed to join the FLN team, then so would the others.[41] A member of the French national team, Zitouni walked away from his dream of playing in the 1958 World Cup finals. "When I was contacted by the FLN in France, and by Boumezrag, I thought that I was being mobilized for my country's revolution," he recalled. "I felt it my duty to be part of the Algerian football team."[42] Three of Zitouni's teammates also left for Tunis: Abdelaziz Ben Tifour (who played for France in the 1954 World Cup), goalkeeper Abderrahmane Boubekeur, and defender Kaddour Bekhloufi. The rest of the group included winger Said Brahimi and midfielder Abdelhamid Bouchouk, both of Toulouse; forward

Amar Rouaï of Angers; and the St. Etienne striker Rachid Mekhloufi. Like Zitouni, Mekhloufi "abandoned the French national team preparing for the World Cup Finals in Sweden and instantly became an Algerian national symbol."[43] By late summer several more France-based Algerians joined the original group in Tunis.

Between April 1958 and December 1961 the FLN team toured North Africa, the Middle East, Eastern Europe, and East Asia. Facing teams of varying quality, the Algerians won sixty-five matches, drew thirteen, and lost thirteen.[44] Putting patriotism ahead of financial self-interest, these professional athletes left behind remunerative careers for a modest monthly salary of 50,000 francs (811 euros in 2008 value).

The anticolonial press and French sport newspapers and magazines pointed out the entertaining style of play of the Algerians. Thanks to Boumezrag's careful management and the professionals' abundant skills, the FLN side developed an approach based on finesse and fluid passing. This approach stood in stark contrast to the mechanistic "scientific football" of Eastern Europeans and the basic, direct game of East Asian sides. "In China and in Vietnam I learned something too," Mekhloufi added: "their joy in playing, their simplicity in approach, qualities we tend to neglect."[45] Tactically, the FLN usually adopted a 4-2-4 system, an attacking, physically taxing approach popularized by the championship Brazilian team led by Pelé. Zitouni anchored the defense. Mekhloufi spearheaded the attack. Boumezrag and Arribi gave players plenty of freedom of movement and tactical flexibility. As a result, the FLN team crafted a spectacular and effective style of play. Years later, Mekhloufi would reflect on the glaring difference between the romantic playing style of the FLN team and the risk-averting defensive approaches that became the norm in the 1970s: "In our day we tried to put on a show, to honor offensive play," he said. "The difference with elite players today is enormous. On the pitch, we had fun. Young guys [today] seem to be performing work routines."[46]

When the Algerians toured Jordan and Iraq, the imagined nation of Algeria was made real for ninety minutes by a team "in national uniform, standing under a national flag, singing an anthem and competing as a recognized nation."[47] The FLN team's anthem, "Kassaman" (We Pledge), written in prison by Moufdi Zakaria in the 1950s, would become independent Algeria's national anthem. The team won all ten matches played in Jordan and Iraq.

At the same time, the FLN, like the antiapartheid South African Soccer Federation (discussed in the next section), applied for membership in FIFA, claiming to represent the majority of the population in Algeria. But the world body, controlled at the time by mostly conservative Western Europeans, angrily rejected the application. So the FLN looked behind the Iron Curtain for support. While the Soviet bloc withheld weapons and other aid from the provisional government of the FLN due to cold war geopolitics, Eastern European countries diplomatically welcomed the Algerian footballers.[48] Because of FIFA's threats of severe penalties for any member nation that played against the FLN team, Western European nations refused to host the Algerians, thereby diluting the political impact of the FLN team.

But the Algerians persevered. In 1959, they organized two major international tours. The first took them to Eastern Europe, where the Algerians played a grueling schedule of twenty-one matches in ten weeks (from May to July) in Bulgaria, Romania, Hungary, Poland, the USSR, and Czechoslovakia. After suffering a first defeat in Plovdiv, Bulgaria, Boumezrag imposed a night curfew to instill tighter discipline in the squad. The highlights of the tour included a pair of 2-2 draws: with Petroleum Bucharest in front of ninety thousand people at the National Stadium, and with a strong Leningrad representative side at the Zenit Stadium. Overall, the Algerians won twelve, drew four, and lost five matches in Eastern Europe.

The second tour of 1959 took the FLN team to China and North Vietnam. In about six weeks in October and November, the team won eight matches, drew one, and lost two. This kind of sport diplomacy lubricated the already positive international relations between the Algerian government in exile, China, and North Vietnam. The FLN delegation was received at the highest level in both Beijing and Hanoi. They met with Zhou Enlai, and with Ho Chi Minh and General Vo Nguyen Giap (of Diem Bien Phu fame). After an easy win (5–0) over the Vietnamese, the Algerians listened to Prime Minister Phan Van Dong's powerful endorsement of sport's role in the quest for national liberation: "We defeated France and you have defeated us, therefore . . . you will defeat France."[49]

Even though the FLN team declined rapidly after this tour, it stood out in the late 1950s (a critical point in the war of independence) as an example of how a political movement, an organizer, and talented athletes came together to form part of a new country and state in the making—Algeria—and had a considerable impact on their country's fight for independence.

The Algerian team could never again match this level of political and national significance. As a result of the tectonic shifts in French policy towards

Algeria under Charles de Gaulle's Fifth Republic,[50] the FLN team essentially stopped playing. Between January 1960 and December 1961 the team embarked on only one overseas tour, to Eastern Europe in the spring of 1961. This final eight-week series saw the Algerians, fielding several new players recruited in France, win nine matches, draw six, and lose six in Yugoslavia, Bulgaria, Romania, Hungary, and Czechoslovakia. As the final round of political negotiations between France and the FLN got underway in Evian, the team bided its time on Tunisian beaches. Some players coached Tunisian clubs, while others resumed training in order to prepare themselves for a return to elite football in France. In the wake of the failed OAS coup in Paris, the FLN team traveled to Libya in December 1961 for its final matches. On June 6, 1962, the FLN "national" team was disbanded, and on July 5 Algerian gained its independence.

Many of the older team members stayed on to assist with growth and development of football in Algeria. Others, like Mekhloufi, returned to play in France. Mekhloufi later offered a sober assessment of his experience with political football. "For four years I became an absent, anonymous footballer, playing matches that were too easy and following a training regime that was not tough enough. I had lost the taste for effort, the necessary fight."[51] Even so, he and Zitouni starred in Algeria's stunning 2–0 victory over West Germany in Algiers on January 1, 1964, another symbol of the footballers' contributions to Algerian nationhood.[52]

South Africa: Football against Apartheid

While Algerian football seemed poised for a future full of possibilities, apartheid South Africa was under attack, at home and abroad.[53] The rise of apartheid in 1948 had opened another front in the struggle against racism and segregation in colonial sport. South Africa was suspended from FIFA in 1961 and remained isolated from world football until 1992 (except for a one-year reprieve in 1963).

Football in South Africa was the leviathan of black sport,[54] while rugby and cricket were the main sports of the white minority. The term "black" refers to people classified as African, Coloured, and Indian (or Asian) by apartheid legislation. The popularity of football in black communities arose from conditions present throughout colonial Africa: economic expansion, massive urban growth, and access to Western education, albeit for a small minority. The antiapartheid South African Soccer Federation (SASF) was founded in Durban in September 1951. Building on the work of the

Transvaal and Natal Inter-Race Soccer Boards, established in 1935 and 1946, respectively, the SASF became the largest football body in the country. It brought together more than forty-six thousand African, Coloured, and Indian players in opposition to apartheid in sport. The emergence of the racially mixed SASF resembled the formation of the antiapartheid Congress Alliance, formed in 1955.

During the 1950s, black athletes, organizers, and nationalists fought a long struggle with the entrenched white interests reinforced by apartheid. The first were organized in the SASF, while the second were represented by the South African Football Association (SAFA). Internationally, the Federation fought a bitter struggle for recognition within FIFA.[55] Led by George Singh, a progressive Indian lawyer from Durban, in June 1954 the group applied for FIFA membership. It claimed to be the legitimate representative of South Africa, with more than three-quarters of its registered players. In November 1954, the Federation rejected the whites' condescending offer of affiliate membership without voting rights. Then, in May 1955, the Federation scored a significant victory when FIFA's Emergency Committee concluded that the white association "does not comprise and control all the clubs and the players in South Africa and therefore it has not the standing of a real national association that can govern and develop football in accordance with provision of article 3 of the Statutes of FIFA." However, FIFA did not accept the Federation's membership application because it did not include whites.

The struggle over the right to represent South Africa in world football was far from over. The first international delegation to visit South Africa for the purpose of addressing apartheid-related disputes was a FIFA commission of inquiry. In January 1956, the Lotsy commission confirmed earlier findings that SAFA represented a minority group and did not properly constitute a national association. However, FIFA agreed with SAFA that segregated football was a South African "tradition and custom." The world body recommended further negotiations in an attempt to defuse the situation.

Meanwhile, in March 1956, the white association deleted the offending racially exclusionary clause from its constitution. In an attempt to create confusion while remaining indifferent to apartheid, SAFA in 1957 renamed itself the Football Association of Southern Africa (FASA), essentially to create the perception of substantive change while maintaining the status quo. In response to this subterfuge, the SASF reiterated its demands for complete racial integration. Pretoria fought back by denying passports to the SASF delegates traveling to the Lisbon FIFA Congress in June 1956. While no sanctions were imposed in Lisbon, the whites were back on the defensive at the FIFA Congress in Stockholm in 1958. Again, the world body advised that SASF and FASA find a compromise.

While this was a setback for the SASF, it allowed the antiapartheid organization to address internal tensions. Some black members were reluctant to desegregate. Notably, the South African Indian Football Association, for example, excluded non-Indians from its competitions well into the late 1950s. Forming a small minority vis-à-vis Coloureds and Africans, some Indian officials feared that opening their football competitions to athletes of all races would weaken a proud tradition of ethnic football established decades earlier. And in Cape Town, the Cape District Football Association, a Coloured organization founded in 1929, explicitly barred Muslims from joining its ranks. As the SASF began to grapple with these thorny issues, Dennis Brutus and a group of weightlifters initiated the formation of the South African Sports Association (SASA) in October 1958. Football provided SASA with most of its membership, roughly fifty thousand of the organization's seventy thousand members. Supported by the ANC and prominent white liberals, including author Alan Paton, the SASA "promoted nonracial sport and lobbied international sports federations to withdraw recognition of whites-only South African affiliates."[56]

Cooperation between SASA and the SASF injected new life into the antiapartheid struggle at FIFA. An example of this relationship was a well-organized campaign that forced the cancellation of a football match in Cape Town in 1959 between a local white team and Portuguesa Santista, a professional Brazilian club en route to Mozambique. The Brazilian club had reportedly agreed to drop several black players and field an all-white side against the South Africans. SASA caught wind of this acceptance of racism and immediately fired off an official protest to the Brazilian consul in Cape Town. The consul, apparently after communicating with Brazilian president Juscelino Kubitschek, prohibited Portuguesa Santista from playing the game—the first official protest against apartheid by the Brazilian government.

Soon the SASF abandoned its attempts to join FIFA and focused its attention instead on isolating white South Africa. This shift in strategy led to two major victories. In August 1960, the FIFA Congress in Rome adopted an antiracism resolution and also demanded that FASA end apartheid in football within twelve months or face expulsion from FIFA. At a separate meeting in Rome, the Confédération africaine de football (described in chapter 4) expelled South Africa. Then came the FIFA suspension of September 1961, which dealt a major blow to the apartheid regime. It was the first time that a major international organization had sanctioned Pretoria. This raised awareness of the injustices of apartheid among sports fans around the world and instilled hope among South African liberation movements at a time of brutal government repression.

Meanwhile, inside South Africa, something remarkable was taking place: a racially integrated and semiprofessional South African Soccer League was underway. Fans of Avalon Athletic, Durban Aces, Cape Ramblers, Orlando Pirates, Moroka Swallows, and other clubs became political actors by virtue of their presence at the grounds. Attendance at SASL matches meant taking a stance against state-enforced racial discrimination and segregation. And people voted with their feet. SASL matches regularly drew crowds of ten thousand people, while marquee matches attracted up to forty thousand crammed into ramshackle grounds. Boosted by the extensive daily coverage of the black popular press, the SASL became immensely popular. It survived for five seasons. Eventually Pretoria came to view this integrated league as an intolerable affront to apartheid orthodoxy. The government conspired with white football organizations and municipal authorities to deny racially mixed teams access to playing facilities, and thus forced the SASL to shut down in 1966. The lesson of the incompatibility of sport and apartheid was not lost on South Africans and the world community, as demonstrated by the sport boycott in the 1970s and 1980s.

In South Africa, as in Nigeria and Algeria, football after 1940 reverberated with political implications, locally and internationally. In all three cases, urban growth, access to Western education, mass media coverage, and passion for the game among cosmopolitan African nationalists strengthened the connections between football and mass politics. Football helped to propel and legitimize the activities of anticolonial movements. As the next chapter shows, independent African states drew on this powerful experience to forge a sense of nationhood, foster African unity, and democratize the world's game.

CHAPTER FOUR

Nationhood, Pan-Africanism, and Football after Independence

THE FORMATION in 1957 of the Confédération africaine de football (CAF) opened a new era in African soccer. The new Republic of Ghana won its independence that same year and together with CAF stimulated an optimistic pan-African vision and bolstered Ghanaian nationalism. With more than thirty African countries in FIFA by the mid-1960s, European domination of world football was challenged by African claims to equal citizenship. African nations democratized the game, at least the male version, and transformed it into a more fully global cultural form by campaigning against apartheid and mobilizing to increase the number of African participants in the World Cup finals.

By 1960, football was certainly deeply rooted in urban African popular culture, and as such, it provided a rare form of "national culture" in post-colonial Africa. The new nations staged matches as part of their independence celebrations and asserted their full membership in the international community by joining FIFA. In 1957, Stanley Matthews, one of England's all-time greats, visited Ghana, the first sub-Saharan country to gain independence, and played a series of matches in Accra and Kumasi. The Ghanaians honored Matthews in a "traditional" ceremony that conferred upon him the title of *Soccerhene* (from the Asante monarch's title of *asantehene*).[1] The following year Ghana became a member of FIFA. Togo's independence festivities in 1960 featured a game between its national team and Nigeria at a packed Municipal Stadium in Lomé. The crowd reportedly chanted *Ablode, ablode* (Freedom) throughout the match, which ended in a 1–1 draw.[2] A few months later, having already joined FIFA, Nigeria marked its independence by hosting the Nkrumah Gold Cup at the new thirty-thousand-seat National Stadium in the Surulere neighborhood of Lagos. Ghana spoiled the party by defeating Nigeria 3–0 in the final. Similar football festivals contests were held throughout decolonizing Africa, including Uganda, Kenya, and Zambia.

The game exposed newly enfranchised Africans to the gravitational pull of the idea of nation. As historian Eric Hobsbawm remarks, "The imagined community of millions seems more real as a team of eleven named people. The individual, even one who cheers, becomes a symbol of his nation himself."[3] For overwhelmingly male African political elites, football projected a vigorously masculine understanding of the nation. The game also carried a relatively small price tag for "territorializing identity" and providing ballast to the idea of the nation-state as a legitimate institution with a monopoly on power.[4]

As part of this political project, many African governments built new football stadiums in their capitals. In a departure from the few colonial-era stadiums, smaller facilities usually with one grandstand and an overall capacity of less than twenty thousand spectators, independent Africa's stadiums were large modern cathedrals of sport: symbols of modernity and national pride. These stadiums quickly became almost sacred ground for the creation and performance of national identities. The ritualized experience of spectatorship, together with "the transcendent characteristics of large gatherings and the emotive capacity of sport,"[5] engendered a commonality among fans, practitioners, officials, and the media that extended beyond the stadiums to include radio listeners and, in later years, television viewers as well. African stadiums became extremely valuable public spaces where, as geographer Chris Gaffney put it, "potentially disaggregated social actors [found] a common symbol, language, history, and purpose."[6]

Government ownership of stadiums directly linked them to nation-building projects, as evidenced by their names. A partial list includes Independence Stadium in Accra and Lusaka; 5 July Stadium in Algiers and 28 September Stadium in Conakry (dates of independence); Stadium of the Revolution in Brazzaville; and simply National Stadium in Lagos, Nairobi, and Dar es Salaam. In Abidjan and Addis Ababa, the national stadiums were named after sitting heads of state, Félix Houphouët-Boigny and Haile Selassie, respectively. Stadiums also advanced the conceptualization and production of nations through the menacing presence of police officers and soldiers. "The smooth functioning of stadiums," Gaffney points out, "requires a militarized control of space and the uninterrupted functioning of state power."[7] So armed forces at football grounds in Africa served more than crowd-control purposes; they conveyed an image of government power and authority just as African nation-states began the arduous work of achieving stability, security, and legitimacy in a postcolonial world.

In the euphoric moment of independence, the mass media captured the excitement of stadium crowds and built enthusiasm for football outside of the main cities. The African press had a long tradition of sports coverage, but with the rapid expansion of literacy and the proliferation of popular dailies, newspapers such as the *Daily Graphic* in Ghana built circulation by selling both the nationalist agenda and football coverage.[8] The broadcasts of matches on radio stations—which were almost exclusively government-owned—intensified the excitement and loyalty of fans. Building on the late-colonial development of radio broadcasting, the newly independent nations invested heavily in radio and to a lesser extent television, and thus reached out to the huge audiences who were not literate. Radio coverage nourished the idea of football as a form of national culture in independent Africa.[9]

Yet newspapers were by no means the province of elites. Since early colonial times, publications had had a wide urban readership. Organs of ethnic associations, political organizations, and religious institutions, as well as the standard press, regularly included coverage of sport, as, for example, Zik's pioneering populist paper, the *West African Pilot,* did in Nigeria. African football fans developed a keen taste for the sporting press; a single copy of a daily paper could reach many readers as well as those who could have stories read to them if they could not read easily themselves. It helped, as has been noted elsewhere, that "the sports section is the most creative and emotive part of the newspaper, rich in imagery and metaphors and employing colorful language."[10] The weekly cycles of news and football were closely intertwined. Monday newspapers sold well partly thanks to the weekend match reports, results, and league standings. Tuesday through Friday, coverage of upcoming matches sustained or manufactured fans' seemingly endless appetite for sport. Coverage of international matches and tournaments tended to equate positive results on the pitch with the success of the nation-state. African newspapers and broadcasters, like their counterparts around the world, could also evoke national identity and pride by denigrating the "Other," be that a neighboring country, controversial referee, or foreign coach.

The media also knew how to appeal to local fans in culturally savvy ways. Football writers and announcers often deployed literary styles, narratives, and imagery that originated in the oral literatures of agrarian societies, thus connecting citizens in town and countryside across the nation. According to the Kenyan scholar Solomon Waliaula, the Swahili commentator Mohammed Juma Njuguna continues to do what writers and announcers did at that time, as he alternates between close accounts of the game and connecting with his audience. Njuguna does this by sending greetings to friends and listeners and using proverbs, riddles, and animal metaphors to describe the action on the pitch. He entertains the audience by dramatically changing his rhythm and tone, drawing on Swahili songs, inventing names for players, cracking jokes, and generally putting himself at the center of attention. Thus, a football commentator resembles the traditional folkteller, who "tries to frighten, delight, worry, and put the listeners on tenterhooks . . . and skillfully builds on the passages which move them the most, expanding the exciting parts and condensing or transforming the ones where the attention of the audience lags."[11]

National Leagues in the Making of Nations: Regional Patterns

Supported by the construction of national stadiums and mass media coverage, the establishment of sovereign football associations and countrywide leagues contributed to the production of nationhood and the centralization of power in independent Africa. "National contests unite towns, cities, and regions; international competitions focus everyone's identity as national citizens. Everyone who resides within the national borders—the countryside as well as the cities—shares the event."[12] In North Africa, the development of national leagues coincided with independence. As was so often the case in African football, Egypt was the first to launch a league championship in 1948–49, won by the Cairo club Al Ahly. In 1956, Tunisia and Morocco gained independence from France, and predictably, in that same year national championships replaced the city-based leagues.[13] Sudan also secured its independence, from Britain, in 1956, but civil war and the existence of the popular Sudan Cup, a playoff tournament pitting regional state champions against each other, ended up delaying the formation of a season-long league until 1963. Having aggressively linked football to the nationalist struggle, the Algerians created a national league in late 1962 soon after independence. Given the bloody eight-year war of liberation against France, it seemed fitting that the first Algerian champion in 1963 was the Union Sportive Militaire, the army team based in Algiers.[14]

National championships in North Africa shared a gaping competitive imbalance that also characterized competitions elsewhere on the continent. Two or three big urban clubs, typically based in the capital city, dominated the local soccerscape. In Egypt, for example, Al Ahly and Zamalek from Cairo won all but one of the league championships between 1949 and 1962. Similarly, Wydad Casablanca and Forces Armées Royales (Royal Armed Forces, FAR) Rabat claimed ten out of the first fourteen Moroccan titles. In Sudan, Al Hilal and Al Merreikh of Omdurman alternated as national champions for decades. Slightly greater competitive balance characterized other Maghrebi leagues. In Tunisia, the hegemony of Espérance Sportive, Club Africain, and Stade Tunisien, all based in Tunis, was only occasionally broken by Club Sportif Sfaxien and Railways Sports of Sfax, Étoile Sportive du Sahel of Sousse, and other clubs as well. In Algeria, the 1960s belonged to clubs from the capital, but in the early 1970s this began to change with the rise of Jeunesse Sportive Kabylie (JSK) of Tizi Ouzou, which won ten league titles between 1973 and 1990, while teams from Oran, Constantine, and Sétif also managed to win championships.

South of the Sahara, Ghana led the way in using football to build a nation.[15] President Kwame Nkrumah fervently believed in the game's capacity to transcend ethnic, linguistic, regional, religious, and generational barriers. He appointed Ohene Djan as "sports czar" in 1958. Djan took over the Ghana Amateur Football Association and organized an eight-team national league. The league's main centers were located in coastal Accra, Sekondi, and Cape Coast, and in the old Asante capital of Kumasi in the interior. From the league's inception, archrivals Hearts of Oak and Asante Kotoko were dominant. In an attempt to show off the government's power and authority, Nkrumah and Djan formed Real Republikans in 1961, a superclub modeled after the legendary Real Madrid side that had won five consecutive European Cups in 1956–60.

This team was intended to represent the best of Ghanaian football at the domestic and international level. Real Republikans obtained the right to poach the two best players from each club in the Ghanaian league, a move that enabled the all-star club to quickly challenge the Hearts/Kotoko domination. Real Republikans won the 1962–63 title, but not without controversy. In the middle of the season, Djan ordered the transfer of Liberian forward Modibo Toe from Sekondi Hasaacas to Real Republikans, even justifying the move as being "in the national interest." Despite Djan's meddling and Nkrumah's growing authoritarianism, Real Republikans never again ascended to the top of the league. In 1966, after a coup ousted Nkrumah and his Convention People's Party, the superclub was disbanded and Hearts and Kotoko quickly reasserted their dominance.

In Nigeria no national league existed until the early 1970s. The federal government's takeover of the Nigerian Football Association in 1962 had augured well for the prospects of establishing a countrywide league. But, as historian Wiebe Boer has shown, the country's enormous size, organizational problems, political and ethnic conflict, corruption, and a vastly inadequate infrastructure undermined Nigeria's chances for success in football as in politics.[16] A military coup in 1966 and the catastrophic Biafran War (1967–70) further delayed the start of a national league until 1972.[17] A few years later, Nigeria finally asserted itself as a dominant power in African football.

Led by Ivory Coast, the former French colonies in West Africa also formed national leagues in the 1960s. President Félix Houphouët-Boigny, leader of the RDA party, had been a key player in forcing the dismantling of French West Africa and securing Ivoirian independence. His government, backed by booming cocoa revenues, had the political will and financial wherewithal to support the creation of a national league at independence in 1960. Clubs from the capital, Abidjan, put their stamp on the domestic game, winning an astounding forty-six out of forty-nine league titles between 1960 and 2008. Abidjan's ASEC Mimosas and Africa Sports have led the way with twenty-two and sixteen titles, respectively. Following in the footsteps of Ivory Coast, Senegal kicked off its national competition in 1964; Guinea, Togo, and Upper Volta (today Burkina Faso) followed suit in 1965; Mali and Niger in 1966; Dahomey (today Benin) in 1969; and Mauritania in 1976.

In contrast to the North African territories, the laborious creation of national sports federations in francophone West Africa had to be done from scratch because until the late 1950s these territories were incorporated within the larger French West Africa colonial federation and thus lacked the "national" infrastructures and sense of identity that had been developed in colonies such as Tunisia or Algeria. The case of Senegal is revealing of the complex relationship between domestic football and nationhood in French Africa.[18] As we saw in chapter 3, the game was so popular locally that in 1946 the first French West Africa Cup was in fact an entirely Senegalese affair. By 1955, an interdistrict championship in Senegal was under way, with teams from Dakar, Saint-Louis, Gorée, Thiès, and Rufique. For unknown reasons, clubs from the southern regions of Casamance and Kaolack did not participate, so the interdistrict tournament was not fully "national." Thanks to its status as the country's capital and headquarters of the Senegalese Football Federation, Dakar benefited disproportionately from the construction of basic playing facilities and the training of coaches, players, and referees.

This highly centralized approach to football development in Senegal had contradictory effects. For example, under the stewardship of Raoul Diagne— the first African professional footballer in Europe (see chapter 5) and the son of Blaise Diagne, the first black African member elected to the French Chamber of Deputies—Senegal won the football tournament at the 1963 Jeux de l'amitié (Friendship Games) in Dakar. This international triumph aroused tremendous national pride in Senegal, although the overrepresentation of players from Dakar lent a metropolitan bias to the "Senegalese-ness" of the victory. Despite teaching the French a lesson on the pitch, Daour Gaye, a wise interpreter of Senegalese football, describes the trajectory of the sport in his country after independence as one of "long, slow painful decline" in the 1960s, followed by "relative stability" in the 1970s and then a deep crisis in the 1980s that was only partially masked by Senegal's solid performances in international competitions.[19]

A similar pattern unfolded in the former colonies of French Equatorial Africa and in the former Belgian Congo. There, too, nations joined FIFA and then inaugurated countrywide leagues. In the Republic of Congo, CARA and Étoile du Congo of Brazzaville stamped their authority on the league, claiming sixteen of twenty-five titles between 1965 and 1989. Other Brazzaville sides, such as Diables Noires and Inter Club, as well as Patronage of Pointe Noire on the coast, also won national championships and had loyal followings. Across the Congo River, in the Democratic Republic of Congo, the colonial inheritance of widespread material poverty and almost complete lack of infrastructure in an economy based on mining exports, together with the country's massive size, made a season-long nationwide competition virtually impossible. Making matters worse, football in DR Congo was held back by the explosive political crisis that began in 1960 with independence, escalated with the Katanga secession and Prime Minister Patrice Lumumba's murder, and ended in 1965 with the Belgian- and American-aided installation of dictator Joseph Mobutu. Yet in spite of terrible turmoil, the country's regional champions organized a postseason tournament for the first Congolese championship in 1963. This format has endured, with Kinshasa and Lubumbashi clubs taking every national title from 1963 through 1982.[20] AS Vita Club and CS Imana (today DC Motema

Pembe) of Kinshasa and Tout Puissant Englebert (today TP Mazembe) of Lubumbashi became the most successful and popular sides in Congo.

The case of Cameroon, with its more complicated colonial past, differed slightly. When Germany lost its African colonies after the First World War, Cameroon was divided into two League of Nations (and later United Nations) mandates, which were administered separately by France and Britain. Francophone East Cameroon established its football association in 1959 and a national championship in 1960—the year of independence. In 1961, East Cameroon (making up two-thirds of the territory) merged with Anglophone West Cameroon to form a federal republic, and in 1962 the Cameroonian Football Federation (FeCaFoot) affiliated with FIFA.[21] Political tensions between the two culturally distinct regions resulted in West and East Cameroon operating separate leagues through the first decade of independence.[22] Clubs from the two leagues faced each other only in the Cameroon Cup. Not until 1972, when Cameroon became a unitary republic, did a national league finally begin play. As in the case of Nigeria, the formation of a domestic league would later lead to the national team's entrance into the pantheon of African football, with memorable performances in the 1982 and 1990 World Cup tournaments.

Metropolitan bias shaped Cameroon's football culture much as it did in other parts of the continent. Clubs like Oryx, Union, Caiman, and Leopards from the port city of Douala, the country's largest city and its economic capital, dominated the league in the 1960s and most of the 1970s. The 1980s ushered in the golden age of Canon and Tonnerre from Yaoundé, the capital city, located in the central province. In the Cameroonian league's first thirty seasons, Douala and Yaoundé teams each won fourteen championships.

The end of British rule in the early 1960s brought several East African nations into FIFA and sparked the launch of national leagues in the region. In Kenya in April 1963, just a few months before independence, ten clubs competed in the inaugural season of the Kenya National Football League.[23] Coached by a white government sports officer, the Nakuru All-Stars from the Rift Valley edged out seven teams from the capital, Nairobi, and two sides from coastal Mombasa. Quickly, however, the familiar pattern of capital city hegemony asserted itself. Between 1965 and 1993, Nairobi's AFC Leopards and Gor Mahia won all but five championships. As we shall see below, these Nairobi clubs drew most of their supporters from rural areas and boasted dramatically different ethnic identifications. Another successful Nairobi club, without ethnic affiliation, was Kenya Breweries (today

Tusker FC), which was owned by East African Breweries and won three league titles in the 1970s. However, commercial forces, as chapter 6 will show, had a limited impact on the game in Africa until the 1980s.

In Tanzania, Dar es Salaam clubs monopolized the league from its inception in 1965. Through 1983, Simba (formerly Sunderland) won nine titles and Young Africans ("Yanga") seven. These two clubs were so powerful that they managed to operate almost autonomously despite growing encroachment in sport by the socialist government of Julius Nyerere and TANU.[24] In Uganda, the national league officially began in 1968, six years after the country's independence from Britain and nine years after it became a member of FIFA. There, too, teams from Kampala, the capital, have won thirty-five of forty titles through 2009.

The story to the south was dramatically different. There, racism, inequality, and segregation in white minority–ruled South Africa, Southwest Africa (Namibia), Southern Rhodesia (Zimbabwe), Angola, and Mozambique precluded the building of new and inclusive nations and developing the nation-football nexus. In southern Africa, only Zambia escaped this predicament. Following the demise of the short-lived Central African Federation (1953–63), which brought together Nyasaland (Malawi), Northern Rhodesia, and Southern Rhodesia, in 1964 the Zambian people achieved majority rule and independence. That year, an African-controlled Zambian Football Association under the leadership of Tom Mtine replaced the former, white-run, Northern Rhodesian Football Association. It joined FIFA, and by 1966 the new body had gained full control over the Zambian National Football League.[25] Mufulira Wanderers and Kabwe Warriors were the clubs to beat in the 1960s and early 1970s; then Nkana Red Devils burst onto the scene in the 1980s along with Power Dynamos. In an exception to the overall trend, clubs from Lusaka, the capital, rarely challenged sides from the towns of the Copperbelt. In fact, aside from Lusaka City Council's 1964 championship, only Green Buffaloes, the Zambian Army team, which made Independence Stadium in Lusaka its home, challenged the mine teams. Between 1973 and 1981, a period of strong central government under Kenneth Kaunda, a keen football supporter, the Green Buffaloes were national champions six times.

Ethnicity and Nationhood

While much was achieved in the first decade of independence, African football struggled to produce a lasting sense of nationhood. This was partly due to the game's paradoxical ability to unite participants while simultaneously dividing them. This inherent quality of team sport complicated nationalist agendas in postcolonial nations that had been artificially created by European powers and continued to be marked by cultural pluralism, class and ethnic divisions, and other social cleavages. Much to the chagrin of African governments, football fostered multiple identities. The national championships allowed citizens to choose to belong to the "imagined community" of the nation, without neglecting individual, local, ethnic, religious, and other identities.[26]

In Ghana, for instance, Asante Kotoko of Kumasi has long been identified with Asante nationalism. Asantehene Prempeh II was named Life Patron of the club in 1935. and the porcupine—the symbol of the Asante army—was adopted as the team mascot. "The name Kotoko evoked not just Asante pride, but a populist form of militant Asante nationalism, which, like the porcupine's quills, is thought to be an inexhaustible source of strength."[27] In the early 1960s, Kotoko's anti-Nkrumah reputation brought it into open conflict with presidential favorites Real Republikans as well as rivals Hearts of Oak, the Accra club, which had alleged ties to the ruling Convention People's Party.[28]

Ethnic chauvinism elsewhere on the continent militated against the construction of nationhood through football. In Algeria, a majority Arab country, JSK Tizi Ouzou, rooted in the Kabylie region, came to represent Berber identities. As a result of JSK's extraordinary success in the 1970s, its fans started to refer to the initials JSK as an acronym for *Je suis Kabylie* (I am a Kabylie). The FLN government did not look kindly upon ethnic nationalist sentiments among the Berber minority, especially at a time of growing political turmoil. It forced the club to change its name to the insipid and de-ethnicized Jeunesse Électronique Tizi Ouzou for most of the 1980s.

In ethnically and culturally diverse Cameroon, parochial affinities continue to shape the game to this day. For example, PWD Bamenda, from the Anglophone west, "carries the hopes and aspirations of most Anglophones," while Canon Yaoundé is linked to people of Beti background, Union Douala with Bamileke migrants, and so on.[29] In Nairobi, Kenya, AFC Leopards is closely tied to Abaluhya people, for whom the leopard is a mythical totem symbolizing martial masculinity and grace under pressure, while Gor Mahia is a club associated with Luo people (the name refers to an invincible Luo diviner and warrior of legendary repute).[30] The

Highlanders of Bulawayo in southern Zimbabwe acquired a reputation as the "national team" of the Ndebele minority in a predominantly Shona-speaking country.[31]

That competitive football in Africa was bound up with ethnicity is hardly surprising, and certainly not a symptom of atavistic tribalism. This was very much a local expression of a global phenomenon. In Britain, for example, the "Old Firm"—the city rivalry between Glasgow Rangers and Celtic—is widely regarded as "one of the most bitter and enduring feuds in world football," as it plays out in political, social, and religious divisions between Protestant Scots and Irish Catholic communities.[32] In Spain, Athletic Bilbao and Barcelona were and still are intimately associated with Basque and Catalan nationalism, respectively.[33] Some club identities can be more "imagined" than real, as in the intriguing case of Ajax Amsterdam's alleged "Jewishness."[34] Football can also express translocal identities, as in the case of the Al Wihdat football club, based in the eponymous Palestinian refugee camp in Jordan.[35] Football is so intimately connected to multiple identities in Africa that "the meaning of sport for national identity and unity, for international visibility and prestige, and for pan-African cohesion and leverage weaves in and out of the history of independent Africa."[36] This latter process was brought into stark relief by the founding of CAF and its most prestigious competition: the African Nations Cup.

The Rise of CAF and African Competitions

Immediately after gaining their freedom, African states, as a way of asserting their status as independent nation states and their membership in the global community, joined the United Nations and a series of transnational institutions, including FIFA, the International Olympic Committee, and other global sports organizations.[37] In 1950, power in world football was firmly in the hands of Europeans, who accounted for 46 percent of FIFA's membership, although South Americans were quite influential and boasted the oldest regional association, formed in 1916. Today, there are six continental confederations that influence the politics of world football.

Egypt, Sudan, Ethiopia, and South Africa—then the only African members of FIFA—discussed a plan for an African confederation at the 1954 FIFA Congress in Bern, Switzerland. At this meeting, FIFA officially recognized Africa as one of its six geographical zones, which automatically carried the right to a permanent seat on FIFA's executive committee. An African confederation seemed both appropriate and necessary to address inequity in world football and to develop the game in Africa on administrative and sporting levels. "It was not an easy task to get this recognition," remembered Abdel Halim Mohammed, the Sudanese representative in attendance. "Argentina kicked against the seats given Africa and Asia arguing that the standard of football in these continents was not good enough," he said.[38] But after "a long and heated argument," the motion passed 24–17. The FIFA Congress elected Egyptian Abdelaziz Abdallah Salem to the executive committee. Africa's challenge to European domination of the sport was underway. By the early 1960s thirty-two of sixty-nine of FIFA members were African, a new reality that reflected the coming of independence and one that would radically transform football's world order.

Crucially, African assertiveness in football's corridors of power coincided with the growth of anticolonial protest movements and decolonization. This frightened FIFA's European members and some Latin American ones too. In fact, according to sociologists John Sugden and Alan Tomlinson, it was "mounting awareness [among Europeans] . . . of the merging threat to their privileged position within world football's power structures" that led to the founding on June 15, 1954, of the Union des associations européennes de football (UEFA) in Switzerland.[39] At the same time, African members of FIFA decided to reconvene at the 1956 FIFA Congress in Lisbon to finalize the creation of a pan-African football body. There, delegates from Egypt, Sudan, and South Africa (represented by a white man) made progress toward that goal. Yidnecatchew Tessema of Ethiopia was unable to travel to Lisbon, but was kept informed about the latest developments. The group agreed to meet in Khartoum in 1957 to formalize the establishment of the Confédération africaine de football (Confederation of African Football, or CAF) and to host the inaugural African Nations Cup.

CAF was a trailblazing pan-Africanist institution in the era of independence. It was one of FIFA's six continental confederations, essentially the ruling body of the game in Africa. Its formation preceded by six years the founding of the Organization of African Unity, the predecessor of today's African Union. The founding meeting of CAF was held on February 8, 1957, at the Grand Hotel in Khartoum, attended by representatives from Sudan, Egypt, Ethiopia, and South Africa.[40] Fred Fell, a white South African, was invited because the South African Football Association (SAFA) had rejoined FIFA in 1952. SAFA, which excluded blacks, initially approved sending a team to Khartoum, although minutes of its meetings and press reports at the time indicated that participation in the tournament "was not received in the Union with much enthusiasm in the first place."[41] As we will see below, African nations would soon come to rally around the issue of apartheid and spearhead a campaign to exclude South Africa from international football.

CAF's main aims were to organize international tournaments and to advance the interests of Africa in world football. FIFA executive member Abdelaziz Abdallah Salem became CAF's first president; he headed an executive committee comprising Tessema, Halim Mohamed, and Fred Fell. Assembled delegates in Khartoum formally approved rules and by-laws, set up several special committees, and created a General Assembly that would meet every two years. French, English, and Arabic were made the official languages of CAF. Over time, three linguistic and regional blocs emerged: Arabophone in the north, Francophone in the west and center, and Anglophone in the east and south.

These regional/cultural blocs demonstrated how internal tensions complicated the quest for African unity and solidarity in the game. Political, ideological, and cultural factors spiked these antagonisms. CAF's decision to locate its headquarters in Cairo rather than Addis Ababa is a case in point. Cold War divisions placed Egypt and Ethiopia in opposite camps. Egyptian president Gamal Abdel Nasser had just acquired heroic status among Third World nationalist movements as a result of the resolution of the 1956 Suez Crisis involving Britain, France, and Israel, while Ethiopian emperor Haile Selassie was a staunch anticommunist who was deeply antagonistic to pan-Arab socialism—or any other kind of socialism. Beyond these ideological and diplomatic issues, perceptions about Arab attitudes of racial and cultural superiority toward darker-skinned Africans caused considerable bitterness. Yidnecatchew Tessema argued vociferously in favor of putting CAF offices in Addis Ababa, but the Egyptians ultimately convinced the Sudanese to accept that the organization's headquarters should be placed in the country of its president, who, conveniently, was Egyptian. So Cairo became the administrative capital of African football.

In sporting terms, CAF's most important task was to organize the African Nations Cup. This tournament aimed to supersede the various regional competitions that had been established earlier, which no longer satisfied fans, players, or administrators. The first Nations Cup took place at the time of CAF's official launch in Khartoum in 1957, three years before the inaugural European Nations Cup.

Before the Khartoum competition kicked off, however, the hot-button political issue of apartheid in South Africa took center stage. CAF demanded that South Africa field a racially integrated team, but SAFA, after consulting with the authorities in Pretoria, refused to do so. The minutes of the meeting were later destroyed in a fire, and there are conflicting accounts about what happened next. CAF officials stated that they promptly excluded South Africa. Fred Fell and SAFA had a different story: they claimed they withdrew the team due to the Suez Crisis and an impending tour to Europe. In any event, South Africa's absence meant that only three teams participated in the inaugural tournament. The South African issue certainly did not disappear, however, and in fact the struggle against apartheid in football would become a powerful bond that united African nations for more than two decades.

In the 1957 African Nations Cup semifinals, with South Africa out of the tournament, Ethiopia received a bye into the final. Egypt nipped hosts Sudan 2–1 and dispatched Ethiopia 4–0 in the final thanks to an astonishing four-goal performance by striker Mohammed Diab El-Attar "Ad Diba." (Nine years later in Addis Ababa, Ad Diba refereed the Nations Cup final won by DR Congo over Ghana.) In 1959, Egypt hosted the tournament and won again. The Pharaohs defeated both Sudan and Ethiopia in a round-robin tournament in front of forty thousand ecstatic Egyptian fans at Cairo's Al Ahly National Stadium. A sporting triumph in an electric atmosphere delighted Nasser. Such victories, of course, help to explain why in independent Africa, as in most of the world, outside of military alliances, it was "in elite sport that modern states came to see the greatest political benefits to participation in international culture."[42]

The independence of sixteen African nations in 1960 increased the size of both CAF and the African Nations Cup. The 1962 tournament introduced qualifying rounds. Uganda and Tunisia advanced, and their teams traveled to Addis Ababa to meet defending champions Egypt and the host nation. Taking advantage of Addis's high altitude (twenty-five hundred meters, or eight thousand feet) and the home crowd in Haile Selassie Stadium, Ethiopia stunned Egypt in a dramatic final. Deploying an attacking 4-2-4 formation popularized by 1958 World Cup champions Brazil, the home side twice tied the game and then went on to win 4–2 in extra time. After the match, Ethiopian captain Luciano Vassalo, an Italo-Eritrean whose brother was also on the team, received the silver trophy from the hands of the emperor himself. It was a powerfully symbolic moment: the "Father of the Nation" sanctioning Ethiopia's greatest sporting victory in the capital's stadium bearing his name.

Since that fateful day, the Addis Ababa stadium, as historian Solomon Getahun has written, has often been transformed into a site for the festive celebration of Ethiopian nationalism; male and female fans belt out "patriotic songs, waving the Ethiopian tri-colors," and proudly displaying their "Ethiopian cultural dress" even as regime changes have promoted dramatic ideological shifts.[43] While the 1962 African Nations Cup was, without question, the most memorable event in Ethiopian football history, it also revealed the contradictory effects of sportive nationalism. Ethiopia's winning team included nine Eritrean players (out of eleven), and so its success bolstered both Ethiopian and Eritrean nationalism. This outcome was especially important given the attempted coup of 1960 and Ethiopia's annexation of Eritrea later in 1962, a decision that begat an independence struggle that found its way into football stadiums.[44]

Not surprisingly, however, it was the great champion of pan-Africanism, Kwame Nkrumah, rather than Haile Selasssie and Nasser, who effectively built national consciousness, patriotic pride, and pan-Africanist sentiments through football. As we saw earlier, Nkrumah empowered his "sports czar," Ohene Djan, to lead the Ghana FA and run the domestic league and Real Republikans. With the game in Ghana on a relatively sound footing, Nkrumah then hosted the six-team 1963 Nations Cup to enhance his position and that of his country as continental leaders. Like the Olympic Games, which struggled to resolve the tension of promoting international solidarity through nationalist rivalries, Nkrumah tried to capitalize on football's potential for pan-African unity while at the same time "mobilizing the youth of the nation around a common identity . . . creating pride and self-respect . . . [and] engendering patriotic sentiments amongst the Ghanaian people."[45] The nickname of Ghana's national side, the Black Stars, was inspired by Marcus Garvey's shipping line of the 1920s, which aimed to take black Americans "back home" to Africa and build transatlantic connections among peoples of African descent.

The carefully orchestrated success of the Black Stars on the pitch boosted Nkrumah's political project. That Ghana played every match in the capital city of Accra, where his Convention People's Party had strong support, surely was not a coincidence, since Kumasi, in the interior, was the heartland of Asante nationalism and opposition to Nkrumah's regime. Ghana advanced to the final against Sudan, winners of the Kumasi group. With more than forty thousand spectators packing the Accra stadium, the Black Stars won decisively (3–0), sparking epic celebrations across the country.

Proving that this victory was neither a fluke nor a gift, the Black Stars successfully defended their title two years later in Tunisia. Nkrumah's financial and political muscle was crucial in helping Ghana win back-to-back African championships. But football victories could not prolong the life of his increasingly authoritarian and corrupt rule. Less than ten weeks after the Tunis victory, a coup ousted Nkrumah. Clearly, there were limits to what football nationalism could do to sustain an unpopular regime.

Four months after the overthrow of Nkrumah, the Supreme Council for Sport in Africa organized the Jeux africains (All-Africa Games) in Brazzaville. Established in Bamako, Mali, and headquartered in Yaoundé, Cameroon, this new pan-African organization had no affiliation to CAF. It sought to foster pan-African unity through sport by capitalizing on the International Olympic Committee's support for the establishment of regional Olympic-style festivals around the world. The All-Africa Games are still in existence, although the Association of National Olympic Committees of Africa, based in Abuja, Nigeria, recently took over responsibility from the moribund Supreme Council. The most popular event at the 1965 Games, in which more than three thousand athletes participated, was the football tournament, which featured nineteen national teams. A huge crowd squeezed into the Brazzaville stadium to watch the final between the host nation and Mali. After a goalless draw, Congo-Brazzaville was declared the winner for having taken five more corner kicks than Mali. Despite this surprising ending, FIFA president Sir Stanley Rous wrote in his official report on the All-Africa Games football competition that "the standard of play was good and the team shewed that they had been well coached in modern methods." Together with IOC president Avery Brundage and other foreign dignitaries in attendance, Rous believed that "progress has been made rapidly to develop sport in Africa and . . . through sport Africa is being united."[46] Large crowds and media coverage of the football tournament at the All-Africa Games temporarily enhanced the status of the Supreme Council for Sport in Africa, an organization that has effectively ceased to exist today, but provided valuable assistance to the antiapartheid sport boycott.

In 1964, CAF launched the African Cup of Champion Clubs, or simply Champions Cup. Modeled after its European counterpart, this African knockout competition pitted domestic league champions against each other in two matches played on a home-and-away basis. Oryx Douala defeated Stade Malien 2–1 in the first final, to the delight of many Cameroonians who, regardless of local loyalties, celebrated it like a "national" victory. Overall, in the first two decades or so of the Champions Cup, clubs from sub-Saharan African nations won fourteen of the first sixteen editions of the Champions Cup, led by Hafia Conakry and Canon Yaoundé (Cameroon) with three each. Only in the 1980s did North African clubs come to dominate the competition, for reasons that will be explored in chapter six. Between 1981 and 2008, Egyptian, Tunisian, Algerian, and Moroccan clubs won twenty-two of twenty-six African club titles.[47] The immense popularity of the Champions Cup inspired CAF to create the Cup Winners' Cup in 1975 and the CAF Cup in 1992; these were merged into the new Confederation Cup in 2004.

CAF competitions afforded African political leaders yet another opportunity to publicly link themselves to major clubs and use enthusiasm for football to build popular support. In 1966, for example, thousands of Ivoirians beamed with pride as Stade Abidjan won the second Champions Cup final against Real Bamako. Houphouët-Boigny, who was present at the match, was quick to cast Stade's victory as a symbol of the political stability and economic prosperity of a country that embraced free-market, capitalist economic policies. It was common for African dictators to bestow gifts of cars, houses, and cash on championship teams, as Mobutu did in the case of Tout Puissant Englebert of Lubumbashi in the late 1960s and Sekou Touré with Hafia Conakry in the 1970s.[48]

In the meantime, the Nations Cup continued to grow. Between 1968 and 1992 the number of nations in the qualifying rounds increased from fifteen to thirty-one, reflecting the expansion in the number of independent African nations. The final tournament expanded from eight teams in 1968 to twelve in 1992, and then to sixteen in 1996. Growth stiffened competition. Between 1968 and 1976, four different nations lifted the Nations Cup for the first time: Congo/Zaire (1968 and 1974), Sudan (1970), Republic of Congo (1972), and Morocco (1976). Nigeria's title in 1980 and Cameroon's in 1984 and 1988 finally heralded the rise of two continental giants. As the Nations Cup settled into a now familiar pattern of West Africa versus North Africa, its commercial potential remained largely untapped. While the rest of the football world in the 1980s veered into the high seas of commercialization, Yidnecatchew Tessema, the Ethiopian boss of CAF, was reluctant to follow in the same path.

Tessema's life story captures the history of Ethiopian football and the trajectory of pan-Africanism in the game. His story also raises questions about the impact of individual moral codes and modus operandi on African football. Tessema's father rose from very humble origins to become a well-known musician and jack-of-all-trades who worked at the palaces of emperors Menelik II and Iyassu. Born in 1921 in the small rural town of Jimma, Yidnecatchew Tessema attended St. George's, an elite Anglican school in Addis Ababa, where he developed a lifelong passion for football. In 1935, he was a founder of Arada Football Club, later renamed St. George's FC, Ethiopia's most accomplished club. After working as a translator in the public works department during the Italian occupation, Tessema cofounded the Ethiopian Sports Office in 1943 and the Ethiopian Football Association in 1948. He continued to play as a striker for St. George's and went on to captain the Ethiopian national team from 1948 to 1954.

A fluent speaker of French, English, Italian, as well as Amharic and other Ethiopian languages, Tessema passionately articulated Africa's case for equality and full citizenship in FIFA, while skillfully brokering tensions within CAF among Anglophones, Francophones, and Arabophones and across the Cold War divide.[49] A founder of CAF, Tessema also served as its general secretary for fifteen years and then as its president from 1972 until his death in 1987. His speech at the CAF General Assembly in Cairo on February 27, 1974, synthesized his most cherished political beliefs: "I'm issuing a call to our general assembly that it affirm that Africa is one and indivisible: that we work towards the unity of Africa together . . . that we condemn superstition, tribalism, all forms of discrimination within our football and in all domains of life." Tessema then emphasized "that we do not accept within our organization the division of Africa into Francophone, Anglophone, and Arabophone. Arabs from North Africa and Zulus from South Africa, we are all authentic Africans. Those who try to divide us by way of football are not our friends."[50] In 1970, Tessema joined the Supreme Council for Sport in Africa, and in 1971 he became a member of the International Olympic Committee. At FIFA he spent much of his career, including a spell on the executive committee in 1966–72, actively supporting antiapartheid initiatives and tirelessly working to expand the number of guaranteed places for African national teams in the World Cup finals. Tessema's unwavering commitment to sport's ideals of merit, fairness, and equality reflected his embrace of the British game ethic learned at St. George and informed his skepticism about the influence of professionalism and commercialism on the game in Africa.

Football and Human Rights: The Fight against Apartheid

The acrimonious struggle to oust racist South Africa from FIFA demonstrated Africa's pivotal role in democratizing football and making it more truly global. The country's exclusion from the African Nations Cup was proof that Cold War rivalries, racial animosities, and cultural differences took a backseat to pan-African unity and solidarity in support of freedom, justice, and equality in South Africa. The apartheid regime's inflexibility strengthened the resolve of Africans and their allies. In a June 1960 letter to the renamed Football Association of Southern Africa (FASA), the minister of the interior, Johannes de Klerk (father of future state president F. W. de Klerk), wrote that

> [while] there is no legislation in this country prohibiting inter-racial competition . . . [and] whilst the Government is sympathetic towards and prepared to help non-White sporting associations which accord with the Government's policy of separate development it will not support non-White sporting activities designed to force the country to abandon the South Africa custom that Whites and non-Whites should organize their activities, in whatever field, separately. . . . Competitions between White and non-White teams within the Republic, will . . . not be tolerated, nor will passport facilities be extended to teams composed of Whites and non-Whites, or teams from abroad, so composed, be allowed to enter the Republic. There is no objection, though, that a non-White team from South Africa competes against a White team abroad.[51]

Matters came to a head three months later at FIFA's 1960 Rome Congress. As we saw in the previous chapter, CAF and its allies in the Soviet bloc and in Asia called for the antiapartheid South African Soccer Federation to be admitted to FIFA and demanded the expulsion of the white FASA. A stalemate ensued that was resolved thanks to the adoption with overwhelming support of an antidiscriminatory clause later integrated into FIFA's constitution. This resolution stated that "a National Association must be open to all who practice football in that country whether amateur, 'non-amateur' or professional, and without any racial, religious or political discrimination."[52] FASA was given one year to change its racist ways. When it failed to do so, in September 1961 the FIFA Executive Committee

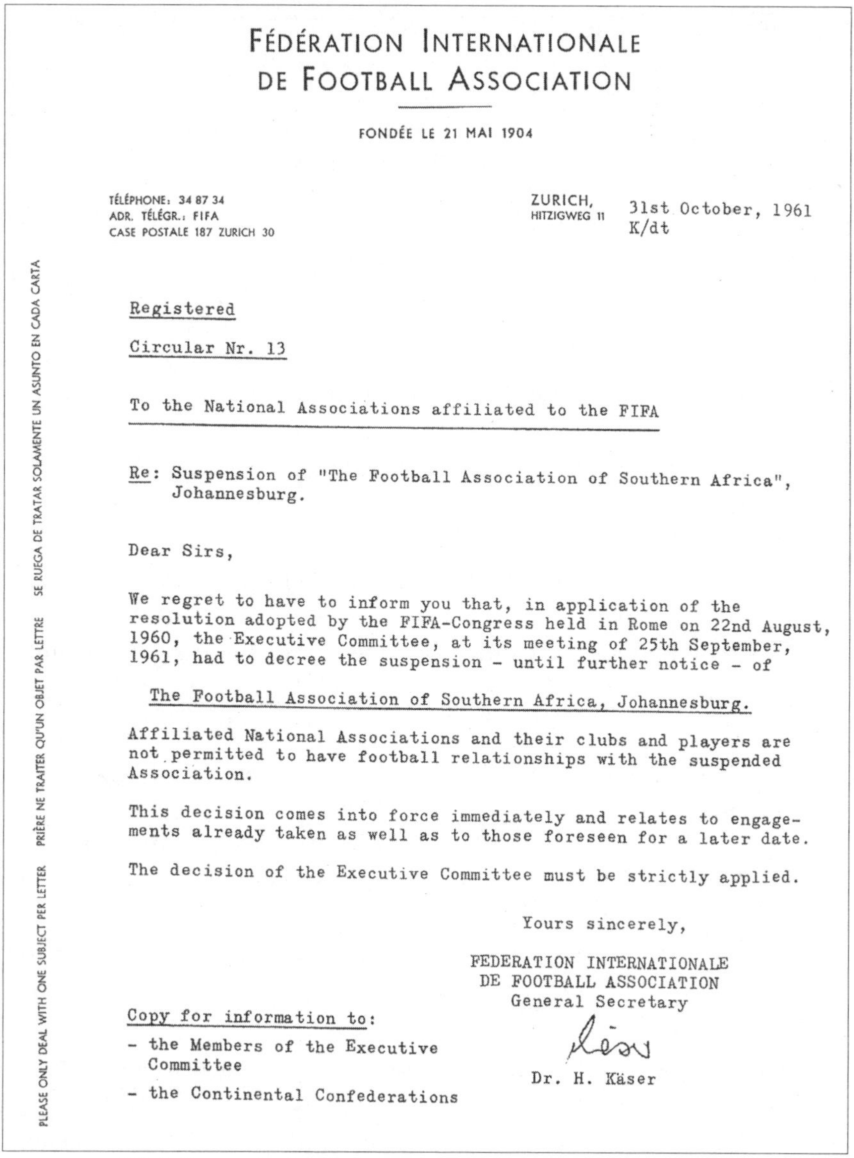

FÉDÉRATION INTERNATIONALE
DE FOOTBALL ASSOCIATION

FONDÉE LE 21 MAI 1904

TÉLÉPHONE: 34 87 34
ADR. TÉLÉGR.: FIFA
CASE POSTALE 187 ZURICH 30

ZURICH,
HITZIGWEG 11

31st October, 1961
K/dt

Registered

Circular Nr. 13

To the National Associations affiliated to the FIFA

Re: Suspension of "The Football Association of Southern Africa", Johannesburg.

Dear Sirs,

We regret to have to inform you that, in application of the resolution adopted by the FIFA-Congress held in Rome on 22nd August, 1960, the Executive Committee, at its meeting of 25th September, 1961, had to decree the suspension - until further notice - of

The Football Association of Southern Africa, Johannesburg.

Affiliated National Associations and their clubs and players are not permitted to have football relationships with the suspended Association.

This decision comes into force immediately and relates to engagements already taken as well as to those foreseen for a later date.

The decision of the Executive Committee must be strictly applied.

Yours sincerely,

FEDERATION INTERNATIONALE
DE FOOTBALL ASSOCIATION
General Secretary

Dr. H. Käser

Copy for information to:

- the Members of the Executive Committee
- the Continental Confederations

PLEASE ONLY DEAL WITH ONE SUBJECT PER LETTER PRIÈRE NE TRAITER QU'UN OBJET PAR LETTRE SE RUEGA DE TRATAR SOLAMENTE UN ASUNTO EN CADA CARTA

FIGURE 3 FIFA Suspends South Africa, October 31, 1961 *(FIFA Archives)*

suspended South Africa. But this by no means indicated strong FIFA support for the campaign against football apartheid.

The election of Sir Stanley Rous as FIFA president in 1961 forced CAF to flex its pan-Africanist muscles once again. An English schoolmaster with three decades of experience as Secretary of the English Football Association and a genuine sympathy for white South Africans, Rous personified the conservative and Eurocentric nature of FIFA. In January 1963, he and Joseph Maguire of the United States made a two-week-long official visit to South Africa to evaluate whether any changes had taken place to justify lifting sanctions. During their stay, Rous and Maguire steadfastly refused to meet with representatives of antiapartheid football organizations, branding them "political agitators." The FIFA dignitaries spent much of their time in the company of white football officials and their supporters. In the end, Rous's official report to FIFA came to the astonishing conclusion that "there is no wilful discrimination on the part of FASA in respect of any organization in South Africa."[53] On the basis of the Rous Report, FIFA's Executive Committee in 1963 reinstated South Africa.

CAF officials were outraged. The organization issued a statement lambasting FIFA and Rous. At a hastily convened special congress in Cairo that year, the pan-African body unequivocally rejected any contact with South Africa and warned FIFA that it would call for South Africa's expulsion unless "its obnoxious apartheid policy [was] *totally* eliminated" at the 1964 Congress in Tokyo. Working with the South African Soccer Federation in Durban and the South African Non-racial Olympic Committee in London, CAF aggressively campaigned for South Africa's expulsion. It received assistance from Asian countries and from the Soviet Union, which was described by a sports official from Guinea as "the first country in which equality of people, regardless of their skin color, social position and religion was proclaimed."[54] At the 1964 FIFA Congress, the CAF motion was downgraded to a suspension, but it passed by a large margin. African unity had won the day. Acknowledging Africa's growing political power, FIFA awarded the African representatives another seat on its executive committee and a vice presidency.

The events at FIFA bolstered the sport boycott against South Africa by demonstrating that racial discrimination violated the constitutions of international sport's governing bodies. In the wake of football sanctions, the boycott movement went on to gain wide support in the court of world public opinion and eventually among sport administrators too. South Africa was not allowed to participate in the 1964 and 1968 Olympics and was then expelled from the Olympic movement in 1970. Sporting isolation stood as a forceful global indictment of apartheid, and the country would not return to world football and the Olympics until 1992.

As the largest voting bloc in FIFA, an organization in which each member nation had one vote, Africans were in a particularly strong position to influence the fight against apartheid in southern Africa. In 1972, for instance, Tessema used the upcoming FIFA presidential election in 1974 to counter Rous's ongoing attempts to get South Africa reinstated. Tessema threatened to deny João Havelange, the Brazilian businessman and sports administrator, the African votes needed to win the election against Rous if he did not withdraw Brazil from the 1973 South African Games, the "apartheid Olympics" organized by Pretoria and sponsored by Shell Oil.[55] Havelange immediately realized that he needed to back the antiapartheid movement to defeat Rous, and so he withdrew Brazil from the Games. By backing the sport boycott against South Africa (and also Rhodesia/Zimbabwe), Havelange secured Africa's votes and won the FIFA presidency in 1974.

African Football Arrives on the World Stage

Africa had arrived as a major power broker in world football, but the struggle for equality and citizenship continued. CAF turned its attention to prying open the doors to the World Cup finals. By 1964 no African nation had played in the tournament since Egypt in 1934. The 1962 World Cup in Chile featured eight European teams and four South American ones. Africa, Asia, North America, and the Caribbean had no guaranteed places in the finals, so the only way they could qualify was via playoffs against European or South American teams. When a terrific Morocco side lost a qualification playoff to Spain in 1962, Africans' patience ran out. With Ohene Djan spearheading the campaign, CAF threatened to boycott the 1966 World Cup in England unless FIFA guaranteed Africa a place in the finals. "'We are not asking this as beggars,' Djan declared. 'We are putting forward just and moderate demands, taking account of the huge progress made in our football.'"[56] FIFA responded by fining CAF five thousand Swiss francs. Tessema had this to say about the governing body's decision: "FIFA has adopted a relentless attitude against the African Associations and its decisions resemble methods of intimidation and repression designed to discourage any further impulses of a similar nature. In our opinion, the African National Associations . . . really deserved a gesture of respect rather than a fine."[57]

An African boycott of the World Cup ensued. The legitimacy of African claims and North Korea's top eight finish in 1966, an excellent result by a nation at the margins of world football, eventually influenced FIFA's decision to finally guarantee Africa a berth in the 1970 World Cup finals in Mexico. As Africa's first World Cup representative in nearly four decades,

Morocco performed respectably. In the next World Cup in West Germany in 1974, Africa was poorly represented by Zaire, which lost all three matches by a combined score of 14–0. As a result of this debacle, Mobutu shunned the side upon its return to Kinshasa and withdrew his financial and political support from the national team. In 1978 in Argentina, Africa's fortune took a positive turn as Tunisia became the first continental side to win a match in the World Cup finals, a decisive 3–1 victory over Mexico. The Eagles of Carthage then narrowly lost to Poland and held world champion West Germany to a scoreless draw.

Outside of the World Cup, African teams performed well in Olympic football tournaments (amateur-only until 1984), where they had three guaranteed places (out of sixteen) beginning in 1964. Some of the most notable African accomplishments in the Olympics include Ghana reaching the 1964 quarterfinals, Nigeria drawing with Brazil in 1968, and Zambia sensationally beating Italy 4–0 in 1988. By the late 1970s and early 1980s, African national teams had proven that they could hold their own on the world's stage. The Olympic triumphs of Nigeria in 1996 (against Argentina) and Cameroon (against Spain) in 2000 would confirm this new reality.

FIFA's new youth competitions further sharpened Africa's image as an emerging power in world football. These tournaments were a key component of Havelange's ambitious plan to develop the game in the poorer countries. This strategy paid political dividends for Havelange and generated financial profits for FIFA and its major corporate partners, Adidas and Coca-Cola.[58] Nigeria won the maiden Under-16 World Championship in China in 1985. This achievement was soon followed by a remarkable three consecutive world titles for sub-Saharan Africa: Ghana won in 1991 (when it became an Under-17 tournament), Nigeria in 1993, and Ghana again in 1995. In 2007, Nigeria claimed its third world crown at this level. Ghana and Nigeria also did well in the Under-20 World Youth Championships, the former finishing second in 1993 and 2001 and the latter matching this result in 1989 and 2005. In addition, Nigeria, Mali, and Egypt have each earned third-place honors on one occasion.

Africa's improving performances on the pitch and growing political influence in FIFA produced a steady increase in the continent's guaranteed berths in the World Cup finals. The 1982 World Cup in Spain was a watershed event. Africa fielded two teams in the twenty-four-team tournament, and Algeria and Cameroon performed admirably. Algeria defeated West Germany to give Africa its first-ever World Cup victory against European opposition, and only a highly controversial result between Germany and Austria kept Algeria from advancing to the second round of the competition.[59] Cameroon surprised the world with an inebriating combination of skill, physicality, and *savoir-faire*. "The Indomitable Lions," as the Cameroonian national team is known, did not lose a match in a tough first-round group with eventual champion Italy and third-place finisher Poland, but were eliminated on goal difference. The African contingent at the World Cup finals grew to three in 1994, the year Nigeria came within a few minutes of defeating Italy in the round of sixteen. When the World Cup expanded to thirty-two finalists in 1998, Africa had five teams: Cameroon, Morocco, Nigeria, South Africa, and Tunisia. In 2010 in South Africa, the first World Cup on African soil will feature six African teams, including the host nation. But growing international respectability for African soccer had an unfortunate side effect: it greatly accelerated player migration overseas, a process analyzed in the next chapter.

CHAPTER FIVE

Football Migration to Europe since the 1930s

MICHAEL ESSIEN and Albert Youmba were talented African players who had decidedly different fortunes in the European football world. Essien, whose father was an elite footballer, grew up in Accra, Ghana. At the age of thirteen he joined Liberty Professionals, and in 1999 he came to the attention of European talent scouts when he proved decisive in Ghana's third-place finish at the Under-17 World Championships in New Zealand. The following year, SC Bastia in France signed him on a free transfer and three years later sold him to Olympique Lyonnais for 8 million euros (approximately 7 million dollars). Essien and Lyon won two consecutive league championships. In 2005, the French club made a huge profit by trading Essien to Chelsea for about 26 million pounds (47 million dollars). At the time this was the largest fee ever paid for an African footballer, and it made Essien a millionaire.

The Cameroonian Albert Youmba had a dramatically different experience.[1] In the 1990s, he met a shady European agent in Cameroon who lured him to Le Havre Football Club, the oldest club in France, with promises of great riches. In pursuit of his dream of playing in Europe, Youmba dropped out of high school against the wishes of his parents and left for France on a tourist visa. After a short trial period, Le Havre did not sign him. Youmba's "agent" disappeared. Penniless, homeless, and without a work permit, the young Cameroonian chose the life of an illegal immigrant rather than face potential embarrassment and shame if he returned home. "When you come back from Europe," said Samuel Ojong, a Cameroonian who recently played in France and Switzerland, "people ask you what you have been up to. You can't stay here for two years and come back empty-handed. Even if you don't have a contract anymore, it's better to stay."[2] Essien and Youmba represent the dramatically different experiences of African footballers overseas.[3]

Football migration was part of a larger movement of labor from Africa to Europe and beyond that has intensified greatly in recent years. From 1981 to 2001, the number of African athletes, musicians, artists, white-collar professionals, entrepreneurs, and manual laborers "living in the European Union increased by about 70 percent, from 700,000 to 1.2 million."[4] According to recent data, more than thirty million Africans live abroad (including other African countries) and send remittances home that contribute crucial income to households and represent on average about 5 percent of national gross domestic product.[5] In the context of Africa's five-hundred-year history of global migration, forced and voluntary, the overseas movement of athletes is not surprising. But the intensity and volume of recent migration are unprecedented, and represent a significant brain drain and muscle drain.

Footballers, like African workers in general, have been part of the increasing flow of permanent migrants, which has "grown in volume and significance since 1945 and most particularly since the mid-1980s."[6] The movement of African players to Europe, and more recently to Asia and North America, has grown exponentially over the last two decades. For example, between 1996 and 2000 the number of Africans playing in European professional leagues increased from about 350 to more than 1,000. Today, there are dozens of Africans playing in leagues in the Persian Gulf states, India, China, Vietnam, and South Korea, and more than 30 competing in Major League Soccer in the United States.

Like many white-collar workers in the African diaspora of the last half century, male footballers were (and are) mainly economic migrants.[7] This muscle drain is a legacy of colonial capitalism, under which imperial powers used colonies as reliable sources of crops and minerals for processing in Europe. Football was no different. "The clearest example . . . during the colonial period," as sport scholar Paul Darby has pointed out, "was the mining and export of indigenous football talent for consumption on the European football market."[8]

The athletes were not passive victims. Migration also represented their effort to find opportunities, economic, educational, and professional, a motivation "common to both colonial and post-colonial African dispersions" in and out of sport.[9] Africans typically migrated to the former metropoles or to countries where they would find themselves more comfortable in terms of culture and language.[10] Most important, African athletes have played a key role in giving the culture of football a global character. Their experiences illustrate some intriguing ways in which Africa has participated in "a transnational revolution that is reshaping societies and politics around the globe."[11]

Football Migration from the Colonial Period to the 1970s

Before decolonization in the 1960s, France received the bulk of African football migrants. From the dawn of professional football in France in the 1930s, francophone Africans found their way to metropolitan clubs. Most migrants were from the French territories of Morocco, Algeria, and Tunisia in North Africa, also known as the Maghreb, where the game had acquired widespread popularity by 1920.[12] In Algiers, for example, there were more registered football players (13,494) in the late 1930s than in Paris (13,448). Both European settlers (*colons*) and indigenous Algerians enjoyed the game, mostly in segregated clubs and leagues, as was common throughout colonial Africa. Several colons played for French clubs and the national team.[13] The special status of Algeria as an overseas department of France, rather than a colony or a protectorate, further encouraged the movement of Algerian workers, students, and footballers to the colonial metropole. There were at least eighteen Algerians in the French first division in 1937.[14]

But the first African professional footballer in France came from Senegal, not the Maghreb. His name was Raoul Diagne, and he was the son of Blaise Diagne (1872–1934), a colonial civil servant who became the first black African member elected to the French Chamber of Deputies in 1914, and a French mother. As a Western-educated young man, Blaise Diagne had hoped to take advantage of France's assimilation policy, but he was repeatedly overlooked for promotion and became a proponent of African civil rights. The French punished him by posting him to faraway places such as Madagascar and French Guyana.

Blaise's son Raoul was born in French Guyana in 1910. He honed his football skills at elite schools in Senegal before immigrating to France at the age of twenty to pursue his studies. A big central defender (six feet, one inch and 175 pounds), Diagne joined the amateur Racing Club de France in 1930. Two years later, Diagne moved up to the professional ranks with Racing Club de Paris, winning the league and cup "Double" in 1936, as well as the French Cup in 1939 and 1940. Most famously, Raoul earned the distinction of becoming the first black player to play for the French national team. He won eighteen caps (denoting the number of international appearances for one's country) and played against Italy and Belgium in the 1938 World Cup, which France hosted.

By including blacks in Les Bleus, France sought to demonstrate the success of its "civilizing mission" and the allegedly positive aspects of colonial rule. The acceptance of black footballers as representatives of the French nation has also been explained in terms of the game's lower status than rugby and cycling, both of which excluded blacks, perhaps they were perceived as more deeply symbolic of French identity and character. During the war Diagne moved to Toulouse and won four consecutive regional titles before closing his professional career with Annecy in 1946. He then returned to Dakar as a player/coach for US Gorée and became active in coaching development programs in French West Africa. After Senegal's independence from France, Diagne was named the first head coach of the national team. In 1963 in Dakar, he coached Senegal to its first victory against France (2–0) in the Jeux de l'amitié (Friendship Games) and thus became a national hero.[15] Diagne oscillated between his Senegalese roots and French cultural identity for much of his life. He returned to France to work as a technical consultant for various football programs into the 1970s.[16]

Unlike Diagne and other early African sporting migrants, Larbi Ben Barek moved to Marseilles in 1938 exclusively to play professional football.[17] Born in Casablanca in 1917, Ben Barek came from humble circumstances—his father repaired boats. He learned the game in the streets like most boys. After kicking about with neighborhood teams, Ben Barek joined second-division club Ideal. He did extremely well against elite teams in the North African Cup, and as a result, the Union Sportive Marocaine (USM), a prestigious Moroccan club, recruited the precocious teenager into its ranks. In 1937–38, Ben Barek led USM to both the local championship and the North African Cup. He caught the attention of French scouts in April 1937 in Casablanca with a dazzling performance for Morocco against the France "B" or second team. Olympique Marseilles quickly signed him to a contract that paid him fifty times more than he earned as a member of the cleaning staff at the gas company.[18] The young Moroccan forward, now known as the "Black Pearl," scored twice in his French league debut.

After less than four months, Ben Barek earned a call up to the French national team. In his first match for France in Naples, on December 4, 1938, Ben Barek played alongside Diagne. Les Bleus lost 0–1 to world champions

Italy. In January 1939, the Moroccan star scored a hat trick (three goals) against Poland in Paris. With war fast approaching, Ben Barek went back to Morocco, where between 1940 and 1945 he and his USM club won four league titles and a North African Cup. At twenty-nine, Ben Barek resumed his pro career in 1946 in Paris, this time with Stade Français. Two years later, Atletico Madrid paid the astonishing sum of 1 million pesetas (thirty-seven thousand dollars) to acquire his services—then the highest transfer fee in the history of Spanish football. It turned out to be a very good investment. Ben Barek's goals guided Atletico to consecutive Spanish league titles in 1949–50 and 1950–51. Two years later, he went back to Marseilles. His stellar career ended with a loss to Nice in the 1954 French Cup final. Ben Barek eventually returned to Morocco, where he was involved with local clubs and the national team. But sadly, he died in 1992 in Casablanca "alone and in squalor."[19] French audiences had mixed, even contradictory reactions to black players. In the case of national team members Diagne and Ben Barek, Laurent Dubois argues that French fans probably saw these Africans as French, though probably not as equals.[20]

The postwar years ushered in a new era of African football migration to Europe.[21] Between 1945 and 1962, 117 North Africans played professionally in France.[22] Nearly two-thirds of the players from the Maghreb were Algerians, almost a third were Moroccans, and a small minority came from Tunisia. Following in the footsteps of Diagne and Ben Barek, twelve North Africans represented France internationally in the 1950s, including Abdelaziz Ben Tifour, Rachid Mekhloufi, and Moustapha Zitouni, all of whom abandoned Les Bleus in favor of the Algerian National Liberation Front's "national team" in 1958 (see chapter 3).

As the stream of migrants grew, the sources of African talent became more numerous and diverse. West Africans played a pivotal role in this process. The scarcity of finances available to many French clubs after the war made players from the French West African federation an extremely attractive source of cheap labor. Also, a new rule prohibiting foreign players in France after 1955 stimulated the migration of colonial subjects, who, as "citizens of empire,"[23] were exempted from the ban to the metropole—a tangible way in which "Greater France" manifested itself. African students in France continued to serve as a reservoir of talent for metropolitan clubs. The lack of professional leagues in Africa also pushed top African players overseas. As a result, the number of sub-Saharan African footballers increased from a handful in 1955 to more than forty by 1960.

Ivory Coast was an especially reliable supplier of talent. The formidable striker Jean Topka of Africa Sports Abidjan joined Montpellier in 1955 at the age of twenty-one; he scored 75 goals in 170 games in his first six seasons (two each with Montpelier, Olympique Alès, and Racing Club Paris). Recurring knee injuries led to a premature retirement and a return to Abidjan, where Topka would coach Africa Sports and then the Ivoirian national team, the Elephants. In 1956, FC Sète signed eighteen-year-old forward Ignace Wognin Otchonou from ASEC Abidjan. In ten seasons with four clubs, the prolific Ivoirian scored 103 goals. Another Abidjan talent was Touré Sekou of Africa Sports. In his fourth season in France, Sekou led the league in scoring in 1962 with twenty-five goals for Montpellier.

Ivory Coast was not the sole West African provider of athletic labor to France. For example, midfielder René Gaulon (originally from Benin but recruited from Sporting RC Dakar) played twelve seasons for Stade Français, Red Star, and Rennes. Oumar "Barrou" Keita and Bassidiki Touré, both from Mali, had long careers (twelve and fifteen seasons, respectively) for various French clubs. Karimou Djibrill from Togo won two league titles and two Cups in eight seasons with AS Monaco. Boubacar Bèye from Senegal had two seasons with AS Monaco in the late 1940s.[24]

Cameroon, like Ivory Coast, was a rich reservoir of low-cost labor for postwar French football. At the time, many players still went to Europe, mainly to study or work, not to become professional athletes. Eugene N'jo Lea, for instance, migrated at the age of twenty and initially played at amateur level while studying for a law degree. That changed in 1954–55 when he signed a professional contract with Saint-Étienne. An athlete with rich and diverse interests and talents, N'jo Lea was fond of jazz, "played the trumpet, loved reading Kafka and managed to receive his PhD in law as well as a league title with St. Etienne."[25] He won the 1956–57 league title with Saint-Étienne, scoring 29 goals in 32 matches. In seven full seasons in France, including two with Olympique Lyonnais, N'jo Lea amassed 93 goals in 182 matches. He also helped to found the French Players' Union in 1961.[26] N'jo Lea's son later played in France, as did José Touré, son of Bakou Touré, French champion in 1980 and 1983 with Nantes and an Olympic champion with France in 1984. In the wake of N'jo Lea's achievements other Cameroonians proved themselves in France, including Yegba Maya "Joseph" (scorer of nearly 150 goals for various teams from 1962 to 1976), Fréderic N'Doumbe Mondo, Samuel Edimo N'Ganga, Emmanuel Koum, Zaccharie Noah (father of tennis champion Yannick Noah and grandfather of professional basketball player Joachim Noah), and Gabriel Abossolo.

The increasing visibility of African players, however, could not mask racial discrimination against them. Racism in France manifested itself in different ways. For example, wage inequities long affected Africans, especially in the first years of their careers. At stadiums across European fans sometimes heaped racial insults on black players, waving bananas and making monkey sounds—a practice that is still far too common today.[27] On the pitch, a culture of "stacking" led to players being disproportionately assigned certain playing positions based on ascribed racial or ethnic characteristics.[28] Black footballers were perceived as fast, agile, and reactive, but lacking in leadership skills, tactical intelligence, and self-control.[29] Much as black players were denied opportunities to play quarterback in American football, stacking in France led to Africans being regularly played in wide positions, or as strikers. In 1937, for example, none of the eighteen, mostly Algerian, Africans who played in France occupied central positions such as goalkeeper, center-half, and inside forward. Data on seventy-five sub-Saharan Africans who competed in the top two divisions in France in the 1950s and 1960s show that forty-nine were strikers (65.3 percent), eighteen were midfielders (24 percent), eight were defenders (10.7 percent), and none were goalkeepers.[30]

While racialized stereotypes about African abilities developed quite early in France, they seem to have appeared later in Britain. "After 1945," football historian Phil Vasili writes, "with the greater number of migrant Black footballers, playing against the backdrop of an increasingly racialized political environment, certain myths emerged as to this 'new' generic type."[31] These myths resembled French and American ones: that Africans and West Indians lacked decision-making ability and were "fast and fancy, but lacking in 'bottle' and unable to perform in the cold." Sociologist John Maguire discovered that in the ninety-two clubs of the English Football League in the mid-1980s the ratio of black goalkeepers, centerbacks, central midfielders, and center-forwards to those occupying noncentral positions was nearly three-to-one, but with white players the ratio was almost one-to-one. Maguire also notes that "whereas blacks make up 7.7 per cent of the total number of players, they make up 4.5 per cent and 10.5 per cent of central and noncentral positions, respectively."[32] Ultimately, stacking harmed generations of black players and European teams; it reproduced racial myths of blacks being "natural" athletes but not intelligent enough to be decision makers, thus precluding many talented individuals from advancing into coaching careers and football administration. Only in 2008, when Blackburn Rovers hired former Manchester United star Paul Ince, did a black manager take the helm of a club in the top flight of English football. "There's an unconscious racism," Viv Anderson, the former England defender, told the *Daily Telegraph* newspaper. "It used to be thought that black players were flair players—that you couldn't be in a position of responsibility. . . . I think there is a preconception now that they can't perform in the boardroom."[33]

Given the challenges of racism and economic inequality, the sporting accomplishments of Africans in France go a long way toward explaining the gradual increase in migration to Europe during the 1970s. François M'Pele (b. 1947) from Brazzaville, Congo, was one of the top strikers in France. He scored 130 goals in 350 first division matches in thirteen seasons for four different teams. M'Pele also married a French (Corsican) woman and acquired dual citizenship. But he chose to represent Congo-Brazzaville in international football, leading his country to its only African Nations Cup title in 1972. After retiring in 1982, M'Pele returned to Brazzaville and opened a French bakery. Another gifted striker of this era was the Ivoirian Laurent Pokou, who made his way from ASEC Abidjan to Rennes in 1973. A crafty dribbler and opportunistic finisher, Pokou arrived having set an African Nations Cup record with fourteen career goals in thirteen matches for Ivory Coast in the 1968 and 1970 tournaments. Unfortunately, a series of knee injuries sharply curtailed his playing time at Rennes and later at Nancy.

If M'Pele and Pokou added to the self-confidence and growing legitimacy of African football, then Salif Keita turned out to be the first African superstar in Europe. Born in 1946 in Bamako, the son of a truck driver, he was plucked from a neighborhood team by the prestigious Real Bamako club. Known by the nickname "Domingo," after a local movie star, Keita made his first division debut at seventeen and was capped soon after. Quick, elegant, and strong, the five-foot, ten-inch Keita asserted himself locally as a prodigious scorer with Stade Malien and Real Bamako, runners-up in the African Champions Cup in 1965 and 1966, respectively. He helped Mali reach the final of the inaugural All-Africa Games in Brazzaville in 1965. Keita's magnificent performances led to a transfer to Saint-Étienne in France in 1967. At Saint-Étienne, Keita joined fellow Africans Rachid Mekhloufi (Algeria) and Frederic N'Doumbé (Cameroon) in a formidable attack.

With Keita, Saint-Étienne won three consecutive league titles (1968–70) and two French Cups (1968, 1970). In 1970, he was named African Player of the Year by the French magazine *France Football*. In 1970–71, Keita scored virtually at will for Saint-Étienne: 42 goals in 38 matches! Olympique Marseilles acquired his services in 1972, the same year that Keita led Mali to second place in the African Cup of Nations (losing the final to M'Pele's Congo-Brazzaville). Keita struggled to adjust to Marseilles's risk-averting tactics and physically aggressive style of play, yet still managed to find the net ten times in eighteen appearances. When Marseilles demanded that he take up French citizenship to make room for another foreign player (only two were allowed), Keita refused. Having amassed 135 goals in 168 matches in France, he was traded for nearly five hundred thousand dollars to Spanish club Valencia in 1973. Keita tallied 23 goals in 74 games over three seasons in Spain, the lower total partly due to his being played out of position on a regular basis. His nomadic journey continued across the border in Portugal with Sporting Lisbon, and finally across the Atlantic for two seasons with the New England Tea Men of the North American Soccer League. Today, Keita is a successful businessman in Bamako and runs the Salif Keita Football Academy (see chapter 6). Keita's outstanding career was built on exceptional scoring abilities and a calm temperament, as well as the achievements of earlier generations of African football migrants.

Postwar Portugal's voracious appetite for African talent resembled France's.[34] The status of Mozambique, Angola, Guinea-Bissau, Cape Verde, and São Tomé and Príncipe as "overseas provinces" of Portugal eased the movement of players out of Africa. Portugal's treatment of its African colonies was similar to France's handling of Algeria and its island colonies in the Caribbean, Indian Ocean, and Pacific. In the 1940s and 1950s, Portuguese clubs regularly toured Mozambique and Angola in the off-season, where they encountered stiff competition from local teams. Metropolitan clubs such as Sporting Lisbon, Benfica, and Porto set up branches in Luanda and Lourenço Marques (now Maputo) to recruit local players and to foster greater interest in and allegiance to Portugal among colonial populations.

While only a few Africans had played in Portugal before the Second World War, more than two dozen arrived in the early 1950s.[35] Probably the pioneer of this new era was FC Porto's eighteen-year-old Miguel Arcanjo, signed from Nova Lisboa (now Huambo) in Angola in 1951. Arcanjo was an educated "son of a colonial civil servant employed in the agricultural division office" and a former seminarian.[36] At first he continued his studies, but by 1953 the defender was a full-time professional. He became a regular starter at Porto and went on to earn nine caps for Portugal. Arcanjo's presence in the heart of the national team's defense had political implications in the sense that it allowed Portugal, like France, to use him as evidence of the so-called positive aspects of colonialism. Arcanjo and other Africans also seemed to legitimize the myth of *lusotropicalism*, the theory that Portugal was unique among colonial powers because its culture naturally produced multicultural societies free of racism and segregation. The gradual Africanization of Portuguese football was symbolized by the inclusion of four Africans in a World Cup qualifier in December 1957, which Portugal lost against Italy in Milan. Sitting out that match was a Mozambican striker named Lucas Sebastião da Fonseca, known as "Matateu," a gifted striker who had scored a goal in Portugal's 3-0 victory over Italy a few months earlier in Lisbon.

Matateu was the first sub-Saharan African to gain widespread notoriety in post-war Europe.[37] Born in Lourenço Marques in 1927 into a working-class family, he was known in Maputo for stellar performances with Primo de Mayo, a local club controlled by Lisbon's CF Os Belenenses. In 1950, a Brazilian scout saw Matateu score for a Lourenço Marques representative side against Benfica, Portugal's glamour club. Impressed with Matateu's scoring instinct, grace under pressure, dynamism, and ability to shoot well with both feet, the scout enthusiastically recommended him to Belenenses. Matateu signed with this Lisbon club in 1951 and endeared himself to fans by scoring twice in his league debut, a dramatic 4–3 victory over city rivals Sporting. In 1953 and 1955, Matateu led the Portuguese league in scoring, with twenty-nine and thirty-two goals, respectively. Between 1952 and 1960 he made twenty-seven international appearances for Portugal, scoring thirteen goals. Injuries and age led to a gradual decline. In 1962, Matateu moved to second-division side Atletico, with whom he would later enjoy a final taste of top-flight football.[38]

Matateu's extraordinary achievements began to soften Portuguese prejudice against black footballers. By the early 1960s there were about thirty Africans playing in Portugal, and more were selected for the national team. This Africanization was made possible because dictator Antonio Salazar granted *assimilado* (assimilated, or "civilized") status to culturally "Europeanized" Africans, such as elite footballers. (In 1961, all colonial subjects were recognized as citizens.) Not all naturalized Africans in Portugal hailed from Lusophone Africa. The unusual case of David Julius, a South African, was particularly interesting. Classified as "Coloured" by the apartheid regime, Julius asserted himself as a top midfielder in the multiracial South African Soccer Federation (see chapter 3). Given the very limited prospects for a black footballer in apartheid South Africa, Julius left for Lourenço Marques in 1956 with the hope of being recruited by a Portuguese club; Sporting Lisbon signed him almost immediately. Julius soon acquired Portuguese citizenship and a new name: Julião. He went on to earn six caps for Portugal. In 1958, Sporting welcomed another mixed-race player from Lourenço Marques: nineteen-year-old Rosario Hilario da Conceiçao ("Hilario"). In thirteen seasons with Sporting, the steady, reliable central defender won three league titles and three cups. Hilario earned forty caps and participated in the 1966 World Cup, which saw Portugal defeat two-time defending champions Brazil and finish a stunning third.

That memorable team featured two black players from Lourenço Marques who raised Portuguese football to unprecedented heights. Recruited through Benfica's feeder team, Desportivo, Mario Coluña (b. 1935) played 715 times for the Lisbon club between 1954 and 1970, winning ten league championships, six national cups, and two European Cup trophies. He scored in both European finals against Barcelona in 1961 and Real Madrid in 1962. Coluña played in two more European finals with Benfica, losses to AC Milan in 1963 and Internazionale in 1965. Capped fifty-eight times (with eight goals), Coluña achieved international recognition as midfield anchor and captain of Portugal's 1966 World Cup team.[39]

But it was Eusebio da Silva Ferreira, known as Eusebio, who captured the imagination of world football. He became the first African player to acquire global fame. Nicknamed the "Black Panther," Eusebio grew up kicking makeshift footballs in the streets of a shantytown on the outskirts of Lourenço Marques. He idolized Coluña, who was seven years older than he. In his teens, Eusebio went for a trial at Benfica's Mozambican club Desportivo, but was rejected because he did not have proper boots. So Eusebio ended up joining Sporting in Lourenço Marques instead. His big break came when he scored twice against Ferroviária de Araraquara from Brazil, which was touring Mozambique. José Carlos Bauer, the Ferroviária coach and a former member of Brazil's World Cup team, recommended Eusebio to Bela Guttmann, the Hungarian coach of Portuguese superclub Benfica. Guttmann was an ardent believer in overseas players and an emigrant himself.

And so in 1961 Benfica signed Eusebio for seventy-five hundred pounds. Fast and strong, he had the rare combination of mobility, long-range shooting ability, and a striker's instinct close to goal that made him "perhaps the archetype of the modern football player."[40] "In 13 seasons with Benfica between 1961 and 1975, Eusebio achieved almost everything the game could offer."[41] His honors included seven league titles, two Portuguese cups, and a European Cup. Eusebio was awarded the prestigious European Footballer of the Year award in 1965—he was the only African so recognized until George Weah in 1995—and was the top scorer, with nine goals, at the 1966 World Cup. He became a national hero in Portugal and was idolized throughout Africa. Eusebio's career numbers were impressive: 317 goals in 301 games for Benfica, and 41 goals in 64 games for the national team—a record yet to be surpassed.

Eusebio was instrumental, together with Pelé, in elevating the status of black players in world football, but the experiences of players like Carlos Alhinho and Fernando Freitas were probably more broadly representative of African migrants in Portugal. Originally from the Cape Verde Islands, Carlos Alhinho signed for Academica de Coimbra in the mid-1960s. He earned a university degree in agrarian engineering, transferred to Sporting Lisbon, and was then called up by the national team. Like many African migrants in Europe, he married a local woman. Alhinho's itinerant career took him to Real Betis in Seville, Spain, and then RWD Molenbeek in Belgium. After a very difficult year in Belgium, he and his family returned to Lisbon, this time to play for Benfica. When his career ended, Alhinho opened a sporting goods store and then coached the Angolan and Cape Verdean national teams.[42] In the late 1960s and early 1970s, Fernando Freitas from Lobito, Angola, played for Porto and Portugal. As in Alhinho's case, football wages rewarded Freitas with a middle-class lifestyle and capital to invest in business ventures after retiring from the game.

Ultimately, just as Portugal's African colonies boosted the country's economic development and helped to bring an end to military dictatorship in 1974, so African labor enriched Portuguese football by providing inexpensive talent and infusing it with greater cultural diversity. As a result of the independence of Angola, Mozambique, Cape Verde, Guinea-Bissau, and São Tomé and Príncipe in 1974–75, "the migration of [African] footballers became more complicated legally but continued at a similar pace and rhythm."[43] By 1984, when Portugal reached the semifinals of the European championships, the top three Portuguese leagues featured 340 foreigners, many of them Lusophone Africans.

The postwar migration of Africans to Europe centered on France and Portugal, but it also reached Britain and Belgium.[44] England had been home to the first black professional footballer in the world: Ghanaian goalkeeper Arthur Wharton at Preston North End in 1886.[45] Several Egyptian student-athletes had followed Wharton in the 1910s and 1920s, including Hassan Hegazi, Tewfik Abdallah, and Mohammed Latif. What Vasili described as the "historic unwillingness of British clubs to consider African players" slowly began to change in the mid-1950s and early 1960s.[46] The first African to sign a professional contract was twenty-seven-year-old Teslim "Thunder" Balogun from Lagos, Nigeria. After touring England with the Nigerian "national" team in 1949 (see chapter 3), Balogun joined Peterborough United of the Midlands League in 1955. His wages were meager, and the club found him a day job as a printer. The powerful six-foot, two-inch forward won the hearts of local fans despite not playing a single first-team match. Traded to Third Division Queen's Park Rangers, he scored in his debut against Watford and added four more in fifteen games in 1956–57. Balogun then spent a season with Holbeach in the Eastern Counties League before returning to Nigeria in 1958 to work as a coach for the Western States Sports Council. He died in 1973, and a stadium in Lagos was recently named after him. In 1960, Tranmere Rovers acquired twenty-one-year-old Elkanah Onyeali. His four goals against Dahomey (now Benin) in 1959 still stand as a single-match record for the Nigerian national team. Like many athletic migrants of this era, Onyeali made education his priority. "My father at home in Nigeria would be very angry with me if he found out I was playing football rather than studying," he once explained to his club after missing a midweek game. In his only English season, Onyeali bagged eight goals in thirteen games, but he then moved to the United States to continue his education. The third Nigerian international to go to England was Francis Feyami, who lasted only three months with Cambridge City in 1961. The same club then signed the Ghanaian John Mensah in 1964. A common thread running through the experiences of all these West African migrants to Britain was that they were temporary migrants and "came primarily to learn a trade or profession, rather than to earn a living from playing football."[47]

Between 1956 and 1961, three black South Africans made it into English football: Steve Mokone, Gerry Francis, and Albert Johanneson. The first to arrive was Mokone in 1956–57. Nicknamed "Kalamazoo" after a popular American hit song, he featured in just four matches (one goal) for Third Division Coventry City, including one against Balogun's Queen's Park Rangers. Mokone's flair and finesse clashed with the dour, direct style of play of the English. "I never did learn to like the British way of playing soccer," Mokone recalled. "It was a kind of 'kick and run' game. For me, soccer was and is an art form in which each individual player can express style and technique."[48] Soon Mokone moved on to Heracles Almelo in the Dutch Third Division. He made an immediate impact: Heracles won promotion into the Second Division, and Mokone became a local hero. He helped to recruit fellow South Africans Darius "Ndaru" Dhlomo and Herbert "Shordex" Zuma from Durban. Both Dhlomo and Zuma remained in the Netherlands at the end of their sporting careers, unwilling to return to the humiliation and indignity of apartheid. Mokone's career continued with brief stints in Britain, Italy, and finally Southern Rhodesia.[49]

The next black South African to go to England was Gerry Francis, a twenty-three-year-old winger classified by apartheid regulations as "Coloured." Signed by Leeds in 1957, Francis took two years to earn the distinction of becoming the first black South African to play in the English First Division. In four seasons he made fifty appearances and scored nine goals. In 1961, Francis moved to York City in the Fourth Division, and he later played at Tonbridge in the Southern League. Although used sparingly at Leeds, Francis paved the way for the arrival, also in 1961, of Albert "Hurry-Hurry" Johanneson, another "Coloured" South African. This fast winger from Germiston, near Johannesburg, broke into the Leeds starting lineup right away. In 1963–64, he led the team in scoring with fifteen goals as Leeds won promotion to the First Division. Between 1964 and 1966, Johanneson scored twenty-four goals in sixty-four games, well above average for a nonstriker. In May 1965, he made history as the first black player to participate in an FA Cup final (Leeds lost to Liverpool 0–1). After that game Johanneson's career entered a steady decline. He played fewer than fifty matches due to a combination of injuries, isolation, and alcohol abuse. After an undistinguished season with York City, in 1970–71, Johanneson retired from football. He died alone and in poverty in a housing project in Leeds at the age of fifty-three.[50] In 1994, Leeds resuscitated its South African connections when it signed striker Phil Masinga and central defender Lucas Radebe, the first South African captain of an elite English club.

The case of South Africans in Britain brings into sharp relief the racial and cultural dynamics that have underpinned the history of football labor migration. It is instructive, for example, to compare the considerable difficulties faced on and off the pitch by African migrants, and black players generally, with the smooth integration of white South Africans into the culture of the British game. White South Africans first came to the attention of the British during tours of South Africa by English and Scottish professional sides in the late 1920s and especially during the Great Depression. In the 1930s, Gordon Hodgson scored 240 goals for Liverpool and played three times for England. At Liverpool Hodgson played with Arthur Riley and several other white South Africans. Charlton Athletic coach Jimmy Seed signed at least thirteen white South Africans after the war.[51] The best known were John Hewie, who played 495 times for Charlton (1949–68) and represented Scotland nineteen times, and Eddie Firmani, who later scored 125 goals for Italian clubs Sampdoria, Inter, and Genoa. The Capetonian's Italian ancestry also allowed Firmani to play three times (scoring twice) for the Italian national team. Several white South Africans also signed with various Scottish clubs.

That many white South Africans either held British citizenship or could easily obtain it allowed them to circumvent the English league's restrictions on foreign players. Moreover, racial and cultural solidarity soldered bonds of friendship among whites. Jimmy Seed, for instance, believed that "white South Africans would fit in to the dressing-room/training-ground environment and settle comfortably in Britain. . . . [The whites] were 'one of us' while their Black countrymen were not."[52] Only in 1979 did black players—Viv Anderson and Laurie Cunningham—finally wear the England jersey at senior level. While France capped African-born players like Jean Tigana and José Toure (Mali) in the 1980s and Basile Boli (Ivory Coast), Marcel Desailly (Ghana), and many others in the 1990s, England had yet to cap an African-born player as of 2009.

African football migration to Belgium resembled trends elsewhere in Europe. By 1960, Belgium's top two divisions counted about thirty Africans in its ranks.[53] As in other European countries, migrants came largely from colonial possessions. Congo's Paul Bonga Bonga, a defensive midfielder from Kinshasa, was possibly the most accomplished. Born in 1933, Bonga Bonga played for Standard Liège between 1957 and 1963, winning three Belgian league titles before moving over to Olympique Charleroi. Julien Kialunda, born in Matadi, Congo, in 1940, earned the nickname "Puskas" (after the legendary Hungarian player) on the pitches of Kinshasa. In the late 1950s, he signed for Royale Union Saint-Gilloise before joining RSC Anderlecht, perhaps the country's most prestigious club, in 1965. By this time the Congo government's restrictions on player exports and the Belgian authorities' ban on foreign players curtailed the number of Africans in Belgium.

After the repeal of the ban on foreign players in 1978, the Belgian league acquired new appeal as a destination for African migrants. Limited finances led local clubs to sign young Africans so as to keep costs down and generate profits through resale in the European market. African footballers were also pulled to Belgium by liberal citizenship laws that allowed any person at least eighteen years of age with three years of residency in Belgium to be naturalized. As a result, between 1985 and 1995 at least 126 Africans, 48 from the Congo, played in the top two divisions. As a less competitive environment than England, Italy, Spain, France, and Germany, the Belgian leagues enabled many young Africans to develop technically, tactically, and physically. They also offered a place in which to cope with culture shock and adjust to European attitudes toward immigrants.[54] "African footballers try to ignore the racial abuse they encounter. . . . Other adjustments are actually more drastic: to a new way of dealing with people, to the weather, to European eating habits and to the different way of playing football."[55] The presence of many Congolese migrants in Belgium suggests the extent to which football relations between the Democratic Republic of the Congo and Belgium are an expression of neocolonialism.

After 1980: Increased Movement of Africans in the Era of Commercial Football

The flow of African footballers to Europe increased in the 1980s and 1990s, a trend some labeled a "New Scramble for Africa."[56] Regulatory changes quickened the pulse of migration. Many European leagues began to allow a small number of foreigners per team, usually no more than two or three (though citizenship rules differed from country to country). In 1981, FIFA introduced a rule that forced all clubs to release their players for international duty. This rule made it easier to implement article 3 of the FIFA constitution, which states that every citizen of a member nation is eligible to play for his (or her) country. Then, in 1982, CAF rescinded a rule imposed in 1965 that limited the number of overseas-based players on national teams to two.

The result of this lowering of barriers to movement to and from Africa was an increase in the number of Europe-based African players in the African Nations Cup, as well as the World Cup and other international tournaments. This oscillating flow of elite players between African nations and European clubs changed the way the African game was played and how it was perceived internationally. Greater access to football via television and video recorders, together with a steady influx of European coaches, aligned African football with global trends, whereby "organization, the avoidance of mistakes, the ability to take chances and the reduction of risk seem to be the aim of all teams in major championships."[57] Suffocating defense, constant running, collective movements, and declining individual creativity tended to standardize styles of play. "I think there was more individual brilliance in my day," said Salif Keita, the former African Footballer of the Year, "but the teamwork and collective movement is so much better now."[58]

A dramatic improvement in African teams' performances in international tournaments nourished Europe's gluttonous demand for players. As noted in chapter 4, the 1982 World Cup proved to be a transformative event for the African game. Global satellite television broadcasts of Algeria and Cameroon's exploits against Germany, Italy, and other top teams displayed Africa's world-caliber technical, tactical, and physical skills. Africa's dazzling success at youth level further stimulated European interest in young African players, as Nigeria and Ghana each won two junior world championships.

Africa's success on the world stage and expanding media coverage of world football prompted an exodus of elite players from the continent after 1982. A review of the list of African Footballer of the Year recipients bears this out. Between 1971 and 1981 every winner of the award played for a club in Africa. Between 1982 and 2007, however, all but two of the winners played in European clubs.[59] The Algerian attacking midfielder Rabah Madjer and the veteran Cameroonian striker Roger Milla reaped immediate rewards. Having scored in Algeria's historic win over West Germany, Madjer played for Racing Club Paris and then FC Porto. He scored a mesmerizing back-heel goal against Bayern Munich in 1987 to help Porto win the European Cup—the first triumph for a Portuguese side since Benfica's twenty-five years earlier.[60]

Roger Milla, more than Madjer, came to embody African football's rising fortunes on the global stage. Born Albert Roger Miller in 1952 in Yaoundé, Milla won national titles with Leopards of Douala in 1972 and 1973. He moved to Tonnerre de Yaoundé in 1974 and led the club to victory in the inaugural African Cup Winners' Cup in 1975. In 1976, Milla was named African Footballer of the Year. By 1978 he was in France, first with Valenciennes and then with AS Monaco. Milla's transfer to Corsican side Bastia in 1980 brought him success. In his first season, he scored a magnificent goal in the final to help Bastia win its only French Cup title. Between 1984 and

1989, Milla had spells with second-division St. Étienne and Montpellier before leaving for well-paid semiretirement with a club in Reunion. In eleven seasons in France, he tallied a respectable III goals in 310 games.

But it was as Cameroon's leader that the charismatic Milla put an indelible mark on the history of the game. He played in three consecutive African Nations Cup finals, twice winning the title in 1984 and 1988. Most impressively, at the 1990 World Cup finals in Italy, the thirty-eight-year-old Milla scored four goals, celebrated with distinctive dances, and spearheaded Cameroon's run to the quarterfinals—the best result by an African team in the competition until it was equaled by Senegal in 2002. Cameroonian president Paul Biya lured Milla out of retirement for the 1994 World Cup tournament in the United States. Despite Cameroon's disappointing performance, Milla broke his own record as the oldest player to score in a World Cup match.

Milla's generation included many other prominent players, including his compatriot and goalkeeper Joseph Antoine Bell; Jules Bocande and Oumar Gueye Sene from Senegal; and Kalusha Bwalya, the greatest Zambian player in history. Bwalya's hat trick against Italy in the 1988 Olympics in Seoul led to very successful years with Cercle Brugges in Belgium and PSV Eindhoven in the Netherlands. Another important Zambian was Charles Musonda, who went to Anderlecht with Stephen Keshi of Nigeria.

The player who arguably had the most impact on European football at the time was Abedi Ayew "Pelé." The Ghanaian attacking midfielder won the African Footballer of the Year three times in a row (1991–93). Born in 1964 into a poor family near Accra, Abedi Pelé began his career in 1978 with Real Tamale United. His nickname celebrated his extraordinary skills and knack for game-breaking plays. He played in Ghana's victorious 1982 African Nations Cup campaign in Libya, then left for the Persian Gulf, which made him wealthy at a young age. He returned to West Africa in 1984, first with Dragons of Ouémé (in Benin) and then back home with Real Tamale. In 1985, Abedi Pelé answered the call from French second-division club Niort, which was followed by a move to Mulhouse. Olympique Marseilles acquired him in 1987 and loaned him to Lille for two seasons. Upon his return to Marseilles, Abedi Pelé became a pivotal member of the prodigious team that won two league championships and the UEFA Champions League in 1993 (a new version of the European Cup). He continued his career with several clubs in France, Italy, Germany, and the United Arab Emirates before hanging up his boots in 2000.

Abedi Pelé's decline coincided with George Oppong Weah's rise to worldwide fame. Born in Monrovia, Liberia, in 1966, he launched his career with the capital's most prestigious clubs, Mighty Barolle and Invincible Eleven. Weah then moved to Cameroon, where he won the 1988 national championship with Tonnerre Yaoundé, notching fifteen goals. After just one season in Cameroon, Weah signed with AS Monaco in France. He would play four seasons with AS Monaco and then three with Paris St. Germain, scoring 79 times in 199 league games. Nineteen ninety-five was a magical year for Weah. Paris St. Germain won the domestic treble (League championship, FA Cup, and League Cup) and reached the semifinals of the glamorous Champions League, and Weah was crowned the undisputed king of world football, winning the African, European, and World Player of the Year awards. A multimillion-dollar deal with AC Milan brought him to Italy, where he went on to win two national titles in the late 1990s. While in Milan, Weah learned a valuable lesson from Silvio Berlusconi, the Italian media magnate-cum-politician and president of AC Milan, about transferring football success and popularity into political power.[61] After his retirement in 2003, following short spells in England, France, and then the United Arab Emirates, Weah embarked on a career in politics in post–civil war Liberia.

Weah's rise to global fame had seemed to bring a glimmer of hope to Liberians suffering from the devastating conflicts of the 1990s. In Weah's words, "football is the only thing that people have to forget the war." Nelson Mandela at the time called the Liberian striker an icon of "African pride."[62] As the civil war finally ended, Weah capitalized on both his heroic status in Liberia and appeal among international NGOs (including FIFA) to announce his candidacy for president in 2004. Taking a page out of Berlusconi's playbook, Weah used his newly established Royal Communications media outlets (a TV channel and radio station) to mobilize support for his new party, the Congress for Democratic Change. The 2005 election results, however, revealed the limits of Weah's football-politics. While the young men who formed the core constituency of football fans voted for their hero, most women and better-educated Liberians supported his opponent, Ellen Johnson-Sirleaf, who won by 20 percentage points.

Finally, Nwankwo Kanu was another West African football star to strike gold in Europe. Born in 1976 in Owerri, Nigeria, Kanu became a pro soccer player at fifteen with Federation Works. Kanu's five goals during Nigeria's triumphant campaign at the 1993 Under-17 World Championships in

Japan earned him a lucrative contract with Ajax Amsterdam, which paid Iwuanyanwu National a transfer fee of about $300,000. Kanu and Ajax won the 1995 UEFA Champions League and three Dutch league titles. Ajax traded Kanu to Inter Milan in 1996 for a sum more than ten times what the Amsterdam club had originally paid. That summer, Kanu also captained Nigeria to the gold medal in the 1996 Atlanta Olympics and was later honored as the African Footballer of the Year. At the peak of his career, a routine medical exam in Milan revealed a life-threatening health problem, a defective heart valve. After a successful operation in the United States, Kanu eventually return to football. But he played just eleven matches in three seasons at Inter. In 1999, Arsenal paid Inter more than 4 million pounds and offered Kanu a princely salary of nine hundred and sixty thousand pounds (after taxes, and excluding bonuses and endorsements). Kanu temporarily revived his predatory ways and was again voted the best player in Africa in 1999. Crowded out of Arsenal's star-studded lineup after six seasons, he transferred to West Bromwich Albion in 2004 and then to Portsmouth in 2006. Kanu scored the only goal in Portsmouth's 2008 FA Cup final win over Cardiff City.

The remarkable accomplishments of Milla, Abedi Pelé, Weah, and Kanu fed Europe's ravenous appetite for African talent precisely at the same time that a commercial boom revolutionized European and world football. This combination greatly accelerated the pace of African migration in the 1990s. The spread of satellite, cable, and digital technology in television and the emergence of private, subscriber-based networks in Europe fueled football's commercial explosion (see chapter 6). The launch of the UEFA Champions League and the English Premier League in 1992, for instance, ended the era of limited live football on television. It vastly increased the value of football broadcasting rights, so that by 2000 "the largest leagues were collectively generating about $2 billion per season from the sale of live rights."[63] Club revenues were no longer generated mainly from sponsors' logos on uniforms, stadium advertisements, and ticket sales. The European Union's 1995 *Bosman* ruling, which eliminated barriers to player movement between member nations and introduced free agency (i.e., freedom to sign with another team upon expiration of previous contract) resulted in huge salary increases for elite players. Among the top players in Africa, *Bosman* further reduced the appeal of spending one's career in local leagues. Even the budgets of relatively wealthy clubs like Al Ahly and Zamalek Cairo, Raja and Wydad Casablanca, Esperance and Club Africain Tunis, Kaizer

Chiefs and Orlando Pirates in Johannesburg often amounted to one-third of those of minor French Ligue 1 clubs.[64]

Deepening financial inequality *within* European football boosted demand for cheap labor from Africa and Latin America. Manchester United, Chelsea, AC Milan, Juventus, Real Madrid, Barcelona, and the other megaclubs that devour nearly 80 percent of football revenues bought formidable foreign players almost at will. But the majority of European clubs, those with smaller fan bases in lower divisions or outside the "Big Five" leagues experienced much more modest revenue growth and struggled to cope with rising operational costs. Under enormous pressure to balance the books and remain competitive, ordinary clubs developed a business strategy focused on cutting costs and generating profits by purchasing inexpensive young talents in Africa (and Latin America) and later reselling them at higher prices on the European market. The vertiginous growth of African migration in the second half of the 1990s was incontrovertible: from about 350 in 1996 to around 1,000 in 2000.[65] The centrality of African players to football economics is reflected in the fact that in 2006 nearly one-fifth of players moving *between* European leagues were Africans.[66] The growing use of immigrant labor and the glaring disparity between elite and ordinary clubs illustrated how "the economics of European football offered a microcosm of the wider transitions and inequalities of twenty-first century capitalism."[67] In this context, African and Latin American football players have had much in common since the 1980s. They fulfill a similar economic function, experience high rates of out-migration, and retain cultural ties to their home countries.

The latest trends in football migration from Africa to Europe reveal two major changes. First, as table 2 illustrates, West Africa has replaced North Africa as the main exporting region.[68] Data from 2002–3 show that the leading exporters were Nigeria and Cameroon, with players in thirty-two and twenty-seven UEFA leagues, respectively.

The second transformation has to do with the declining age of migrants. In 2002–3, the average age of 708 Africans listed in the top eight UEFA leagues was 19.2 years, compared with 24.5 for European migrants. (In earlier times, immigrants had tended to be in their early twenties.) Younger Africans like Albert Youmba, cited at the beginning of this chapter, are extremely vulnerable and more likely to be exploited by agents and coaches.[69] According to a 1999 report of the United Nations Commission on Human Rights, the situation had turned so grim at the dawn of the millennium

TABLE 2   COUNTRY OF ORIGIN AND NUMBER OF
AFRICAN PLAYERS IN UEFA LEAGUES (2002–3)

Nigeria	214 (18.6%)
Cameroon	145 (12.6%)
Ghana	106 (9.2%)
Senegal	92 (8%)
Ivory Coast	71 (6.2%)
Morocco	48 (4.2%)
Guinea	44 (3.8%)
DR Congo	44 (3.8%)
South Africa	43 (3.7%)
Angola	37 (3.2%)
Rep. Congo	28 (2.4%)

"that there was a danger of effectively creating a modern day 'slave trade' in young African footballers."[70] This disturbing reality led to a new FIFA rule in 2001 that imposed age limits on international transfers. However, the rise of football academies and other avenues of trade enabled individuals to circumvent these well-meaning regulations, thus adding to the talent drain and the weakening of domestic football in Africa (see chapter 6).

Even with these recent transformations, colonial legacies endured. France, Portugal, and Belgium remain the largest importers of African players, although Germany has joined this group. France continues to lead Europe with 207 Africans in the professional ranks (18 percent of the total number of Africans in Europe). Germany, due to its liberal immigration policy and labor needs, is second with 157 Africans (13.6 percent), although more than 80 percent play in lower-division clubs as compared to only 53 percent in France. Belgium has consolidated its position as a leading importer: 131 Africans (11.4 percent) make up close to half of all foreigners in Belgium, and most compete in the First Division. Portugal is fourth with 92 Africans (8 percent), half of them in the top flight. Former colonial powers Italy, England, and Spain import Africans as well. In 2003, Italy had 82 (7.3 percent), but only 10 were in top clubs; England 48 (4.2 percent), with half in the Premier League; and Spain 21 (1.8 percent), but just 5 in the elite league.[71]

Television, radio, print, and electronic coverage of the extremely wealthy English Premier League and the UEFA Champions' League, and to a lesser extent leagues in Spain, Italy, and France, has created the perception that the relatively small number of highly paid and prominent players is typical of the broader impact of Africans on European football. Constant broadcasts of matches and highlights feature stars like Freddy Kanouté (Mali/Sevilla), Samuel Eto'o (Cameroon/Inter), Emmanuel Adebayor (Togo/Manchester City), and Didier Drogba (Ivory Coast/Chelsea) perforating defenses and stylishly celebrating goals. Global television audiences regularly enjoy watching midfielders like Michael Essien (Ghana/Chelsea), Yaya Touré (Ivory Coast/Barcelona), and Mohamed Sissoko (Mali/Juventus) perform alongside many of the best players in the world. African media feed into the image of migration to Europe as the way to material riches and professional success. By reporting extensively on Africans in European clubs and showing the celebrity lifestyles of Eto'o, Drogba, and other millionaire athletes, local media fuel young Africans' aspirations to "make it" overseas.

What the media overlook is the existence of a soccerscape in which most African players labor in middle- and lower-tier European leagues. As the work of sociologist Raffaele Poli has demonstrated, Africans make up the majority of foreigners in Romania and Malta; [72] they represent nearly a third of the foreigners playing in Switzerland, Turkey, Ukraine, Sweden, and Denmark. Africans are also increasingly present in the Netherlands, Finland, Austria, Greece, Israel (a member of UEFA), Russia, and Norway. The diversification of destinations signals the growing importance of multistage migration within Europe. This internal circulation, according to Poli, "can be defined as a sequence of short stays in different clubs in order to take advantage of geo-economical discrepancies existing between country leagues, in a context of a labour market in which the ability to move is a capital to be exploited." [73]

Today, a globally recognized and extraordinarily well-paid elite group of millionaire African superstars in Europe coexists with "a kind of professional-football *lumpenproletariat* with career patterns and privileges as distinct from [the superstars] as the movie extra is from the Hollywood star." [74] Football and society in the age of migration are inextricably linked. "Linkages between global cities and distant hinterlands create paradoxes," Lanfranchi and Taylor note, "wherein enormous wealth and highly skilled and remunerated professional employment uneasily coexist with growing low-paid and unskilled service industry employment and developing world-like employment conditions in underground industries." [75]

It is possible to estimate that for about one-third of Africans, multiple transfers in Europe have led to upward mobility and, in a small number of highly visible cases, great success. Mahamadou Diarra from Mali is a case in point. Born in Bamako in 1981, this defensive midfielder arrived as a teenager at OFI Crete and went on to spend three years at Vitesse Arnhem in the Netherlands. His next stop was Lyon, where he won four consecutive French titles. In 2006, Real Madrid paid Lyon 26 million euros for Diarra, an investment immediately rewarded with consecutive national championships in 2007 and 2008.

But American journalist Franklin Foer's story of Edward Anyamkyegh is probably more representative of the latest trends.[76] A Nigerian from the southeastern part of the country, Anyamkyegh represented his country in the 1995 Under-17 World Cup and in the 1999 African Youth Championship. An agent from Ivory Coast organized a trial for him at Bordeaux, which ended with Anyamkyegh's return home, while the intermediary pocketed five thousand dollars intended for the player. After suffering a serious thigh injury, he revived his dream of European football by scoring the winning goal for BCC Lions in the 1997 Nigerian Challenge Cup final. Buoyed by an older brother's success at Queen's Park Rangers in London, Anyamkyegh signed an eighteen-month contract with Sheriff Tiraspol, a team in the former Soviet Republic of Moldova, which already had two Nigerians on its payroll. Before his contract expired, Sheriff sold him to Karpaty Lviv in Ukraine for five hundred thousand dollars and a tidy profit. An eighteen-year-old compatriot, Samson Godwin, soon joined the twenty-three year-old Anyamkyegh in Lviv.

The two Nigerians had difficulties integrating into the team and adjusting to life in a city of eight hundred and fifty thousand people with only fifty Africans. News reporters, fans, and even children on the streets made audibly offensive remarks; teammates "complained to team officials 'that they didn't want to play with monkeys.'" Beyond crude racism, the Nigerians also had to cope with Lviv's inhospitable climate. "It's hard for the African players to adapt," said the Serbian coach, "especially when you have training sessions at minus 25. It's hard for us continental people. I can't imagine for them." Anyamkyegh eventually left Ukraine for Finland, where he currently plays for Palloseura Kemi Kings in the Second Division. The thirty-year-old Nigerian adapted to the modest lifestyle of a Scandinavian semiprofessional rather than return home. Anyamkyegh exemplifies the resilient migrants who survive in Europe by playing for minor clubs in marginal leagues. Players unable to sign such contracts usually vanish from European football altogether.

By the late 1980s and early 1990s, "it [became] almost every aspiring African footballer's dream: to catch the eye of a foreign scout and be called to the riches and glories of the European professional game."[77] Today, Nigeria, the colossus of West Africa, is the leading feeder nation to the European market. It specializes in exporting under-twenty players to peripheral nations. Cameroon is a major exporter as well. Senegal, Ivory Coast, and Ghana are influential suppliers at the intermediate level. Morocco, the main North African provider, sends a disproportionate number of older and slightly more expensive players to upper-tier clubs.[78] The commercial revolution and the Bosman ruling of the mid-1990s resulted, among other things, in a massive influx of African players into Eastern and Central Europe and parts of the Mediterranean. Small clubs in these regions acquire Africans to improve their competitiveness, lower operational costs, and generate profits. Consequently, the internal circulation of Africans in Europe has increased dramatically.

Migration brought about a partial Africanization of the European game that blurred the boundaries of race, citizenship, and national identity. It is no longer extraordinary for players of African origin to represent a European nation in the World Cup or European championship. Unlike earlier migrants, many Afro-European footballers, like the recently retired Zinedine Zidane, were born and raised in Europe. Some Africans have been fast-tracked to citizenship and have represented Poland, Germany, and Russia— teams without any prior association with African football.

Migration has also transformed the composition of Africa's national teams.[79] While no foreign-based players were included in the squads of the first four African teams at the World Cup—Egypt (1934), Morocco (1970), Zaire (1974), and Tunisia (1978)—today the vast majority of national team members are based in Europe. Changes in the makeup of Cameroon's World Cup squads clarify this point: the number of Europe-based players increased from four in 1982 to nine in 1990 to sixteen (out of twenty-two) in 1998.[80] In the 2006 World Cup finals, only about one in five African players came from African clubs.[81]

The departure of legions of young prospects, as much as established names, has been a major factor in the deterioration of domestic football in Africa. The best players now spend their entire careers in European clubs, thus deskilling African leagues. "Ghana league football is getting weaker and weaker because the best players are leaving," said Ghanaian legend Charles Kumi Gyamfi.[82] "There's not much entertainment left for the public." Issa Hayatou, president of CAF, concurred: "After the flight of brains Africa is confronted with the muscle exodus. The rich countries import the raw material—talent—and they often send to the continent their less valuable technicians. The inequality of the exchange terms is indisputable. It creates a situation of dependence and . . . the pauperization of some clubs . . . and national championships."[83] As the stories of Essien and Youmba mentioned at the beginning of this chapter suggest, African migration overseas, like the privatization of the game examined in the next chapter, reveals how "specific forms of 'global' integration on the continent coexist with specific—and equally 'global'—forms of exclusion, marginalization, and disconnection."[84]

CHAPTER SIX

The Privatization of Football, 1980s to Recent Times

AS THE accelerating movement of leading African players to Europe illustrates, world football became increasingly commercialized, and globalized, during the 1990s. The advent of professional football in Britain in the 1880s and in continental Europe between the wars underscored the game's economic implications from its earliest days. But even in the consumer society of postwar Europe, commercialization of football remained quite limited. Only in the 1980s did Western European clubs move decisively toward maximizing revenues and turning themselves into brands.[1] Stadium advertising expanded, corporate logos adorned team uniforms, and ticket prices rose dramatically. Rising costs, partly due to players' wages, kept profits down until the epochal changes of the 1990s, when "football was transformed into a booming post-industrial service sector awash with money and hubris."[2] Television deregulation and the rise of new global communication technologies triggered this revolution.

The development of digital signals and compression technology, which allowed the transmission of multiple channels without costly bandwidth expansion, powered the rise of cable television and direct broadcast satellite (DBS) via small "dish" receivers in Europe and North America. The global reach and astounding profit potential of subscription-based TV, as historian Walter LaFeber notes, "blew apart governmental regulations and geographical boundaries."[3] Almost overnight, hugely lucrative broadcasting deals became the norm for European football. The newly formed English

Premier League (EPL) spearheaded this process in 1992, when it sold rights to live matches to Rupert Murdoch's BSkyB television for 304 million pounds over five years. As the value of the EPL escalated and competition for TV rights intensified, Murdoch's company (later renamed Sky) renewed its contracts for 670 million pounds in 1996 and a breathtaking 1.1 billion pounds in 2003. The EPL/Sky agreement became a model for leagues in Italy, Spain, France, and Germany, all of which experienced exponential growth in revenues. FIFA too filled its coffers with television money as it transformed itself from a nonprofit sports body to a multinational corporation with increasingly financial goals. Sale of World Cup broadcasting rights skyrocketed from 84 million pounds in 1998 to 1.16 billion pounds for both the 2002 and 2006 tournaments. Though on a much smaller scale, African soccerscapes underwent a comparable transformation.

Commercialism and CAF Competitions

As shown in previous chapters, the goals of organizers, players, and coaches had not been exclusively sporting and social, but in the 1990s individuals, clubs, national associations, and CAF increasingly prioritized financial profits. Changes in the African Nations Cup, the continent's most venerable competition, clearly illustrate this shift. The final tournament had expanded to eight teams in 1968 (when it adopted a biennial schedule), twelve in 1992, and then sixteen in 1996. At the time of writing, the African Nations Cup had been staged twenty-six times and produced thirteen different winners: Egypt led the way with six titles (including the last two); Ghana four; Cameroon three; Nigeria and the Democratic Republic of Congo two; and Tunisia, South Africa, Ivory Coast, Algeria, Morocco, Sudan, Republic of Congo, and Ethiopia one each. The competition also recorded the largest crowd ever to watch a football match in Africa: more than one hundred thousand fans filled the International Stadium in Cairo in 1986 to witness Egypt's dramatic penalty shoot-out victory over Cameroon in the final. No other soccer tournament in Africa could match the Nations Cup popularity.

Between 1980 and 1988 the quasi-amateur form and ethos of the Nations Cup gave way to the forces of commercialism. In 1982, CAF rescinded the two-player limit on foreign-based professionals on each national team, and in 1984, private sponsors and commercial advertisements were allowed for the first time. The influx of overseas-based players improved the play of national teams, but it obscured the declining quality and health of African leagues. Also, European clubs routinely expressed dissatisfaction with the departure of players for Nations Cup qualifying matches and finals staged every two years in January and February, critical months in the European football calendar. Africans in Europe continue to struggle with the difficult decision of whether to take care of their patriotic duties or stay at the club that pays their wages.

After Yidnecatchew Tessema's death in 1987, the new CAF president, Cameroonian Issa Hayatou, adopted a far more sympathetic approach to commercialism. Adidas and Coca-Cola, FIFA's main corporate partners, jumped at the chance to conquer new markets and turn millions of African fans into consumers of soft drinks, sports shoes, and sports clothing. Alcohol and tobacco companies, previously excluded under Tessema's regime, began advertising at the Nations Cup to turn more football fans into consumers of cigarettes, beer, and spirits. As a result of the influx of corporate sponsorships, CAF's premier competition began to look more and more like sporting megaevents in North America and Europe. But the enduring popularity and prestige of national football teams preserved the importance of the Nations Cup as a cultural vehicle for representing the "nation" and expressing patriotic pride.

As in Europe, television in Africa propelled the commercial development of football. Deregulation and technological improvements set off an explosion in the size of TV audiences in the 1990s.[4] While Nigeria had launched the first station on the continent in 1959, an example followed by the establishment of state TV services in many independent countries in subsequent decades (in some cases only in the 1980s), television in Africa had a history of being a medium for urban elites. As late as 1987 in Ivory Coast, for example, 82 percent of Abidjan residents had access to TV, compared with 22 percent in the rural areas. Access to TV in Africa was much more limited than in the industrialized world. By the mid- to late 1980s, there were just 160 transmitters on the entire continent and only one television set per hundred people. Europe, by comparison, had 21,800 transmitters, and Oceania's twenty-three million people had nearly seven million TV sets!

The new technologies brought DBS to Africa. The launch of new satellites (e.g., PanAmSat's PAS-4 in 1995 and PAS-7 in 1999, and Eutelsat's W4 in 2000) provided coverage to sub-Saharan Africa, thus giving viewers potential access to dozens of new television channels. These technological innovations, coupled with "external pressures for economic restructuring and democratization, and increasing commercial interest in Africa as a television market,"[5] broke down government media monopolies.

Multichoice, a South African company owned by Naspers, the media conglomerate of the Afrikaner National Party during apartheid, rapidly emerged as the dominant satellite provider in Africa. Its DSTV business in South Africa alone grew at an astonishing rate: from forty-four thousand subscribers in 1998 to 1.7 million in 2008.[6] DSTV Africa is now available in nearly fifty countries. As part of its business strategy, Multichoice went to the extent of purchasing Pretoria City FC in 1994 and renamed it Supersport United. "The future of decoder purchases lies with the emerging market," stated the company's Web site, "and soccer is beyond doubt the most popular sport in South Africa. [We intend] to use the team as a marketing tool for the Supersport Television Channel that broadcasts sport into Africa."[7] The arrival of privately owned satellite television in Africa boosted entertainment and sports programming at the expense of news and educational programming—the pillars of state-owned free-to-air TV broadcasting. Given that a hefty proportion of the new content was imported, critics contended that television acted as a force for Western cultural domination and neocolonialism.

There was, in fact, a huge increase in the number of hours of European football available on television as satellite providers relied on the game's massive popularity on the continent to sell subscriptions.[8] Transnational channels like Supersport (in English) and Tv5 and Canal Horizon (in French) inundated Africa with continuous coverage of European games and highlight shows. The presence of African players and aggressive marketing enticed African viewers to watch the English Premier League and the European Champions League, as well as France's Ligue 1, Italy's Serie A, and Spain's La Liga. These factors, combined with the "gap between African football and European football in terms of performance, [TV] production level, equipment and facilities," resulted in European football (especially English) quickly replacing local football in the hearts and minds of millions of African fans. "The trouble started back in the early 1990s," commented a Nigerian sportswriter. "When you look at the stadiums you'll find that the stands are virtually empty, while the bars and the joints that have satellite TV are full. People will pay to watch the Premier League on TV but not to watch Nigerian football live."[9] Glamorous, revenue-generating leagues and clubs are marginalizing various forms of nonelite football around the world, but the game in Africa is so acutely affected that sport scholar Gerard Akindes labeled it a form of "electronic colonialism."[10]

Due to widespread poverty in Africa and the market dominance of European football, African spectators are being transformed into consumers of imported football commodities. In South Africa, the continent's largest economy, local commodification of fandom is visible in the sale of Kaizer Chiefs and Orlando Pirates merchandise, ranging from replica jerseys, scarves, and caps to cell phones and life insurance. But many African football fans with disposable income express their status and identity as consumers of football by wearing European, not African, team jerseys, both the expensive branded originals and inexpensive knockoffs. Minibuses are highly public symbols of increasingly Eurocentric fandom in African cities. These private forms of public transport are often adorned with slogans, flags, pennants, scarves, photographs, and team colors of Manchester United, Liverpool, Arsenal, and the like. While fans in Europe are also being exposed to and even exploited by capitalist football, in Africa the neocolonial undertones of this process are distinctive: "It is the final triumph of a system of domination when the dominated start singing its virtues," writes the influential Kenyan writer Ngugi wa Thiong'o.[11]

CAF's response to such tumultuous cultural and economic change was to transform the Nations Cup and the Champions League into commodified "sport products." To begin with, CAF sold both competitions' TV broadcasting rights to the highest bidder, whereas previously it had made them available for a nominal sum to African public broadcasters. In doing so, CAF followed in the footsteps of European football leagues and other sport cartels such as the National Football League and Major League Baseball in the United States. The first sale took place soon after Cameroon's outstanding performance at the 1990 World Cup. CAF signed a multiyear contract with MediaFoot, a subsidiary of the Darmon group (a major French sports marketing company) to manage the sale of TV rights for the African Nations Cup. A key player in the commercialization of French football in the 1970s and 1980s, Jean-Claude Darmon used market opportunities in Africa to "globalize" his company before taking it public in 1996 on the Paris stock exchange.[12]

CAF and the Darmon group reinvigorated their mutually profitable business relationship by striking a deal to manage the sale of broadcasting and marketing rights for the African Champions League (successor to the Champions Cup). "It was an act of faith by the Confederation of African Football and Jean-Claude Darmon's French-based marketing group Media Foot that launched the new-look tournament in 1997," reported *African Soccer* magazine, published in London from 1992 to 2004, "with guaranteed prize money of $2.1m for the first time bringing serious money to the African club scene."[13] To keep these figures in perspective, others have noted that the African Champions League "received TV rights income of less than 1 percent of its European equivalent and less than a quarter of the Arab Champions League."[14] Modeled after the European Champions League, an expanded version of the Champions Cup, the CAF version sought to professionalize elite clubs and provide incentives for top footballers to stay in Africa. The competition opened with preliminary qualifying matches for clubs based in countries with low CAF rankings, followed by two knockout rounds played on a home-and-away basis, from which eight teams were divided into two minileagues, the winners of which contested the two-leg final.

Commodification was most obvious in the Champions League's introduction of unprecedented sums of prize money. For the first time, sporting success was given a hard cash value. For example, qualification to the mini-league stage was worth $150,000, with clubs standing to gain $11,500 for each point earned (one for a draw, three for a win). Obuasi Goldfields (Ghana) and Raja Casablanca (Morocco) each received $225,000 for reaching the inaugural final. Raja won on penalties and received the $450,000 winners' bonus. Prize money increased to $3 million in 1998. In 2001, the Champions League was expanded to sixty-four teams. Twelve countries entered two teams (the league champion and runner-up) based on results from CAF club competitions in the previous five years. Semifinal matches were introduced after the group stage, and the winners' share reached $1 million.[15]

By 2000, CAF and Darmon were sufficiently pleased with their business relationship that they signed a new $50 million contract, thereby extending the French company's marketing and media rights to the African Nations Cup through 2008. Fortified by its African football operations, the Darmon group then merged in 2001 with Vivendi-owned Canal Plus and Bertelsmann-owned RTL to form Sportfive, a sports media and marketing giant that "would manage the rights of 320 clubs around the world, more than 40 national football associations and leagues."[16] Sportfive and CAF recently prolonged their agreement until the 2016 African Nations Cup.[17]

The leadership of CAF was not the only African interest group shaping the partial privatization of football. For example, Christian Laginde, a former footballer and founder of La Cellule 2 (LC2), a private TV station in Benin, acquired the rights from Sportfive to show the African Nations Cup in Africa. In 2006, the perils of privatization became clear when state broadcasters in Guinea Bissau, Malawi, Republic of Congo, and several other countries were unable (or unwilling) to pay high provider fees to LC2. As a result, millions of viewers in those countries who had previously had access to the matches on free-to-air TV could not watch the tournament. This episode illustrates how provider fees are far more important in sub-Saharan Africa, a region where, unlike Europe, there are few middle-class consumers who can pay for home subscriptions and thus generate advertising revenues for the media companies. The changing mediascape also reveals the extent to which African sport and media organizations are willing participants in a global business that aims to sell its product to smaller but far more profitable pay-TV audiences.

The television revolution established the dominance, if not the legitimacy, of commercial football in Africa. In addition to selling broadcasting rights to its competitions, CAF also signed lucrative sponsorship deals with transnational corporations. Coca-Cola, for instance, was named official sponsor of the finals in South Africa in 1996 and in Burkina Faso in 1998. Cellular phone manufacturer Nokia took over the role in 2004. South African companies also entered the market. Most notably, between 2002 and 2004 MTN, Africa's leading cell-phone provider in terms of revenue (owned by Naspers like Multichoice/DSTV), acquired naming rights to both the Champions League and the Nations Cup. The latter deal was reportedly worth $12 million through 2008. MTN's corporate branding of Africa's premier football competitions calls attention to South Africa's increasingly subimperial role on the continent. In 2001, South Africa's export-import ratio with countries of the Southern African Development Community was 9:1, and it continues to grow. "South African corporations have moved with speed into Uganda, Swaziland, Lesotho, Tanzania, and Rwanda," scholars Ashwin Desai and Goolam Vahed note, "where they are running railroads, managing airports, providing cell phone services, or controlling banks, breweries, supermarkets and hotels."[18]

African Football as a Global Business: Impact and Aftermath

The commercial imperatives of mass media and corporate sponsors, assisted by football administrators at various levels, have integrated Africa more fully into the networks of global capitalist sport. In the words of Lucas Radebe, former captain of South Africa and Leeds United: "Football is not a pastime for us. It's big business."[19] But is this a "good thing"?

Privatization exacerbated the problem of competitive imbalance at both national team and club level. The list of champions is illustrative. Since the Nations Cup's initial opening to commercial influences in 1984, Egypt and Cameroon have each won it four times (61 percent), while five nations (Algeria, Tunisia, Ivory Coast, Nigeria, and South Africa) have won it once. The hegemony of a few wealthy and popular teams extended to club football. During the Champions Cup era (1964–96), eleven nations produced twenty-three different winners. West and Central Africa produced the most champions in the 1960s and 1970s, while North African sides won fourteen times (out of sixteen) in 1981–96, including a streak of eleven consecutive titles (1984–94). In the Champions League era, however, just three clubs claimed eight of eleven titles (73 percent): Al Ahly (2001, 2005, 2006, 2008), Raja Casablanca (1997, 1999), and Enyimba (2003–4).

Satellite TV coverage of the African Nations Cup and Champions League exposes talent to a vast global audience, links Africans abroad, and further accelerates migration overseas.[20] In recent years, the biennial Nations Cup has attracted large numbers of foreign coaches, talent scouts, and sports agents who are eager to recruit the next Michael Essien or Emmanuel Adebayor. Unsurprisingly, many Africa-based players have come to view the tournament mainly as a platform to launch overseas careers. In response, CAF launched the new biennial African Nations Championship, reserved for home-based players. DR Congo won the first eight-team competition in 2009 in Ivory Coast, and Sudan is scheduled to host an expanded sixteen-team edition in 2011. It remains to be seen whether the Nations Championship will help to curtail the exodus of players overseas or whether it will become another platform to showcase African talent for export. In the end, the rapid commercialization of elite football signals the paradox of incorporation into world capitalist sport for African fans, athletes, and organizers, whereby their "economic and political dependence on industrialized nations is both their best hope for the future and a leading cause of their underdevelopment."[21]

The growing influence of business interests in the African game has widened inequalities in wealth and worsened the long-running problem of competitive imbalance in African leagues. In South Africa, for instance, where the Premier Soccer League in 2007–8 secured multiyear TV and marketing deals worth 1.6 billion rand (approximately $200 million), Kaizer Chiefs and Orlando Pirates and, to a lesser extent, Mamelodi Sundowns and Supersport United are dominant clubs. "These are drawn principally from Gauteng [Johannesburg/Pretoria area], by far the richest province," comments sociologist Merryman Kunene, "which reaps the largest crowds and most lucrative sponsorships, leaving teams from the other metropoles—and particularly from the more rural areas of the country—in their wake."[22]

The effect of commercialization on football administration cannot be overlooked. As national football bureaucracies lost their quasi-absolute grip on power and revenues, corruption and graft hardly diminished. "Football clubs and associations are places of clientelist pervasion, and of criminal acts. Scandals about embezzled money are very common," observes political scientist Andreas Mehler.[23] As in the past, individuals enter football administration to create and maintain patronage networks and launch political careers. What is markedly different in contemporary Africa is how privatization offers unprecedented opportunities for cashing in on the game. In South Africa, the executive committee of the Premier Soccer League awarded itself a 50-million-rand "fee" for securing a huge new sponsorship deal worth ten times that amount. In many countries, it is widely believed that club patrons bribe referees to gain favorable treatment for their side. Elsewhere, coaches are known to expect payment from players in exchange for a place in a top club or the national team. With so much money at stake, it is no wonder that political meddling in football administration has intensified and even led to suspension from FIFA in the case of Kenya, Ethiopia, Cameroon, Madagascar, and Chad. Greed, shoddy organization, and callous indifference toward spectator safety were major causal factors in a series of stadium disasters that cost the lives of more than two hundred fans in Accra, Johannesburg, and Lubumbashi in 2001, and in Abidjan in 2009.[24]

The entrance of local business tycoons and the greater involvement of domestic and foreign companies at the elite level in some cases did challenge old hierarchies and encourage the professionalization of sport management. Increasingly, top clubs in Africa today are owned by private interests, although government ownership, in full or in part, remains common. In South Africa, billionaire Patrice Motsepe bought Pretoria-based Sundowns FC in 2003, gaining total control of the club in 2004. A lawyer by training, Motsepe became astronomically rich after the end of apartheid as chairman of African Rainbow Minerals, the country's first black-owned mining company. The involvement of "big men" in soccer was not a new phenomenon in South Africa. In the turbulent 1980s, for example, Kaizer Motaung, owner of Kaizer Chiefs, and Jomo Sono, owner of Jomo Cosmos, were football entrepreneurs who symbolized growing black power in sport and society.[25] But unlike Motaung and Sono, Motsepe was not a famous former footballer building a sport business empire. Motsepe's acquisition of Sundowns was a personal extravagance that symbolized the rise of a new black capitalist class in postapartheid South Africa.

In Cameroon, the arrival of private capital in football coincided with the rise of Coton Sport, a club founded in 1986 in Garoua, a city of three hundred thousand inhabitants. Backed by the financial muscle of a large agricultural corporation in North Province, Coton Sport gained a reputation for being a well-managed, professional club. In 1993, it won promotion into the top tier of Cameroonian football. It paid decent wages and boasted good stadium and training facilities, which made it an attractive club for top Cameroonian players. A mere four years later, Coton Sport was national champion, a feat it repeated in 1998 and seven more times after that, including a run of five consecutive titles (2004–8). Coton Sport ended the decades-long dominance of clubs from Yaoundé and Douala and returned Cameroonian clubs to international respectability when it reached the final of the 2003 Confederation Cup and the 2008 Champions League.

A revealing case from Nigeria draws attention to the impact and aftermath of privatizing government-owned clubs. Orji Uzor Kalu, an ambitious local businessman elected governor of Abia State in 1999, transformed Enyimba International FC into a hugely successful club with a demonstrably entrepreneurial ethos. Founded in 1976 in the southeastern city of Aba (population 867,000), Enyimba was taken over by the Abia State government in 1991. After a decade of unremarkable achievements, between 2001 and 2007 the club suddenly won five Nigerian league championships, consecutive CAF Champions League titles (2003, 2004) and CAF Super Cups (2004, 2005). Kalu backed the construction of a floodlit twenty-five-thousand-seat stadium with covered grandstands. The governor then turned the former government-owned club into a commercial vehicle. "Enyimba has become a brand, well equipped to become part of the broader entertainment industry," states the club's official Web site. "Any advertising partnership with one of Africa's best known and most popular soccer brands will enable you [a potential sponsor] to achieve significant economic results, increase profitability and maximize shareholders value."[26] Enyimba's astounding sporting success powered Kalu's "big man" politics.[27] He expanded his network of patron-client relationships and made a bold but ultimately unsuccessful run for the country's presidency in the flawed elections of 2007. The connections between football and his political career ended abruptly with Kalu's arrest on money-laundering charges.

By the time private business interests came to dominate twenty-first-century African football, the game at the grassroots level had suffered a dramatic decline. Governments disengaged from "social sport" in the 1980s, a time of acute economic crisis and political change in Africa. The proximate causes could be traced back to the global oil shocks of the 1970s, which ushered in anemic economic growth, spiraling foreign debt, huge budget deficits, and political instability. In exchange for desperately needed loans to fund basic functions of government, the World Bank and International Monetary Fund imposed strict conditions on African countries under the rubric of Structural Adjustment Programs (SAPs). These programs required African governments to make drastic cuts in social spending (military spending was exempt) and to open their markets to competition from foreign private corporations. For African nation-states, "by the end of the 1980s, the freedom of action which seemed to come with independence had narrowed to the point of becoming a virtual fiction."[28] Massive cuts in government spending for health care and education mandated by the SAPs had dire social consequences. Most Africans experienced a tangible deterioration in their standard of living, and many struggled to get by. Many state-funded sport programs at school, youth, and amateur levels simply disappeared.

Football Academies

The vacuum created by the sudden withdrawal of the public sector from social sport was a critical factor in the establishment of football academies.[29] As we saw in the previous chapter, Africa had a long history of clubs, coaches, and programs operating locally such as the Portuguese feeder teams in Angola and Mozambique, and of exporting football labor to Europe. Darby, Akindes, and Kirwin describe four types of academies in Africa: those founded and operated by African clubs and football associations; Afro-European joint ventures; privately sponsored academies; and ad hoc academies.[30]

The most successful African club academy is MimoSifcom of ASEC Mimosas (Académie Sportive des Employés de Commerce, established 1948) Abidjan. Founded in 1994 by Roger Ouégnin, President of ASEC, and French coach Jean-Marc Guillou, the academy was conceived as a joint venture between ASEC Mimosas and AS Monaco (the latter eventually pulled out). The original arrangement showed, among other things, how privatization in the 1990s sparked the creation of transnational networks of coaches, scouts, and administrators.[31] The academy provides both specialized football training and an education for select teenagers from the ages of thirteen to seventeen. Guillou, a former coach of AS Monaco, offered this explanation for moving to Ivory Coast: "I wanted to work with talented youngsters rather than in France with calculating and unmotivated young Frenchmen. Football is about passion and that is what makes Africa so special."[32] The goal of MimoSifcom, whose Sol Béni campus is in M'pouto near Abidjan, was to produce elite players for Mimosas' professional team and the Ivoirian national team (the Elephants). Financing for the project came from the sale of top players to European clubs and from annual private sponsorships of four hundred thousand dollars. The academy has yielded tremendous results. Since its launch, ASEC Mimosas has won eleven national titles (seven in a row in 2000–2006), seven Ivoirian Cups, the African Champions League (1998), and the African Super Cup (1999). This last triumph came with a team comprising eleven teenagers who defeated an experienced Espérance of Tunis in the final.

The academy has earned ASEC an international reputation as a major exporter of players to Europe. Among the most notable are brothers Kolo and Yaya Touré of Manchester City and Barcelona, respectively. "We learned football well, and I think there's a lot of proof of that," said Kolo Touré, the older brother. "It formed me a lot as a player, and as an adult. After I was spotted playing in my home town I was picked up by the academy, where I stayed for five years, attending five days a week. It wasn't just football, we went to school there as well. Everything was given to us, we didn't have to pay for anything, which was fantastic."[33] The Touré brothers went to KSK Beveren, ASEC's Belgian partner, before moving on to England and Spain. Other high-profile "academicians" (as ASEC alumni are called in Ivory Coast) currently in Europe include Emmanuel Eboué of Arsenal (again via Beveren), Salomon Kalou of Chelsea (via Feyenoord Rotterdam in the Netherlands), and Aruna Dindane of Lens (via Anderlecht in Belgium).

Ghana's youth development, which has depended on underresourced under-seventeen "Colts" leagues since the 1970s, relies on local clubs as well as academies. In 1996–97, businessman El Hadj Sly Tetteh founded Liberty Professionals in Accra, which competes in the Premier Division. Tetteh's main goal was to produce players for Ghana's junior and senior national teams and for export. Today, former Liberty players compete at the highest level in England (e.g., Michael Essien), France, Italy, the Netherlands, and Greece.

Ghana also hosts the second type of academy in Africa: the Afro-European partnership. Feyenoord Fetteh Football Academy outside Accra opened its doors in 1999. With the approval of the Ghanaian government and local chiefs in Fetteh, the Dutch club "Feyenoord adopted a classic neo-colonial industrial strategy . . . that would provide a steady stream of raw talent."[34] Feyenoord Fetteh borrowed from the ASEC model to provide aspiring professional footballers with schooling.[35] "The boys are up by 5:30am. They train between 6:00 and 7:30am and by 9am they are in classes for serious academic work," said Technical Director Sam Arday. "They return for lunch and siesta. Between 3:00 and 5:00pm they are back on the field training. Then they take a shower, have dinner, do their homework, watch TV and by 9:00pm—it is bedtime."[36] But ultimately the academy is geared towards exporting players, a strategy that keeps costs down for European clubs and helps create a transnational identity for them. In the words of business writer Gideon Rachman, "A good geographical spread of players helps to build a global brand."[37]

The first West African academy set up in cooperation with a European side was the Centre Aldo Gentina in Senegal, named after an elderly Italian pastry shop owner, football fan, and Dakar resident since the 1930s who convinced AS Monaco to fund the project with annual grants of one hundred thousand pounds. El Hadj Malick Sy, president of the Senegalese Football Federation, formally established the Gentina academy in 1992–93 as a joint venture between venerable Dakar club Jeanne D'Arc and AS Monaco. "I decided something ought to be done to develop football," said Malick Sy. "Kids just played in the street, like in Brazil, and when you watch them you can see how much potential there is." "The academy has changed my life," said AS Monaco and Senegal goalkeeper Tony Sylva. "You can't imagine how difficult life can be—going to train when you are hungry, walking home without a penny in your pocket. Being in the academy, you immediately felt you were privileged."[38] Over the years, the Gentina academy has become a key source of talent for clubs in the Senegalese first division, the national team (Lions), and French clubs as well. Five members of the 2002 World Cup Senegal side that famously defeated France, its former colonial master, came from Gentina. Ironically, every Senegalese starter in that match was employed by a French club.

Ajax Cape Town in South Africa stands out as another kind of Afro-European partnership. Founded in 1999 after the merger of two Cape Town clubs, Seven Stars and Cape Town Spurs, this club is jointly owned and operated by Ajax Amsterdam and a South African group led by business-man John Comitis. It has been moderately successful in domestic competi-tions, winning the 2007 ABSA Cup and 2000 Rothmans Cup and finishing second twice in the Premier Soccer League. So far, only Steven Pienaar has made the move from Cape Town to Amsterdam (later joining Everton in England). So despite its efforts to function as a feeder team for the metro-politan club, Ajax Cape Town has not been as successful as some of its West African counterparts.

In West Africa, privately run academies are significant. Among the for-mer professional players who have opened academies, the most successful has probably been Salif Keita (see chapter 5), who returned to Mali in 1985 after a great career overseas and took up a coaching director position with the national football federation. Exasperated by the lack of cooperation from federation officials, Keita resigned and set out on his own. In 1993, he launched the Salif Keita Football Center (SKFC). Like Guillou at ASEC, Keita built working relationships with French clubs (Auxerre and Angers). But he continued to directly control the academy himself. In 1995, SKFC entered a team in Mali's top league as part of its strategy to nurture the growth and development of local football and groom players for the na-tional team. Another West African academy organized by former profes-sionals is the Diambars Institute in Senegal. Bernard Lama and Jimmy Adjovi Boco (later joined by Patrick Vieira and Saer Seck) used a grant of about thirty-seven acres of land from Senegalese President Abdoulaye Wade to create a football school. It opened in 2004 and now receives funding from public and private sources, including UNESCO, the governments of Nor-way and France, Cadbury, and Adidas. The impact of educational programs at academies awaits future research.

Private individuals without a past as professional footballers have also opened academies. For example, French entrepreneur Philippe Ezri developed Planète Champion Internationale in Ouagadougou, Burkina Faso. When Paris Saint-Germain FC, the original partner, ended its participation in the mid-1990s, Ezri funded it personally with the assistance of Burkinabé president Blaise Compaoré, a self-declared football aficionado. The focus of Planète Champion, others have noted, "is very much on nurturing the recruits' football abilities and selling them to the highest overseas bidder. As a result, the school-ing that the students at the academy receive is often far from rigorous."[39]

Corporate-sponsored centers are another group of privately run football academies. In a suburb of Lagos, Nigeria, Kashimawo Laloko founded a football school in 1992 with state government funding. Two years later, the school obtained corporate sponsorship and became the Pepsi Football Academy. Today, the Pepsi Football Academy today comprises a national network of fourteen centers with fifty-four coaches training more than three thousand boys from the ages of six to eighteen. Graduates of the Pepsi Academy system currently play in a dozen European countries, as well as in Nigeria, Ghana, Ivory Coast, and Tunisia. In 2006, Laloko launched the Football College in Orile Imo in western Nigeria, which combines secondary school education with football development. A similar model has existed in South Africa since 1994 at the Transnet/SAFA School of Excellence, a social responsibility initiative by the government-owned transport giant. Another example of a prominent company-sponsored academy is the Brasseries Academy in Cameroon, funded by the national brewery.

Ad hoc academies are the largest, most problematic, and least documented group of Africa's football cottage industry. These have been aptly described as "private, nonaffiliated academies [that] expose young Africans to the greed of noncertified agents who are able to acquire recruits cheaply and convince them to sign exploitative contracts if they are successful during their trials."[40] There are hundreds of these informal academies across the continent: 150 in Senegal alone! A group of them from seven African countries recently came together to form an unofficial Confederation of African Football Academies, which organizes tournaments to showcase young talents to coaches, scouts, and agents. Clearly, the ad hoc academies are the most dangerous for young players because they are unregulated, underresourced, and highly susceptible to abuse.

Despite some ambivalence, African governments have generally welcomed the rise of the football academy industry. Political leaders and parties appreciate how academies partially offset government cuts in social services as they train top players who often end up strengthening national teams. By doing so, the academies can enhance the prestige of nation-states and keep alive the construct of the proud and unified "nation." However, the social costs of academies deserve scrutiny.

The football academy has been criticized as a modern-day plantation. It is "a form of neo-colonial exploitation in that it involves the sourcing, refinement, and export of raw materials, in this case African football talent, for consumption and wealth generation in the European core. The process results in the impoverishment of the African periphery."[41] For the thousands of young boys not good enough for admission to the academies or unable to reach the professional ranks, the future looks bleak. The exclusionary process inherent in the football business has serious consequences for football and society. "For every Aruna Dindane who makes the leap from ASEC to Anderlecht in the Belgian top division," writes Chadian football journalist Emmanuel Maradas, "there are thousands of others investing millions of hours of practice—time that could be spent on school work or learning another trade—without even reaching the first hurdle. Only a handful out of each year's intake to the top schools will ever make a living from football. The rest are destined to be turned loose at 18 to fend for themselves."[42]

Women's Football

Although football has always been dominated by men, this has become even more true as the sport in Africa has commercialized. The hypermasculine nature of today's football has curtailed opportunities for girls and women to play, coach, referee, and administer the game. Until the 1990s, governments, businesses, and football associations dominated by men did not support women's football in Africa. This marginalization stood in dramatic contrast to the situation in track and field, netball, basketball, team handball, and other sports where women became very active and their participation very popular.

Scholarly analysis of the history and culture of the female game on the continent is greatly complicated by a lack of documentary sources and publications.[43] Even the FIFA-sponsored 383-page *Le Football en Afrique* (published in December 2008) devotes just one paragraph to the women's game! Scarcity of data notwithstanding, social scientists Martha Saavedra and Cynthia Pelak have produced groundbreaking studies that allow us to chart a basic chronology and to identify key issues and themes in selected African countries. "Women's football has been met with skepticism, neglect and sometimes outright hostility. Yet women's football has nonetheless emerged," Saavedra shows.[44]

Pelak's periodization of African women's football is helpful: emergence and development (1970s–1980s), growth and transition (1990s), and institutionalization (2000–present). This chronology does not mean that informal matches did not take place prior to the 1970s. Women in Nigeria were playing as early as 1943, according to a report published in the *Nigerian Spokesman* newspaper on October 20, 1943:

> In response to the demand of the people of Onitsha, the Sierra
> Leonean friendly Society has started to make arrangements for

the replay of the ladies' football match which so thrilled the township recently. Good news for football enthusiasts. . . . It was the first of its kind to be staged in Onitsha. Fine show but not up to the standard of boys soccer. It seemed odd to some to see our women in shorts kicking a football about the field, or clashing with one another after the manner of men . . . but the game itself, when it came to be played, exploded all the fantastic theories some malevolent individuals had concocted about it, and it was a colossal success both in the fun that it provided and on the financial side of it.

By 1960 and Nigeria's independence, there were women's teams in Jos, Lagos, Calabar, Onitsha, Kanu, Enugu, and other towns.[45] In South Africa in 1962, a group of high school girls in Soweto, led by Jessie Maseko, made an unsuccessful attempt to run an Orlando Pirates Women's Football Club. A similar short-lived effort took place in Cape Town, where Mother City Girls played before men's matches and competed successfully against boys' teams. It was not until the 1970s, at the same time that the women's game in the West expanded considerably, that some women in Senegal and South Africa began regularly playing football, and that in Nigeria official leagues got underway. In general, countries with larger populations and economies were more likely to have women playing football. As in Europe, the male-dominated football establishment in Africa showed little, if any, interest in the women's game, so it was left up to the perseverance and passion of male and female fans to organize the first teams.[46]

The case of the Dakar Gazelles illustrates this trend. According to Saavedra, Eliot Khouma, a football coach at the Sacre Coeur (Sacred Heart) school, organized a girls' team in 1974. With the help of an Italian friend, Khouma brought a women's side from Milan to Dakar that year. The Gazelles practiced for one month and lost 2–5 to the Italians, but gained a degree of respect for the female game in Senegal. As a result, the Gazelles received funding from the Dakar municipality (as well as a symbolic sum from the Senegal Football Federation) that enabled them to play a series of matches around the country against boys' teams. This tour popularized women's football and led to the founding of new teams. In 1979, the Gazelles defeated visiting Guinea 3–1 in what may have been the first international women's match between Africans. A decade later the Senegalese team traveled to tournaments in Italy and Ivory Coast.

Organized women's football in Nigeria developed along similar lines. Individual initiatives led to the rise of teams and competitions with little, if any, assistance from the Nigerian Football Association. As in the case of Khouma's Gazelles, a male coach, Christopher Akintunde Abisuga, founded a pioneering club called the Sugar Babes Ladies FC in Lagos in 1978. Lacking local female opposition, the Sugar Babes played against boys' teams in Lagos and elsewhere in the country. These games spawned many new women's teams across southern Nigeria. Despite passionate and enthusiastic players, as well as sponsorship from Abisuga's employer, Nigeria Hotels Limited, the Sugar Babes lasted only a few years. According to their coach, "Nigeria was not ready for women's football and FIFA was not supportive."[47]

By 1989, however, there were twenty-eight women's clubs active in Nigeria, including Jegede Babes, founded and operated by Princess Bola Jegede, as well as a Nigerian Female Football Organizers Association. Princess Jegede, a wealthy entrepreneur, financed the first major women's tournament in 1990 in Lagos with the seal of approval of the Nigerian FA. This historic tournament led to the selection of the first national team, nicknamed the Super Falcons, which was Africa's representative at the first Women's World Cup in 1991.

Developments in the women's game in South Africa in the late 1960s and 1970s differed from those in West Africa in that apartheid afforded affluent young white women opportunities to play football while denying all but a few "black" (which is to say, African, Coloured, and Indian) women the chance to do so.[48] Within the privileged context of white society, football reconfigured notions of femininity and led to new forms of female empowerment. "Like their counterparts in North America and Europe, during the 1970s," Pelak points out, "South African women of European ancestry challenged gender expectations and forged new opportunities and identities in soccer." These developments inspired the formation of the South African Women's Football Association (SAWFA). With an initial membership of about six hundred players, SAWFA was more than 80 percent white, with some African and Coloured players distributed among the white-run teams. The apartheid government permitted this limited racial mixing for two reasons: the small number of participants involved and South Africa's desire to reenter international sport. In 1975, SAWFA launched a national interprovince women's tournament variously staged in Johannesburg, Durban, and Cape Town. Natal won twelve of sixteen national titles through 1990.

The women's game in Africa and around the world grew by leaps and bounds in the 1990s as it transitioned from its takeoff stage toward institutionalization.

In Nigeria, women's football flourished.[49] Commercial sponsorships were unusually plentiful, including such corporate brands as. Pepsi-Cola and 7Up, and many players signed professional contracts. Such a vibrant national female football culture stemmed from the involvement of women at all levels of the sport, as players, referees, administrators, fans, club owners, and sponsors. The only region of the country where the game was held back was in two deeply conservative areas of the predominantly Muslim north, where official bans were imposed on women playing football. Interestingly, Islamic identity brought no similar restrictions in Senegal, which is 90 percent Muslim. In fact, Dakar, St. Louis, Thiès, Mbacke, and Kaolack and other towns in Senegal saw women's clubs, tournaments, and leagues develop in spite of very limited material and moral support from the Senegal Football Federation. In 1994, the Gazelles won the first national tournament. In Kenya, where a dozen teams had come to life in the 1980s, two local women, Fridah Shiroya and Rebecca Olela, established the Kenya Women's Football Federation in 1993. It sponsored a national team that competed in various international tournaments until 1996, when the male-controlled Kenya Football Federation, in accordance with FIFA demands, created a subcommittee for women's football and forced the KWFF to cease operations.

In South Africa, where apartheid finally gave way to democracy, more women were playing the game than ever before: about 67,000 in 1997. The demographics of the sport also underwent a seismic shift. Black African women became the majority of players, as "their new sense of freedom encouraged them to challenge male dominance in sports in their own local communities."[50] The democratization of women's soccer in South Africa sparked a mass exodus of white women out of the game. By 1998, no whites played for Banyana Banyana, the women's national team (although some have returned recently). As in the Kenyan case, the male-run South Africa Football Association (SAFA) absorbed the women's game into its structures in the mid-1990s and relegated it to second-class status. For feminist practitioners and scholars, this move reflected how the "growth of women's soccer poses a significant challenge to the gender status quo and men's collective sense of entitlement to control the sport."[51]

The boom in women's soccer around the world in the 1990s and 2000s fueled the creation of women's leagues and clubs and the further strengthening of the game in Africa. In Senegal, the SFF finally changed its approach. It charged Françoise Seck, a tireless advocate for women's football, with the task of setting up a national women's league. Thanks to the belated support of the SFF, the league expanded from ten teams in 2001 to twenty in 2003. In Kenya, too, there were positive developments as ten-team women's leagues began play in Nairobi in 2002 and two years later in Mombasa, where the sponsor was the auto dealership Lota Motors. In Nigeria and South Africa, corporate sponsorships have increased substantially. In 2008, the telecom firm Etisalat reportedly paid the Nigerian Football Federation $3.3 million to sponsor the National Women's League. In 2009 in South Africa, the ABSA Women's League was launched thanks to the sponsorship of a financial services giant actively involved in men's football. It remains to be seen whether these sponsorships will lead to women's leagues' long-term sustainability.

At the continental level, CAF organized the first official African Women's Championship in Nigeria in 1998 with strong encouragement from FIFA and corporate sponsors. Having won unofficial tournaments in 1991 and 1995, the host nation took the first of what would become five consecutive continental crowns, a streak interrupted in 2008 by Equatorial Guinea. Nigeria also participated in five FIFA Women's World Cup finals, with its best result a quarterfinal finish in 1999. Striker Mercy Akide symbolized Nigeria's success. FIFA rated her "the most famous name in African women's football, and one of the most dangerous attacking players of the past decade."[52] Born in Port Harcourt in 1975, Akide learned to play the game with neighborhood boys. Her parents, she told *African Soccer,* "rather than scold me, . . . gave me all their support and encouragement. In fact, my dad bought me my first pair of boots."[53] Akide joined a local team and subsequently moved to Lagos to play for Jegede Babes. Her performances in the 1999 World Cup in the United States earned Akide a four-year scholarship to Milligan College in Tennessee along with Super Falcon teammate Florence Omagbemi. In 2003, Akide joined the San Diego Spirit of the WUSA professional league. In 2004, she was invited to play on a FIFA Women's All-Star Team against Germany as part of the world body's centenary celebrations. Akide put African women on the global football map.

In the first decade of the twenty-first century, CAF's commitment to the women's game has deepened. In 2002, it organized the first Under-20 Women's Championship, and in 2008 it launched the Under-17 Women's Championship, two competitions that Nigeria has dominated so far. The creation of the CAF Female Player of the Year award was another milestone. In 2008, the honor went to nineteen-year-old South African striker Noko Alice Matlou.

While the private sector contributed to the growth of women's football at the elite level in several countries, the game's future development requires moral support and financial assistance from governments and the football establishment. "Most African women have overwhelming and intensive household reproductive obligations that leave little time to regularly play and develop skills in football," Saavedra notes, a problem compounded by "the lack of minimal resources [that] also prohibits participation in and organization of football."[54] Attitudes are changing, albeit very slowly. "On the executive level there is recognition that women's football has to be treated a whole lot more seriously than it had been in the past," a male official of the South African Football Association told Cynthia Pelak. "But, how to translate that into real action is another matter. Because, you know, we are not quite sure if everyone is as committed to that as they say they are on paper."[55] This political commitment to gender equity is crucial to put the women's game on firm institutional footing: "Organizing sport needs strong, well-managed institutions run by committed and skilled people who want a fair system that gives all young players the chance to represent their country and play at the highest level."[56]

The rollback of government assistance in sport in the 1990s paved the way for nongovernmental organizations (NGOs) and community-based organizations, as well as corporate social responsibility initiatives, to step in as providers of basic needs and services, including sport and physical education. One of the most prominent NGOs active in sport and development projects is the Mathare Youth Sports Association (MYSA), based in a huge slum of Nairobi, Kenya.[57] In 2006, it organized 250 girls' teams with over thirty-five hundred players.[58] Football affords some girls in the slum an opportunity to enliven their dull daily routines and also gain "access to the dynamic, action-oriented world typically reserved for boys."[59] This pioneering program, founded in 1992 by Bob Munro, a Canadian, is currently funded by local and international sources. It also fields professional teams in both the men's and women's national leagues. In the absence of a national football development agenda, MYSA also acts as a feeder program for Nairobi's other female teams, as well as the national team. This sport development program enjoys the support of most Mathare parents. As one mother put it:

> "I saw there was no need to stop her, since she thought it was good for her and it was a new thing, this sports. Who knows

FIGURE 4   Author coaching in Khayelitsha, South Africa, 1993

maybe this sport may help her in [the] future." She continued by highlighting the integration of sport with health and environmental programs: "What I like is the way take these young children and not only train them in football but they are also taught about many things. For example, Lydia told me that there are usually programs where they are taught about AIDS, how they can take care of themselves as young girls . . . [They also] participate in clean-up activities and picking up rubbish."[60]

Another NGO in Kenya that works with girls' football is Moving the Goalposts (MTG), based in Kilifi, Coast Province. Founded in 2000 by Sarah Forde, a former reporter and soccer coach from England, MTG currently has three thousand girls playing, coaching, refereeing, and administering football clubs, tournaments, and leagues. Like MYSA, it espouses a sport for social uplift mission, with a special focus on issues related to reproductive health.

MYSA, MTG, and other NGOs in Africa are demonstrating how the future of African women's football hinges less on commercial leagues or supposed cultural barriers and more on the need to develop infrastructure, expand funding and access, and struggle for greater gender equality. As Sarah Forde argues, without this kind of "significant change" the women's game faces an insecure future at best. Even a top player, writes Forde, may well "end up living in one of the slums in Mombasa or Nairobi, scraping together a living, playing football at weekends, maybe playing for the national team, squabbling over allowances and feeling demoralized by the game she loves so passionately."

IN THE era of commodified sport and diminishing opportunities for voluntary leisure, as opposed to the "forced" leisure caused by long-term unemployment, neighborhood games and school sport are important vehicles for young people's socialization and recreation. In contemporary urban Senegal, for example, *nawetaan* youth clubs operate area soccer teams and championships outside government control. Through nawetaan football, Senegalese "young people foster a sense of social commitment, public spirit, and democratic process, but also participate in riots and violent acts. . . . They are citizens and anti-citizens."[61] While commercial and civic football exist side by side, the sustainability of both high performance and grassroots football in Africa requires government funds and political support. "Only in recent times have private companies begun to show an interest in football because they have twigged that there is a lot of reflected success in football," said Michael Chiti, the former chairman of the Zambian Football Association. "There will, however, never be a situation in which the involvement of the government is superfluous. After all, football is a matter of national pride. And when national pride is at stake then the involvement of the government is necessary."[62] Nowhere is this more evident than in South Africa's hosting of the 2010 World Cup.

South Africa 2010

The World Cup Comes to Africa

THE END of apartheid and the advent of democracy in South Africa in 1994 seemed to infuse soccer with the spirit of what Nobel Peace laureate Archbishop Desmond Tutu called "rainbow nationalism"—the idea that "South Africa belongs to all who live in it, black and white," to borrow from the Freedom Charter, the blueprint for the liberation struggle adopted in 1955. This inclusive vision of South African citizenship and identity was a founding principle of the National Soccer League in 1985, a league that desegregated the professional game in the midst of a tumultuous decade many feared would lead to racial bloodshed and civil war. Then formerly antagonistic football associations from across the color line came together in a lengthy "unity process" that culminated in the formation of a nonracial South African Football Association (SAFA) on December 8, 1991, a few days before the Convention for a Democratic South Africa held its first session to write the country's new constitution.

As the "negotiated revolution" progressed, the sport boycott ended and South Africa re-entered international sport. In January 1992 in Dakar, the Confédération africaine de football (CAF) welcomed South Africa back into the fold, thus paving the way for readmission to FIFA. To celebrate the occasion, on July 7, 1992, at Durban's King's Park stadium, South Africa's first integrated national team, nicknamed Bafana Bafana (Zulu for "the Boys") defeated visiting Cameroon 1–0. Later that month, in Barcelona, Spain, South African athletes participated in the Olympics for the first time in thirty-two years. On April 27–28, 1994, millions of black South Africans

127

voted in a national election for the first time, and the African National Congress (ANC) won a resounding victory as Mandela became the country's first black president.

Like Kwame Nkrumah and others before him, Mandela and the government of national unity turned to sport to build a new and inclusive sense of "South African-ness" in a sports-obsessed country with eleven national languages and deep racial and economic divisions. From a symbolic standpoint, football received close government attention. For instance, the official festivities for Mandela's presidential inauguration on May 10, 1994, featured a football match at a sold-out Ellis Park in Johannesburg between South Africa and Zambia, where the ANC-in-exile had its headquarters for two decades. Rainbow nationalism received a tremendous lift in February 1996 when Bafana Bafana triumphed in the African Nations Cup in front of a delirious home crowd of ninety thousand people at FNB Stadium, outside Soweto. Africans and Coloureds made up most of the team, but there were whites too, including the coach, the captain, and a burly midfielder whom black fans nicknamed "Mandela" in the spirit of national unity and racial reconciliation. After the final against Tunisia, South Africans poured into the streets of cities and townships across the country in a collective explosion of peaceful sportive nationalism.

Bafana Bafana's victory came just a few months after the South African Springboks' memorable victory in the 1995 rugby World Cup (also on home soil), a cathartic moment that persuaded rugby-obsessed conservative white men to accept, if not embrace, democracy and a "new South Africa."[1] The social and political significance of the rugby and soccer triumphs entrenched a desire among increasingly self-confident South African leaders to host sporting megaevents for the purpose of bolstering the quest for national unity and triggering faster economic growth.[2] Over the next few years, South Africa successfully staged the 1999 All-Africa Games, the 2003 Cricket World Cup, and several other international sporting competitions. It also narrowly failed in bids to host the 2004 Olympics (in Cape Town) and the 2006 FIFA World Cup.[3] The new South African president, Thabo Mbeki, who succeeded Mandela in 1999, responded to FIFA's controversial decision to award the 2006 finals to Germany by giving a prime-time speech on television in which he stated in a determined tone that "next time we will win." Four years later, his prediction came true.

Under Mbeki's stewardship, the 2010 World Cup became a massive national project designed to enhance the status of the nation-state and globally market

"Brand South Africa"—an image of a country as a modern, technologically advanced, democratic, business-friendly, and exotic tourist destination. That only a few countries possess the infrastructural and economic capacity to stage the World Cup meant that emerging powers, like Mexico (in 1970 and 1986) and South Korea (2002), could acquire quasi–Great Power status. Another critical factor behind the national government's firm commitment to the World Cup was the influence of the philosophy of the "African Renaissance"—the belief that modernity and globalization, combined with African cultural heritage, can be harnessed to reinvigorate the continent economically and politically. "This is an African journey of hope," Mbeki emphasized in his speech at FIFA House the night before the decision about 2010 hosting rights. "Nothing could ever serve to energize our people to work for their and Africa's upliftment more than to integrate among the tasks of our Second Decade of Democracy and the African Renaissance our successful hosting of the 2010 Soccer World Cup."[4] In a 2003 letter to FIFA president Joseph "Sepp" Blatter, Mbeki had underscored the "African" nature of South Africa's enterprise: "We want, on behalf of our continent, to stage an event that will send ripples of confidence from the Cape to Cairo—an event that will create social and economic opportunities throughout Africa. We want to ensure that one day, historians will reflect upon the 2010 World Cup as a moment when Africa stood tall and resolutely turned the tide on centuries of poverty and conflict. We want to show that Africa's time has come."[5] As in previous decades, football was being used to advance a pan-Africanist cause.

Blatter never wavered in his plan to bring the World Cup to Africa. As FIFA general secretary in 1998, he had won the presidential election thanks to the votes of African delegates, who represented nearly one-quarter of the votes in the FIFA Congress. Blatter's campaign promised Africans a larger slice of football's expanding economic pie and the opportunity to stage the World Cup finals on African soil for the first time. A few months before the 1998 FIFA presidential election, South Africa officially launched its bid for the 2006 World Cup with Blatter's blessing. After Germany edged out South Africa, Blatter orchestrated a maneuver to rotate the World Cup finals—source of about 90 percent of FIFA's revenue through sale of broadcasting and marketing rights—on a continental basis, beginning with Africa in 2010. The rule was approved in 2002, and South Africa found itself in the pole position. Compared to Morocco and Egypt, the other serious contenders from Africa, South Africa boasted better infrastructure and had experience hosting major sporting events. It also had a trump card: the ability to bring FIFA officials in personal contact with Nelson Mandela, probably the most popular and respected person on the planet.

The 2010 World Cup finals will be staged from June 11 to July 11 in nine cities in eight of South Africa's nine provinces. The Local Organizing Committee claims that the tournament's economic impact will create 129,000 jobs, attract 500,000 tourists, and contribute the equivalent of 2 percent of the gross domestic product. The government is spending substantial public funds on stadiums, media facilities, transport and communications infrastructure, and security arrangements. Five new taxpayer-subsidized stadiums are under construction: two 70,000-seat arenas in Cape Town and Durban, and three 40,000-seat facilities in Nelspruit, Polokwane, and Port Elizabeth. Five existing stadiums are under renovation, including a complete overhaul of Soccer City outside Johannesburg—the venue for the opening match and the final—to expand its capacity to 94,000 and encase the facility with an eye-catching gourd-shaped shell. The costs for building stadiums and related infrastructure doubled from 14.9 billion rand in 2006 to 30 billion rand in mid-2009.

Some football commentators questioned the utility of huge, expensive stadiums that will probably depend on rugby for their long-term sustainability: "It would have been more sensible to have built smaller stadiums nearer the football-loving heartlands," argued former PSL chief Trevor Phillips, "and used the surplus funds to have constructed training facilities in the townships."[6] But because South Africa is parading on a "global catwalk" to increase tourist revenues and foreign direct investment,[7] the government willingly pays for stadiums that stand as architectural symbols of a technologically sophisticated, proud, modern African nation. The new stadiums are among the most powerful and effective means to achieve an Eiffel Tower–like branding effect. The new sports arenas can help debunk stereotyped images of Africa as a primitive, tribal, wild, sick, conflict-ridden, chaotic place populated by kleptocratic tyrants and faceless victims in need of Western help.

I believe South Africa will host a successful World Cup. Preparations are at an advanced stage, and the 2009 FIFA Confederations Cup was held in Johannesburg, Pretoria, Bloemfontein, and Rustenburg without major problems. Blatter applauded South Africa's handling of the eight-team tournament by giving the host nation a 7.5 rating (out of 10). While the 2010 World Cup is richly funded and professionally organized, its long-term legacy must be discussed. From an economic perspective, the megaevent is extremely unlikely to turn a financial profit due to spiraling costs, overly optimistic economic projections, and the fallout from a brutal global recession. Even so, some large construction companies involved in 2010 projects privatized profits while South African taxpayers assumed most of the financial risks as well as responsibility for eventual losses.[8] For ordinary workers, the long-term economic benefits are uncertain at best, partly due to organizers' reliance on volunteers for many tournament-related services and partly due to the short-term nature of newly created jobs in an economy where 80 percent of companies employ temporary workers and about half use contract labor. The effects of World Cup spending on government funding of social programs are another serious concern, especially at the local level, given that half of South Africans are poor, almost that many are unemployed, millions lack adequate housing and schooling, and three hundred and fifty thousand people die of AIDS every year. Finally, some analysts warn that 2010 could reinforce South Africa's lopsided economic relationship with the rest of Africa.[9]

From a cultural standpoint, many ordinary South Africans (and their African neighbors generally) cannot afford World Cup tickets and thus may be reduced to adding "African" flavor to this corporate event by dancing in the streets, singing, making music, and showcasing "traditional" clothing and jewelry for foreign visitors and television audiences. That 2010 has yet to produce a coherent development plan for the youth, school, and amateur game, male and female, also points to how global capitalist sport "is a growing threat to the development of sport in underprivileged and economically poor communities," according to Yusuf Ebrahim, former president of the antiapartheid South African Council on Sport.[10] In the end, the most likely positive outcomes from 2010 World Cup's will be emotional ones, and thus intangible and unquantifiable. These include enjoyable memories for a soccer-obsessed nation, short-term feelings of pride and unity, greater confidence among some foreign investors, and an improved image of Africa and Africans.

This last point returns us to the themes I have interwoven throughout this book. For the 2010 World Cup in South Africa is very much about the changing relationship between sport, race, nationhood, and big business. Within an international framework dominated by FIFA and transnational corporations accountable mainly to themselves, South Africa's hosting of the World Cup represents the latest and most ambitious attempt by an

African country to use football to showcase its political achievements, ac-celerate economic growth, and assert the continent's global citizenship. In the words of Danny Jordaan, CEO of the 2010 Local Organizing Com-mittee: "This is an African World Cup, this is a world-class event. There is no contradiction between being African and being world class."[11] The 2010 World Cup signals that the continent is likely to continue shaping the culture and history of the global game for many years to come.

NOTES

Prologue

1. Ahmed Kathrada, *Memoirs* (Cape Town: Zebra Press, 2004), 371.

2. *Mercury*, March 16, 2007.

3. See William James Murray, *The World's Game: A History of Soccer* (Champaign: University of Illinois Press, 1996); and David Goldblatt, *The Ball Is Round: A Global History of Soccer* (New York: Riverhead Books, 2008).

4. Paul Dietschy and David-Claude Kemo-Keimbou, *Le football et l'Afrique* (Paris: EPA, 2008), 336.

5. I have borrowed the term "soccerscape" from Richard Giulianotti, *Football: A Sociology of the Global Game* (Cambridge: Polity Press, 1999), 24. Giulianotti uses *soccerscape* to refer to the geographic and cultural "circulation of players, coaches, fans and officials, goods and services, or formation and artifacts." As per Michael Schatzberg's suggestion, indigenous cultures of power should be included in an expanded definition of soccerscapes; see Schatzberg, "Soccer, Science and Sorcery: Causation and African Football," *Afrika Spectrum* 41, no. 3 (2006), 351–69.

CHAPTER ONE   "The White Man's Burden"
Football and Empire, 1860s–1919

1. Stephen Hardy, "Entrepreneurs, Structures, and the Sportgeist: Old Tensions in a Modern Industry," in *Essays on Sport History and Sport Mythology*, ed. Donald G. Kyle and Gary D. Stark (College Station: Texas A & M University Press, 1990), 45–82.

2. William J. Baker and James A. Mangan, eds., *Sport in Africa: Essays in Social History* (New York: Africana, 1987), viii. For more on this topic, see Peter Alegi, *Laduma! Soccer, Politics and Society* (Scottsville: University of KwaZulu-Natal Press, 2004), 7–14; Laura Fair, "Ngoma Reverberations: Swahili Music Culture and the Making of Football Aesthetics in Early Twentieth-Century Zanzibar," in *Football in Africa: Conflict, Conciliation and Community*, ed. Gary Armstrong and Richard Giulianotti (Basingstoke: Palgrave Macmillan, 2004), 103–13; and John Blacking, "Games and Sport in Pre-colonial African Societies," in Baker and Mangan, *Sport in Africa*, 3–22.

3. John Bale and Joe Sang, *Kenyan Running: Movement Culture, Geography and Global Change* (London: Frank Cass, 1996), 49–50.

4. *Eastern Province Herald*, May 23, 1862; *Cape Argus*, August 21, 1862.

5. These early forms of the modern game resembled both the football of British public schools and universities and the preindustrial "folk" game of artisans and farmers; see John Goulstone, "The Working-Class Origins of Modern Football," *International Journal of the History of Sport* 17, no. 1 (2000), 135–43. On early football, see also James Walvin, *The People's Game: A History of Football Revisited* (Edinburgh: Mainstream, 1994), 41–43.

6. SAFA withdrew from the world body in 1924, along with the British associations, before regaining full membership in 1952. See chapter 4 on the subsequent suspension of SAFA (later renamed FASA) in the early 1960s.

7. Paul Dietschy and David-Claude Kemo-Keimbou, *Le football et l'Afrique* (Paris: EPA, 2008), 57.

8. See Bernadette Deville-Danthu, *Le sport en noir et blanc: Du sport colonial au sport africain dans les anciens territoires français d'Afrique occidentale, 1920–1965* (Paris: Harmattan, 1997).

9. This paragraph is based on Bénédicte Van Peel, "Aux débuts du football congolais," in *Itinéraires croisés de la modernité au Congo Belge, 1920–1950*, ed. Jean-Luc Vellut (Paris: Karthala, 2001), 141–87. Additional information is from Dietschy and Kemo-Keimbou, *Le football et l'Afrique*, 67. Note that the Katanga association did not affiliate with the Belgian FA.

10. Allen Guttmann, *Games and Empires: Modern Sports and Cultural Imperialism* (New York: Columbia University Press, 1994), 68.

11. Ibid., 64.

12. Deville-Danthu, *Le sport en noir et blanc*; and Phyllis Martin, *Leisure in Colonial Brazzaville* (Cambridge: Cambridge University Press, 1995), 100.

13. According to Alice Conklin, the French believed their civilizing mission stemmed from the fact that "France's colonized subjects were too primitive to rule themselves, but were capable of being uplifted. It intimated that the French were particularly suited, by temperament and by virtue of both their revolutionary past and their current industrial strength, to carry out this task. . . . [France] had a duty and a right to remake 'primitive' cultures along lines inspired by the cultural, political, and economic development of France." Alice L. Conklin, *A Mission to Civilize: The Republican Idea of Empire in France and West Africa, 1895–1930* (Stanford: Stanford University Press, 1997), 1–2.

14. *Le Courrier d'Afrique*, November 22–23, 1936, cited in Van Peel, "Aux débuts du football congolais," 164.

15. Stephen Borquaye, *The Saga of Accra Hearts of Oak Sporting Club* (Accra: New Times Press, 1968), 27.

16. Details about Nigeria in this paragraph are from Wiebe Boer, "Nation-Building Exercise: Sporting Culture and the Rise of Football in Colonial Nigeria" (PhD diss., Yale University, 2003), 238–49.

17. Nnamdi Azikiwe, *My Odyssey: An Autobiography* (New York: Praeger, 1970), 402.

18. Laura Fair, *Pastimes and Politics: Culture, Community, and Identity in Post-abolition Urban Zanzibar, 1890–1945* (Athens: Ohio University Press; London: James Currey, 2001), 228–33.

19. Ibid., 231.

20. Ahmad Alawad Sikainga, *"City of Steel and Fire": A Social History of Atbara, Sudan's Railway Town, 1906–1984* (Portsmouth, NH: Heinemann, 2002), 82–83.

21. Soter Tsanga, *Le football camerounais: Des origines à l'indépendence* (Yaoundé: Centre d'Édition et de Production de Manuels, 1969), 52–54.

22. Anthony Clayton, "Sport and African Soldiers: The Military Diffusion of Western Sport throughout Sub-Saharan Africa," in Baker and Mangan, *Sport in Africa,* 114–37.

23. Ibid., 120.

24. Ibid., 122–23.

25. Richard Holt, *Sport and the British: A Modern History* (Oxford: Oxford University Press, 1989); James A. Mangan, *Athleticism in the Victorian and Edwardian Public School: The Emergence and Consolidation of an Educational Ideology* (Cambridge: Cambridge University Press, 1981).

26. Holt, *Sport and the British,* 93.

27. James A. Mangan, *The Games Ethic and Imperialism* (New York: Viking, 1986).

28. Ibid., 35–36. See also Brian Stoddart, "Sport, Cultural Imperialism, and Colonial Response in the British Empire," *Comparative Studies in Society and History* 30, no. 4 (1988): 649–73.

29. Alegi, *Laduma!* 22–24.

30. For further details, see Peter Alegi, "Sport, Race, and Liberation: A Preliminary Study of Albert Luthuli's Sporting Life," in *Sport and Liberation in South Africa: Reflections and Suggestions,* ed. Cornelius Thomas (Alice: NAHECS and Sport SA, 2006), 66–82.

31. On rugby and cricket in South Africa, see David Ross Black and John Nauright, *Rugby and the South African Nation* (Manchester: Manchester University Press, 1998); Albert Grundlingh, André Odendaal, and S. B. Spies, *Beyond the Tryline: Rugby and South African Society* (Johannesburg: Ravan Press, 1995); André Odendaal, *The Story of an African Game: Black Cricketers and the Unmasking of One of Cricket's Greatest Myths, South Africa, 1850–2003* (Cape Town: David Philip, 2003); and Bruce K. Murray and Christopher Edmond Merrett, *Caught Behind: Race and Politics in Springbok Cricket* (Johannesburg: Wits University Press; Scottsville: University of KwaZulu-Natal Press, 2004).

32. Efiong U. Aye, *Old Calabar through the Centuries* (Calabar: Hope Waddell Press, 1967), 146.

33. William H. Taylor, "Missionary Education in Africa Reconsidered: The Presbyterian Educational Impact in Eastern Nigeria, 1846–1974," *African Affairs* 83, no. 331 (1984): 201.

34. Cited in Boer, "Nation-Building Exercise," 145.

35. Ibid., 135.

36. Borquaye, *Saga of Accra Hearts of Oak,* 27.

37. Francis Agbodeka, *Achimota in the National Setting: A Unique Educational Experiment in West Africa* (Accra: Afram, 1977), 160 (on sport see 124–27).

38. James A. Mangan, "Ethics and Ethnocentricity: Imperial Education in British Tropical Africa," in Baker and Mangan, *Sport in Africa,* 148.

39. Heather Sharkey, *Living with Colonialism: Nationalism and Culture in the Anglo-Egyptian Sudan* (Berkeley and Los Angeles: University of California Press, 2003), 44.

40. A. E. M. Anderson-Morshead, *The History of the Universities' Mission to Central Africa, 1859–1909* (London: Office of the Universities' Mission to Central Africa, 1897), 249.

41. Ibid., 287.

42. Mangan, "Ethics and Ethnocentricity," 154.

43. Ibid., 152.

44. Ibid., 147. Mangan also notes the role of individual educational administrators in propagating the game ethic across colonial boundaries. Alexander Garden Fraser did so, for instance, as headmaster at King's in Uganda and then at Achimota in the Gold Coast.

45. James A. Mangan, "Soccer as Moral Training: Missionary Intentions and Imperial Legacies," *Soccer and Society* 2, no. 2 (2001), 53.

46. J. Arthur, "A Great Football Match," *Kikuyu News,* January 1909, 9. Thanks to Derek Peterson for bringing this source to my attention.

CHAPTER TWO   The Africanization of Football, 1920s–1940s

1. Peter Alegi, *Laduma! Soccer, Politics and Society in South Africa* (Scottsville: University of KwaZulu-Natal Press, 2004), 65.

2. Ibid., 125–30.

3. See, for example, Lisa A. Lindsay and Stephan F. Miescher, eds., *Men and Masculinities in Modern Africa* (Portsmouth, NH: Heinemann, 2003); Stephan F. Miescher, *Making Men in Ghana* (Bloomington: Indiana University Press, 2005); Robert Morrell, ed., *Changing Men in Southern Africa* (Pietermaritzburg: University of Natal Press; London: Zed Press, 2001).

4. Andreas Eckert, "Cultural Commuters: African Employees in Late Colonial Tanzania," in *Intermediaries, Interpreters, and Clerks: African Employees in the Making of Colonial Africa,* ed. Benjamin N. Lawrance, Lynn Osborn, and Richard L. Roberts (Madison: University of Wisconsin Press, 2006), 251.

5. John Iliffe, *Honour in African History* (Cambridge: Cambridge University Press, 2005), 299–300.

6. Heather Sharkey, *Living with Colonialism: Nationalism and Culture in the Anglo-Egyptian Sudan* (Berkeley and Los Angeles: University of California Press, 2003), 46–47.

7. Wiebe Boer, "A Story of Heroes, of Epics," in *Football in Africa: Conflict, Community and Conciliation,* ed. Gary Armstrong and Richard Giulianotti (Basingstoke: Palgrave Macmillan, 2004), 63.

8. Bassirou Sanogo, *La longue marche du football burkinabé* (Ougadougou: Éditions Sidwaya, 1998), 11–12. Other French firms active in Bobo included Compagnie Française de l'Afrique Occidentale and Société Commerciale de l'Ouest Africain.

9. Rémi Clignet and Maureen Stark, "Modernisation and Football in Cameroun," *Journal of Modern African Studies* 12, no. 3 (1974): 409–10; Phyllis Martin,

Leisure and Society in Colonial Brazzaville (Cambridge: Cambridge University Press, 1995), 102–3; Adolphe Ogouyon, "Le football au pays de Vodouns: Le cas du Bénin," *Sociétés et Répresentations* (December 1998): 163–65.

10. Hyder Kindy, *Life and Politics in Mombasa* (Nairobi: East African Publishing House, 1972), 94.

11. Excellent overviews of urban studies and urban historiography in Africa are Bill Freund, *The African City: A History* (Cambridge: Cambridge University Press, 2007); David M. Anderson and Richard Rathbone, eds., *Africa's Urban Past* (Oxford: James Currey; Portsmouth, NH: Heinemann, 2000); Catherine Coquery-Vidrovitch, "The Process of Urbanization in Africa (from the Origins to the Beginning of Independence)," *African Studies Review* 34, no. 1 (1991): 1–98; and Frederick Cooper, "Urban Space, Industrial Time, and Wage Labor in Africa," in *Struggle for the City: Migrant Labor, Capital, and the State in Urban Africa*, ed. Frederick Cooper (Beverly Hills: Sage, 1983), 7–50.

12. See Peter Alegi with Robert Vassen, "Moonlighters Football Club: A History," http://www.overcomingapartheid.msu.edu/sidebar.php?id=15 (April 15, 2009).

13. A similar process unfolded in Zanzibar, see Laura Fair, *Pastimes and Politics: Culture, Community, and Identity in Post-abolition Urban Zanzibar, 1890–1945* (Athens: Ohio University Press; London: James Currey, 2001), chap. 5.

14. Soter Tsanga, *Le football camerounais: Des origines à l'indépendence* (Yaoundé: Centre d'Édition et de Production de Manuels, 1969), 56.

15. Charles Van Onselen, *Chibaro: African Mine Labor in Southern Rhodesia, 1900–1933* (London: Pluto Press, 1976), 191.

16. Hikabwe D. Chipande, "The Introduction and Development of Competitive Football in Zambia, 1930–1969" (Master's thesis, Norwegian School of Sports Science, 2009), 60–61.

17. Peter Alegi, "Katanga v Johannesburg: A History of the First Sub-Saharan African Football Championship, 1949–50," *African Historical Review* 31 (1999): 55–74.

18. The discussion in this section draws heavily from Wiebe Boer, "Nation-Building Exercise: Sporting Culture and the Rise of Football in Colonial Nigeria" (PhD diss., Yale University, 2003), 272–83.

19. Quoted in ibid., 271.

20. Ibid., 277.

21. Tadasu Tsuruta, "Simba or Yanga? Football and Urbanization in Dar es Salaam," in *Dar es Salaam: Histories from an Emerging African Metropolis*, ed. James R. Brennan, Andrew Burton, and Yusuf Lawi (Dar es Salaam: Mkuki na Nyota, 2007), 200.

22. Kindy, *Life and Politics*, 97.

23. Fair, *Pastimes and Politics*, 247.

24. Author interview with Sitsila, Langa, July 27, 1995.

25. Fair, *Pastimes and Politics*, 262.

26. FIFA.com, "Al-Ahly: Spirit of Success," February 23, 2009, http://www.fifa .com/classicfootball/news/newsid=1031856.html (accessed March 19, 2009); see

also David Goldblatt, *The Ball Is Round: A Global History of Soccer* (New York: Riverhead Books, 2008), 485.

27. Ahman Alawad Sikainga, *"City of Steel and Fire": A Social History of Atbara, Sudan's Railway Town, 1906–1984* (Portsmouth, NH: Heinemann, 2003), 84.

28. Seth Mataba Boois, *An Illustrated History of the Game of Football in Namibia, 1900–2000* (Windhoek: Namibia Economic Development Services, 2000), 6.

29. Martin, *Leisure and Society*, 112.

30. Fair, *Pastimes and Politics*, 244–46.

31. Alegi, *Laduma!* 31.

32. Ossie Stuart, "Players, Workers, and Protestors: Social Change and Soccer in Colonial Zimbabwe," in *Sport, Ethnicity and Identity*, ed. Jeremy MacClancy (Oxford: Berg, 1996), 177–78.

33. Alegi, *Laduma!* chap. 5; Tsuruta, "Simba or Yanga?" 201, n31; Marissa Moorman, *Intonations: A Social History of Music and Nation in Luanda, Angola, from 1945 to Recent Times* (Athens: Ohio University Press, 2008), 71–77.

34. See Bénédicte Van Peel, "Aux Débuts du football congolais," in *Itinéraires croisés de la modernité au Congo Belge, 1920–1950*, edited by Jean-Luc Vellut (Paris: Karthala, 2001), 168; Martin, *Leisure and Society*, 100–101; Théophile Muka, *Évolution du sport au Congo* (Kinshasa: Okapi: 1970), 19–27; Alegi, "Katanga v Johannesburg."

35. As a general rule, taxes levied on Africans contributed a significant portion of funds for African sport and leisure.

36. Stephen Borquaye, *The Saga of Accra Hearts of Oak Sporting Club* (Accra: New Times Press, 1968), 33.

37. Boer, "Nation-Building Exercise," 282–83.

38. In 1939, King Leopold III awarded the ASC the honorific title of "Royal Society"; in 1958 it merged with the football association in the Belgian colonies of Rwanda and Burundi to form the Association royale sportive congolaise et du Ruanda-Urundi (ASCRU). See Van Peel, "Aux débuts du football congolais."

39. Alegi, "Katanga v Johannesburg."

40. Martin, *Leisure and Society*, 104. For more information on the institutional history of sport in French Africa, see Bernadette Deville-Danthu, *Le sport en noir et blanc: Du sport colonial au sport africain dans les anciens territoires français d'Afrique occidentale, 1920–1965* (Paris: Harmattan, 1997).

41. Tsanga, *Le football camerounais*, 59–68.

42. Tsuruta, "Simba or Yanga?" 199. According to Leseth, the Tanganyika FA was formed in 1935. Anne Leseth, "The Use of *Juju* in Football: Sport and Witchcraft in Tanzania," in *Entering the Field: New Perspectives on World Football*, ed. Gary Armstrong and Richard Giulianotti (Oxford: Berg, 1997), 159–74.

43. Fair, *Pastimes and Politics*, 240–44.

44. Ibid., 237.

45. Clignet and Stark, "Modernisation and Football in Cameroun," 410.

46. Ossie Stuart, "The Lions Stir: Football in African Society," in *Giving the Game Away: Football, Politics and Culture on Five Continents*, ed. Stephen Wagg (London: Leicester University Press, 1995), 32–33.

47. Chipande, "Competitive Football in Zambia," 57–72; see also Ridgeway Liwena, *The Zambian Soccer Scene* (Lusaka: LIPPUHO, 2006).

48. Nuño Domingos, "Football and Colonialism, Domination and Appropriation: the Mozambican Case," *Soccer and Society* 8, no. 4 (2007): 478–94.

49. Martin, *Leisure and Society*, 107.

50. Christian Bromberger, *La partita di calcio: Etnologia di una passione* (Rome: Editori Riuniti, 1999), 244–45.

51. This section draws heavily on my *Laduma!* chap. 5.

52. *Bantu World*, August 23, 1941.

53. Martin, *Leisure and Society*, 122. Subsequent quotes in this paragraph are from this source.

54. Deville-Danthu, *Le sport*, 301.

55. *Gazette du Cameroun*, June 15, 1936, cited in Tsanga, *Le football camerounais*, 78.

56. Martin, *Leisure and Society*, 121.

57. Terence Ranger, "Pugilism and Pathology: African Boxing and the Black Urban Experience in Southern Rhodesia," in *Sport in Africa: Essays in Social History*, ed. William J. Baker and James A. Mangan (New York: Africana, 1987), 205–6.

58. Arnold Pannenborg, "How to Win a Football Match in Cameroon" (Leiden: African Studies Centre, 2008), 147.

59. Patrick Royer, "The Spirit of Competition: *Wak* in Burkina Faso," *Africa* 72, no. 3 (2002): 466.

60. Pannenborg, "How to Win," 120, and chaps. 6–7; and Michael Schatzberg, "Soccer, Science and Sorcery: Causation and African football," *Afrika Spectrum* 41, no. 3 (2006), 351–69.

61. Leseth, "Use of *Juju* in Football"; Schatzberg, "Soccer, Science and Sorcery"; and Pannenborg, "How to Win."

62. Fair, *Pastimes and Politics*, 238–39.

63. Tsuruta, "Simba or Yanga?" 200.

64. Moorman, *Intonations*, 67–77.

65. Elizabeth Gunner and Mafika Pascal Gwala, eds., *Musho! Zulu Popular Praises* (East Lansing: Michigan State University Press, 1991), 3–4.

66. Alegi, *Laduma!* 52.

67. Interview with P. Sitsila, July 27, 1995.

68. "Amalaita Attack Sportsmen," *Umteteli Wa Bantu*, April 1, 1933.

69. Martin, *Leisure and Society*, 124.

70. Pierre Lanfranchi, Christiane Eisenberg, Tony Mason, and Alfred Wahl, *100 Years of Football: The FIFA Centennial Book* (London: Weidenfeld and Nicolson, 2004), 156.

71. Ranger, "Pugilism and Pathology," 209.

72. Njabulo Ndebele, *South African Literature and Culture* (Manchester: Manchester University Press, 1994), 46.

73. Author interview with Stuurman, Factreton, February 25, 1998.

74. Alegi, *Laduma!* 67.

75. Igor Follot and Gérard Dreyfus, *Salif Keita: Mes quatre vérités* (Paris: Chiron, 1977), 15.

76. Tsanga, *Le football camerounais*, 103.

77. "Highlanders Football Club Copies Motherwell Style of Play," *Bantu World*, May 14, 1932.

78. Martin, *Leisure and Society*, 119. Nicknames are also from this source.

79. Van Peel, "Aux débuts du football congolais," 166–67.

80. Fair, *Pastimes and Politics*, 237.

81. Alegi, *Laduma!* 62.

CHAPTER THREE   Making Nations in Late Colonial Africa, 1940s–1964

1. By way of example, see Prosser Gifford and William Roger Louis, *Decolonization and African Independence: The Transfer of Power, 1960–1980* (New Haven: Yale University Press, 1988); Robert L. Tignor, *Capitalism and Nationalism at the End of Empire: State and Business in Decolonizing Egypt, Nigeria, and Kenya, 1945–1963* (Princeton: Princeton University Press, 1996); and Frederick Cooper, *Decolonization and African Society: The Labor Question in French and British Africa* (Cambridge: Cambridge University Press, 1996).

2. This section is based on Wiebe Boer, "Nation-Building Exercise: Sporting Culture and the Rise of Football in Colonial Nigeria" (PhD diss., Yale University, 2003); and Wiebe Boer, "A Story of Heroes, of Epics: The Rise of Football in Nigeria," in *Football in Africa: Conflict, Conciliation and Community*, ed. Gary Armstrong and Richard Giulianotti (Basingstoke: Palgrave Macmillan, 2004), 59–79.

3. Nigerian census data cited in Lisa A. Lindsay, *Working with Gender: Wage Labor and Social Change in Southwestern Nigeria* (Portsmouth, NH: Heinemann, 2003), 64.

4. Ibid., 134–36.

5. Karin Barber, *The Generation of Plays: Yoruba Popular Life in Theater* (Bloomington: Indiana University Press, 2000), 23.

6. James A. Mangan, *The Games Ethic and Imperialism: Aspects of the Diffusion of an Ideal* (New York: Viking, 1986). For a terrific synthesis, see Allen Guttmann, *Games and Empires: Modern Sports and Cultural Imperialism* (New York: Columbia University Press, 1994).

7. Nnamdi Azikiwe, *My Odyssey: An Autobiography* (New York: Praeger, 1970), 406–7.

8. Laura Fair, *Pastimes and Politics: Culture, Community, and Identity in Post-abolition Urban Zanzibar, 1890–1945* (Athens: Ohio University Press, 2001), 261–62.

9. Ahmad Alawad Sikainga, *"City of Steel and Fire": A Social History of Atbara, Sudan's Railway Town, 1906–1984* (Portsmouth, NH: Heinemann, 2003), 82–88, 105.

10. John Sugden and Alan Tomlinson, *FIFA and the Contest for World Football: Who Rules the People's Game?* (Cambridge: Polity Press, 1998), 129.

11. Boer, "Nation-Building Exercise," 308. Boer points out how after the war Azikiwe became more radical and, following in the footsteps of the goodwill tours, he toured Nigeria to build support for the new NCNC party, which he

had just founded with Herbert Macaulay, the elder statesman of Nigerian nationalist politics.

12. Phil Vasili, "Colonialism and Football: The First Nigerian Tour of Britain," *Race and Class* 36, no. 4 (1995): 60.

13. Railway won in 1946, 1948, 1949, 1951, 1956 and 1957; see Boer, "Nation-Building Exercise," 347; and "A Story of Heroes, of Epics," 67; and also Vasili, "Colonialism and Football," 58–59.

14. Benedict Anderson, *Imagined Communities: Reflections on the Origin and Spread of Nationalism*, rev. ed. (London: Verso, 1991), 44. On Azikiwe's journalistic ventures, see Louise M. Bourgault, *Mass Media in Sub-Saharan Africa* (Bloomington: Indiana University Press, 1995), 155–56.

15. See Vasili, "Colonialism and Football."

16. Ibid., 64.

17. Okere is believed to have been Swindon Town's first black player, though he failed to make the first team. Balogun played thirteen League matches (three goals), and two FA Cup matches (two goals) for QPR in 1956–57; cited in Phil Vasili, *Colouring over the White Line: The History of Black Footballers in Britain* (Edinburgh: Mainstream, 2000), 113. For more details on African players' migration to Europe, see chapter 5.

18. Boer, "Nation-Building Exercise," 358–59.

19. Vasili, *Colouring over the White Line*, 86–90. Uganda also toured England in 1956.

20. Information on the French West Africa Cup is from Bocar Ly, *Foot-ball, histoire de la Coupe d'A.O.F.* (Dakar: Nouvelles Editions Africaines du Sénégal, 1990). After the independence of Mali in 1960, the fusion of Jeanne D'Arc with Espérance formed Stade Malien and the fusion of Foyer de Soudan with Africa Sports created Djoliba.

21. Ibid., 89.

22. On the history of sport and imperialism in French West Africa, see Bernadette Deville-Danthu, *Le sport en noir et blanc: Du sport colonial au sport africain dans les anciens territoires français d'Afrique occidentale, 1920–1965* (Paris: Harmattan, 1997).

23. Frederick Cooper, *Africa since 1940: The Past of the Present* (Cambridge: Cambridge University Press, 2002), 77–78.

24. Phyllis Martin, *Leisure and Society in Colonial Brazzaville* (Cambridge: Cambridge University Press, 1995), 125.

25. Ibid.

26. Peter Alegi, "Katanga v Johannesburg: A History of the First Sub-Saharan African Football Championship, 1949–50," *African Historical Review* 31 (1999): 55–74.

27. The main source for this section is Rabah Saadallah and Djamel Benfars, *La glorieuse équipe du FLN* (Algiers: ENAL; Brussels; GAM, 1985). For a useful overview, see Youssef Fates, "Football in Algeria: Between Violence and Politics," in Armstrong and Giulianotti, *Football in Africa*, 41–58. For English-language works on Algeria's political and diplomatic history, see, for example, John Ruedy, *Modern*

Algeria: The Origins and Development of a Nation (Bloomington: Indiana University Press, 1992); and Matthew Connelly, *A Diplomatic Revolution: Algeria's Fight for Independence and the Origins of the Post–Cold War Era* (Oxford: Oxford University Press, 2002).

28. Maouche served several months in prison before resuming his career at Reims and then transferring to Red Star Paris. He joined the FLN team in 1960.

29. Saadallah and Benfars, *La glorieuse équipe*, 136

30. *New York Times*, April 16, 1958. Interestingly, the Times identified the men as "French athletes" in the headline and as "Algerian Moslems" in the body of the article.

31. *Time*, April 28, 1958.

32. *New York Times*, April 16, 1958.

33. Fates, "Football in Algeria," 49.

34. Curiously, Toulouse FC won the Cup with important contributions from Abdelhamid Bouchouk and Said Brahimi, both of whom joined the FLN side in spring 1958. It should also be noted that the French policy of assimilation resulted in Maghrebi teams being allowed to participate in the French Cup beginning in 1956.

35. El-Asnam is located 120 miles southwest of Algiers. In 1954 and 1980, two catastrophic earthquakes devastated the city.

36. Ruedy, *Modern Algeria*, 166.

37. Hocine Seddiki, *Rachid Mekhloufi: L'imagination au bout de pied* (Algiers: SNED, 1982), 14. Ferhat Abbas founded the Popular Union of Algeria in 1938 and expanded it into the AML in 1945, which Ruedy describes as "the second and last effort before the Revolution to create a broadly based national movement" (*Modern Algeria*, 150). In 1946, Abbas created the Union démocratique du manifeste algérien (UDMA), calling for an Algerian Republic within the French Union. Abbas joined the FLN in 1956.

38. Paul Darby, *Africa, Football, and FIFA: Politics, Colonialism, and Resistance* (London: Frank Cass, 2002), 29.

39. Philip Dine, "France, Algeria, and Sport: From Colonisation to Globalisation," *Modern and Contemporary France* 10, no. 4 (2002): 498.

40. Youssef Fates, "Sport en Algérie," in *Geschichte der Leibesübungen*, ed. Horst Überhorst, vol. 6, *Perspektiven des Weltsports* (Berlin: Bartels and Wernitz, 1989), 301, quoted in Guttmann, *Games and Empires*, 69.

41. Saadallah and Benfars, *La glorieuse équipe*, 69.

42. Ibid., 366.

43. Pierre Lanfranchi and Alfred Wahl, "The Immigrant as Hero: Kopa, Mekloufi and French Football," in *European Heroes: Myth, Identity, Sport*, ed. Richard Holt, J. A. Mangan, and Pierre Lanfranchi (London: Frank Cass, 1996), 119.

44. Saadallah and Benfars, *La glorieuse équipe*, 391–93. Overall, the FLN team scored 385 goals and conceded 127.

45. Lanfranchi and Wahl, "Immigrant as Hero," 123.

46. Faouzi Mahjoub, *Le football africain* (Paris: ABC, 1977), 10. For detailed analyses of changes in tactics and styles in world football, see Richard Giulianotti,

Football: A Sociology of the Global Game (Cambridge: Polity Press, 1999), 127–45; Pierre Lanfranchi, Christiane Eisenberg, Tony Mason, and Alfred Wahl, *100 Years of Football* (London: Weidenfeld and Nicolson, 2004), 152–68; Jonathan Wilson, *Inverting the Pyramid: A History of Football Tactics* (London: Orion, 2008).

47. Mike Cronin, *Sport and Nationalism in Ireland: Gaelic Games, Soccer and Irish Identity since 1884* (Dublin: Four Courts Press, 1999), 55.

48. See Connelly, *Diplomatic Revolution,* 226.

49. Saadallah and Benfars, *La glorieuse équipe,* 241.

50. Connelly, *Diplomatic Revolution,* 232.

51. Lanfranchi and Wahl, "Immigrant as Hero," 122.

52. In 1982 in Spain, Mekhloufi was the manager of the Algerian side that earned its first World Cup finals victory against West Germany.

53. This section summarizes material from several chapters of my *Laduma! Soccer, Politics, and Society in South Africa* (Scottsville: University of KwaZulu-Natal Press, 2004).

54. "Race" is a historical and social construction bound up with apartheid history, but racial identities were (and continue to be) crucial in South African life. Use of such racial terms does not imply an endorsement. On racial classification in South Africa, see Deborah Posel, "Race as Common Sense: Racial Classification in Twentieth-Century South Africa," *African Studies Review* 44, no. 2 (2001): 87–113.

55. For further analysis, see Alegi, *Laduma!* chaps. 6–8; and Paul Darby, "Stanley Rous's 'Own Goal': Football Politics, South Africa and the Contest for the FIFA Presidency in 1974," *Soccer and Society* 9, no. 2 (2008): 259–72.

56. Douglas Booth, *The Race Game: Sport and Politics in South Africa* (London: Frank Cass, 1998), 75–76.

CHAPTER FOUR   Nationhood, Pan-Africanism, and Football
             after Independence

1. "Soccerhene" photo in *Daily Graphic,* May 23, 1957; and Stephen Borquaye, *The Saga of Accra Hearts of Oak Sporting Club* (Accra: New Times Press, 1968), 50.

2. *West African Pilot,* April 28, 1960. Two days after the Togo-Nigeria match, Cameroon played Nigeria, but the game ended prematurely (with the score tied 0–0) when the Cameroonians stormed off the pitch in the second half in protest over a penalty awarded to Nigeria.

3. Eric Hobsbawm, *Nations and Nationalism since 1780: Programme, Myth, Reality* (Cambridge: Cambridge University Press, 1990), 143.

4. Crawford Young, *The African Colonial State in Comparative Perspective* (New Haven: Yale University Press, 1994), 25–40.

5. Christopher T. Gaffney, *Temples of the Earthbound Gods: Stadiums in the Cultural Landscapes of Rio de Janeiro and Buenos Aires* (Austin: University of Texas Press, 2008), 26. For a recent history of stadiums in the United States, see Ronald Trumpbour, *The New Cathedrals: Politics and Media in the History of Stadium Construction* (Syracuse: Syracuse University Press, 2007).

6. Gaffney, *Temples of the Earthbound Gods*, 26.

7. Ibid., 29.

8. See Louise M. Bourgault, *Mass Media in Sub-Saharan Africa* (Bloomington: Indiana University Press, 1995).

9. On the links between popular culture, broadcast media, and nationhood in colonial Africa, see Marissa Moorman, *Intonations: A Social History of Music and Nation in Luanda, Angola, from 1945 to Recent Times* (Athens: Ohio University Press, 2008).

10. Tamir Sorek, *Arab Soccer in a Jewish State* (Cambridge: Cambridge University Press, 2007), 82.

11. Jan Vansina, *Oral Tradition as History* (Madison: University of Wisconsin Press, 1985), 34; Solomon Waliaula and Basil Okong'o, "The Contemporary Oral Performance: The Case of the Radio Football Commentator" (unpublished manuscript, Moi University, 2009). My thanks to Solomon Waliaula for sharing his excellent work on Kenyan football.

12. Janet Lever, *Soccer Madness: Brazil's Passion for the World's Most Popular Sport* (Prospect Heights, IL: Waveland Press, 1995), 19.

13. Cf. Gareth Stanton, "Chasing the Ghosts: Narratives of Football and Nation in Morocco," in *Football in Africa: Conflict, Conciliation and Community*, ed. Gary Armstrong and Richard Giulianotti (Basingstoke: Palgrave Macmillan, 2004), 150–66.

14. African governments' "national development" strategies strengthened the relationship between football and articulations of nationhood. In the 1960s and 1970s, for instance, new sport and physical education programs in schools relied heavily on football due to its low cost and boys' passion for the game. Soviet use of "soft" power in Africa during the Cold War encouraged the use of sport as an "important element of national pride and social development, and an important factor of national unity." Baruch A. Hazan, "Sport as an Instrument of Political Expansion: The Soviet Union in Africa," in *Sport in Africa: Essays in Social History*, ed. William J. Baker and James A. Mangan (New York: Africana, 1987), 267.

15. Information on Ghana comes mainly from Ken Bediako, *The National Soccer League of Ghana: The Full Story, 1956–1995* (Accra: Bediako, 1996); Kevin S. Fridy and Victor Brobbey, "Win the Match and Vote for Me: The Politicisation of Ghana's Accra Hearts of Oak and Kumasi Asante Kotoko Football Clubs," *Journal of Modern African Studies* 47, no. 1 (2009): 1–21; and Paul Darby, *Africa, Football, and FIFA: Politics, Colonialism, and Resistance* (London: Frank Cass, 2002), 35–38.

16. Wiebe Boer, "Nation-Building Exercise: Sporting Culture and the Rise of Football in Colonial Nigeria" (PhD diss., Yale University, 2003).

17. A historic visit by Santos and Pelé in 1969 brought Nigeria to a standstill. The matches led to a temporary ceasefire between federal troops and Biafran forces.

18. This discussion of Senegal is based on Daour Gaye, *Crises et perspectives du football sénégalais* (Saint-Louis: Xamal, 1999).

19. Ibid., 22, 36–37.

20. Bangela Lema, "Sport in Zaire," in *Sport in Asia and Africa: A Comparative Handbook*, ed. Eric A. Wagner (Westport, CT: Greenwood Press, 1989), 229–47.

21. Arnold Pannenborg, *How to Win a Football Match in Cameroon* (Leiden: African Studies Centre, 2008), 23.

22. Ibid., 23.

23. Hyder Kindy, *Life and Politics in Mombasa* (Nairobi: East African Publishing House, 1972), 104. Additional information gleaned from Godia in *Sport in Asia and Africa,* and Solomon Waliaula, "Wrangling in Kenyan Football: A Symptom of Displaced Identity" (unpublished manuscript).

24. Dean E. McHenry, "The Use of Sports in Policy Implementation: The Case of Tanzania," *Journal of Modern African Studies* 18, no. 2 (1980): 237–56; Tadasu Tsuruta, "Simba or Yanga? Football and Urbanization in Dar es Salaam," in *Dar es Salaam: Histories from an Emerging Metropolis,* ed. James R. Brennan, Andrew Burton, and Yusuf Lawi (Dar es Salaam: Mkuki na Nyota, 2007), 198–212.

25. Ridgeway Liwena, *The Zambian Soccer Scene* (Lusaka: LIPPUHO, 2006).

26. Bea Vidacs, "Football in Cameroon: A Vehicle for the Expansion and Contraction of Identity," in *Football Culture: Local Contests, Global Visions,* ed. Gerry G. T. Finn and Richard Giulianotti (London: Frank Cass, 2000), 100–117.

27. Fridy and Brobbey, "Win the Match and Vote for Me," 5.

28. For example, Asante Kotoko claims that in 1962 Hearts and Real Republikans played a "fixed" 0–0 match that denied the Kumasi club the title by a single point. Earlier in the season, Kotoko had almost withdrawn from the league as a result of losing its star players Dogo Moro and Baba Yara to Real Republikans. On the controversy, see Bediako, *National Soccer League of Ghana,* 13–14.

29. Vidacs, "Football in Cameroon," 61.

30. Solomon Waliaula, "The Role of Football Cultures in Performing/Constructing Identities to Foster Peace and Stability in the 21st-Century Kenyan Society" (paper presented at the Kenya Oral Literature Association Symposium, 2008), 10–12.

31. Richard Giulianotti, "Between Colonialism, Independence and Globalization: Football in Zimbabwe," in Giulianotti and Armstrong, *Football in Africa,* 80–99.

32. Quotation is from David Goldblatt, *The Ball Is Round: A Global History of Soccer* (New York: Riverhead Books, 2008), 70. For more details, see William James Murray, *The Old Firm: Sectarianism, Sport and Society in Scotland* (Edinburgh: John Donald, 1984); and *The Old Firm in the New Age: Celtic and Rangers since the Souness Revolution* (Edinburgh: Mainstream, 1998).

33. Phil Ball, *Morbo: The Story of Spanish Football* (London: WSC Books, 2001); John Walton, "Basque Football Rivalries in the Twentieth Century," in *Fear and Loathing in World Football,* ed. Gary Armstrong and Richard Giulianotti (Oxford: Berg, 2001), 119–33; Jeremy MacClancy, "Nationalism at Play: The Basques of Vizcaya and Athletic Club de Bilbao," in *Sport, Ethnicity and Identity,* ed. Jeremy MacClancy (Oxford: Berg, 1996), 181–99; Jimmy Burns, *Barca: A People's Passion* (London: Bloomsbury, 1998).

34. Simon Kuper, *Ajax, the Dutch, the War: Football in Europe during the Second World War* (London: Orion, 2003).

35. Sorek, *Arab Soccer in a Jewish State,* 1–2.

36. William J. Baker, "Political Games: The Meaning of International Sport for Independent Africa," in *Sport in Africa: Essays in Social History*, ed. William J. Baker and James A. Mangan (New York: Africana, 1987), 274.

37. John Sugden and Alan Tomlinson, *FIFA and the Contest for World Football: Who Rules the People's Game* (Cambridge: Polity Press, 1998), 9.

38. "CAF Is Born," *CAFoot* 88 (February 2007): 15.

39. Sugden and Tomlinson, *FIFA and the Contest for World Football*, 29.

40. Those in attendance were Ahmed Rahma, Ahmed Ali Singawi, Ahmed Aidrous, Abdel Rahim Sheddad, and Abdel Halim Mohamed (all from Sudan); Mostafa Kamel Mansour, Galal Koreitem, Mourad Fahmy, Abdallah Abdelaziz Salem, and Youssef Mohamed (Egypt); Yidnecatchew Tessema, Aman Andom, and Gegeyehu Dube (Ethiopia); and Fred Fell (South Africa).

41. SAFA, *Minutes of Special General Meeting*, October 27, 1956; "S.A. out of Khartoum Tournament: Now Rangers Can Ask for Tour of Europe," *Rand Daily Mail*, December 29, 1956, cited in Chris Bolsmann, "White Football in South Africa: Empire, Apartheid and Change, 1892–1977," in *South Africa and the Global Game: Football, Apartheid and Beyond*, ed. Peter Alegi and Chris Bolsmann (London: Routledge, forthcoming).

42. Barbara Keys, *Globalizing Sport: National Rivalry and International Community in the 1930s* (Cambridge: Harvard University Press, 2006), 179.

43. Solomon Getahun, "Introduction: A Short History of Sport in Ethiopia," (unpublished manuscript, 2008).

44. Alex Last, "Containment and Counter-Attack: A History of Eritrean Football," in Giulianotti and Armstrong, *Football in Africa*, 27–40.

45. Darby, *Africa, Football, and FIFA*, 36.

46. "Report by the President on the First African Games," July 1965, FIFA Archives, Zurich. I am indebted to Chris Bolsmann for sending me a copy of this document.

47. For various reasons, clubs from eastern and southern Africa never established a winning tradition, the 1995 champion Orlando Pirates from South Africa proving the exception to this trend.

48. Mobutu also bankrolled the national team, known as the Leopards, which won two African Nations Cup titles and qualified for the 1974 World Cup finals in Germany. Mobutu also sponsored the 1974 heavyweight championship boxing match in Kinshasa between Mohammad Ali and George Foreman, known as the "Rumble in the Jungle."

49. Biographical information on Tessema from http://www.tessemas.net (accessed February 17, 2009) and Paul Dietschy and David-Claude Kemo-Keimbou, *Le football et l'Afrique* (Paris: EPA, 2008), 196–97.

50. CAF Minutes, cited in Dietschy and Kemo-Keimbou, *Le football et l'Afrique*, 197.

51. Ministry of the Interior (South Africa), letter to FASA, June 20, 1960.

52. FIFA, Minutes of the XXXIInd Ordinary Congress, cited in Paul Darby, "Stanley Rous's 'Own Goal': Football Politics, South Africa and the Contest for the FIFA Presidency in 1974," *Soccer and Society* 9, no. 2 (2008): 263.

53. FIFA, "Report of the Visit of Sir Stanley Rous and Mr. J. Maguire to South Africa," (1963), 4; Rous Papers, University of Brighton. My thanks to Alan Tomlinson for access to this document.

54. Baruch A. Hazan, "Sport as an Instrument of Political Expansion: The Soviet Union in Africa," in Baker and Mangan, *Sport in Africa*, 267.

55. Darby, "Stanley Rous's 'Own Goal,'" 268. For an overview of the 1973 South African Games, see Douglas Booth, *The Race Game: Sport and Politics in South Africa* (London: Frank Cass, 1998), 99–104.

56. M. Katimia, "The Fight for Recognition," *African Soccer*, no. 35 (June 1998): 54.

57. Darby, *Africa, Football, and FIFA*, 53.

58. For details, see Andrew Jennings, *Foul! The Secret World of FIFA: Bribes, Vote Rigging and Ticket Scandals* (London: HarperCollins, 2006); and Barbara Smit, *Pitch Invasion: Adidas, Puma and the Making of Modern Sport* (London: Penguin, 2007).

59. Germany scored early and won a famously uneventful match 1-0, thus ensuring that both teams advanced to the second round. In response to widespread allegations of a "fix," FIFA decided to kick off the last round of World Cup matches in each group simultaneously.

CHAPTER FIVE   Football Migration to Europe since the 1930s

1. Evariste Tshimanga Bakadiababu, *Le commerce et la traite des footballeurs africains et sud-américains en Europe* (Paris: Harmattan, 2001), 114–15.

2. Raffaele Poli, "Migrations and Trade of African Football Players: Historic, Geographical and Cultural Aspects," *Afrika Spectrum* 41, no. 3 (2006): 411.

3. Tshimanga Bakadiababu, *Le commerce et la traite;* and Joseph Arbena, "Dimensions of International Talent Migration in Latin American Sports," in *The Global Sports Arena: Athletic Talent Migration in an Interdependent World,* ed. John Bale and Joseph Maguire (London: Frank Cass, 1994), 99–111.

4. T. J. Hatton and Jeffrey G. Williamson, *Global Migration and the World Economy: Two Centuries of Policy and Performance* (Cambridge, MA: MIT Press, 2005), 264. These recent numbers are far larger than those of the colonial era, as discussed in Emmanuel K. Akyeampong, "Africans in the Diaspora: The Diaspora and Africa," *African Affairs* 99 (2000): 198, 200.

5. For data on remittances, see United Nations International Fund for Agricultural Development (IFAD), "Remittances Forum: Africa," http://www.ifad.org/events/remittances/maps/africa.htm (accessed June 1, 2008); and Cerstin Sander and Samuel Munzele Maimbo, "Migrant Labor Remittances in Africa: Reducing Obstacles to Developmental Contributions," Africa Region Working Paper Series No. 64, World Bank, November 2003, http://www.worldbank.org/afr/wps/wp64.pdf (accessed June 1, 2008). Countries like Ghana are estimated to have 12 percent of their population living abroad; cited in Akyeampong, "Africans in the Diaspora."

6. Joseph Maguire and John Bale, "Introduction: Sports Labour Migration in the Global Arena," in Maguire and Bale, *Global Sports Arena*, 2; Patrick Manning, *Migration in World History* (Routledge, 2005); Akyeampong, "Africans in the Diaspora."

Quote is from Stephen Castles and Mark J. Miller, *The Age of Migration: International Population Movements in the Modern World* (New York: Guilford Press, 1993), 4.

7. Philip Curtin, *Why People Move: Migration in African History* (Waco, TX: Markham Press Fund, 1995). I am unaware of any academic study on the history of African women's football migration. There is no serious discussion of Africans in Jean Williams, *A Beautiful Game: International Perspectives on Women's Football* (Oxford: Berg, 2007).

8. Paul Darby, "Out of Africa: The Exodus of Elite African Football Talent to Europe," *Working USA* 10 (2007): 445–46. On African players in Asia, see Projit Bihari Mukharji, "'Feeble Bengalis' and 'Big Africans': African Players in Bengali Club Football," *Soccer and Society* 9, no. 2 (2008): 273–85.

9. Akyeampong, "Africans in the Diaspora," 199.

10. Darby, "Out of Africa," 446.

11. Castles and Miller, *Age of Migration*, 5.

12. David Goldblatt, *The Ball Is Round: A Global History of Soccer* (New York: Riverhead Books, 2008), 489.

13. The number of registered players is cited in Pierre Lanfranchi and Matthew Taylor, *Moving with the Ball: The Migration of Professional Footballers* (Oxford: Berg, 2001), 172. See also Youssef Fates, "Football in Algeria: Between Violence and Politics," in *Football in Africa: Conflict, Conciliation and Community*, ed. Gary Armstrong and Richard Giulianotti (Basingstoke: Palgrave Macmillan, 2004), 41–58; and Barry G. Baker, *A Journal of African Football History, 1883–2000* (Rijmenam: Heart Books, 2001), 16–23.

14. William James Murray, *The World's Game: A History of Soccer* (Champaign: University of Illinois Press, 1996).

15. Biographical information on Raoul Diagne comes from Bocar Ly, *Foot-ball, histoire de la Coupe d'A.O.F.* (Dakar: Nouvelles Editions Africaines du Sénégal, 1990), 14–16; Mauro Valeri, *La razza in campo: Per una storia della Rivoluzione Nera nel calcio* (Rome: Edizioni Psicoanalisi Contro, 2005), 92–94; and Lanfranchi and Taylor, *Moving with the Ball*, 172.

16. Diagne died in November 2002 in France.

17. "Death of a Star: Larbi Ben Barek," *African Soccer* (December/February 1992/93): 22; Faouzi Mahjoub, *Le football africain* (Paris: ABC, 1977); and Valeri, *La razza in campo*, 94–96, 262–63.

18. Lanfranchi and Taylor, *Moving with the Ball*, 173.

19. "Death of a Star: Larbi Ben Barek."

20. Laurent Dubois, *Soccer Empire: The World Cup and the Future of France* (Berkeley and Los Angeles: University of California Press, forthcoming 2010), 59 (manuscript). My thanks to Laurent Dubois for sharing portions of his book manuscript in process.

21. Lanfranchi and Taylor, *Moving with the Ball*, 174.

22. Marc Barreaud, *Dictionnaire des footballeurs étrangers du championnat professionnel français, 1932–1997* (Paris: Harmattan, 1998); and Lanfranchi and Taylor, *Moving with the Ball*, 173.

23. This is a phrase used by Dubois in *Soccer Empire*, chap. 2.

24. Bernadette Deville-Danthu, *Le sport en noir et blanc: Du sport colonial au sport africain dans les anciens territories français d'Afrique occidentale, 1920–1965* (Paris: Harmattan, 1997), 292; and Barreaud, *Dictionnaire des footballeurs étrangers.*

25. Lanfranchi and Taylor, *Moving with the Ball,* 177.

26. Ibid., 175; Barreaud, *Dictionnaire des footballeurs étrangers,* 125. As a citizen of newly independent Cameroon, and therefore a foreigner in France, N'jo Lea could not join the union. In his final season in 1961–62, N'jo Lea played only one match for Lyon and two for Racing Club de Paris.

27. Among many recent incidents in Europe, see "[Barcelona Striker] Eto'o Makes Anti-racism Protest," BBC Sport, February 26, 2006, http://news.bbc.co .uk/sport2/hi/football/europe/4751876.stm (accessed May 23, 2008); and "[Messina's Ivoirian Defender] Zoro Suffers More racist Abuse," BBC Sport, http://news .bbc.co.uk/sport2/hi/football/africa/4476412.stm (accessed May 23, 2008).

28. For analysis of racism in European football, see Udo Merkel and Walter Tokarski, eds., *Racism and Xenophobia in European Football* (Aachen: Meyer and Meyer Verlag, 1996); and Sir Norman Chester Centre for Football Research, "Factsheet 6: Racism and Football," http://www.le.ac.uk/footballresearch/resources/ factsheets/fs6.html (accessed May 10, 2008).

29. There is a rich interdisciplinary literature on "stacking" in the United States. For a pioneering study, see J. W. Loy and J. F. McElvogue, "Racial Discrimination in American Sport," *International Review of Sport Sociology* 5 (1970): 5–24. For a historical perspective, see David Kenneth Wiggins, "'Great Speed but Little Stamina': The Historical Debate over Black Athletic Superiority," in *Glory Bound: Black Athletes in a White America* (Syracuse: Syracuse University Press, 1997), 177–99. On stacking in British football, see Joseph Maguire, "Race and Position Assignment in English Soccer: A Preliminary Analysis of Ethnicity and Sport in Britain," *Sociology of Sport Journal* 5 (1988): 257–69; and "Sport, Racism, and British Society: A Sociological Study of England's Elite Male Afro-Caribbean Soccer and Rugby Union Players," in *Sport, Racism, and Ethnicity,* ed. Grant Jarvie (London: Falmer, 1991), 94–123.

30. According to data reported in *Dictionnaire des footballeurs étrangers,* the numbers were as follows: Cameroon (twenty-four players): fifteen strikers, seven midfielders, and two defenders. Ivory Coast (fifteen): eleven strikers, two midfielders, two defenders. Senegal (ten): five strikers, four midfielders, one defender. Togo (eight): four strikers, two midfielders, two defenders. Republic of Congo (seven): six strikers, one midfielder. Mali (four): four strikers. Guinea (three): two strikers, one defender; Gabon (two): one striker; one midfielder. Benin (one): midfielder. Chad (one): striker. This evidence also suggests that the careers of African midfielders tended to be shorter and less successful than those of strikers and defenders.

31. Phil Vasili, *Colouring over the White Line* (Edinburgh: Mainstream, 2000), 116.

32. Maguire, "Race and Position Assignment in English soccer," 264.

33. Kick It Out, "Telegraph Report on Black Managers in England," http:// www.kickitout.org/513.php (accessed June 30, 2009).

34. Nuño Domingos, "Football and Colonialism, Domination and Appropriation: The Mozambican Case," *Soccer and Society* 8, no. 4 (2007): 478–94; and Paul Darby, "African Football Migration to Portugal: Colonial and Neo-colonial Resource," *Soccer and Society* 8, no. 4 (2007): 495–509. See also Valeri, *La razza in campo*, 240–61.

35. Some of the earliest African-born players who arrived in Portugal in the 1920s were white: defender José Bastos (Benfica) and midfielder Martinho de Oliveira (Sporting). The latter was the first "African" to be capped (1928), but Guilherme Espirito Santo was probably the first black African player to play for Portugal (1937). See João Coelho and Francisco Pinheiro, *A Paixão do Povo: História do futebol em Portugal* (Porto: Ed. Afrontamento, 2002).

36. Lanfranchi and Taylor, *Moving with the Ball*, 179.

37. Angelo Oliveira, *Isto de futebóis* (Maputo: Ndjira, 1998), 8; Lanfranchi and Taylor, *Moving with the Ball*, 179.

38. Matateu scored 218 goals in 289 first-division matches. He moved to Canada in the early 1970s, where he died in November 2000.

39. Valeri, *La razza in campo*, 249–57. As Portugal captain, Coluña was granted a special exemption from the racist law that prevented blacks from serving in the armed forces.

40. Goldblatt, *Ball Is Round*, 425.

41. Gary Armstrong, "The Migration of the Black Panther: An Interview with Eusebio of Mozambique and Portugal," in Armstrong and Giulianotti, *Football in Africa*, 252.

42. Biographical information on Carlos Alhinho is from Lanfranchi and Taylor, *Moving with the Ball*, 181.

43. Ibid., 182.

44. Vasili, *Colouring over the White Line;* and Valeri, *La razza in campo*, 277–86.

45. Phil Vasili, *The First Black Footballer: Arthur Wharton, 1865–1930* (London: Frank Cass, 1998). Wharton's career continued with Rotherham Town, Sheffield United, and other clubs until 1902. He was a fiercely tenacious and talented multisport athlete. In addition to being an elite footballer, he also held the first world record in the hundred-yard dash and played professional cricket.

46. Vasili, *Colouring over the White Line*, 111–17.

47. Ibid., 115; Wiebe Boer, "Nation-Building Exercise: Sporting Culture and the Rise of Football in Colonial Nigeria" (PhD diss., Yale University, 2003), 392–95.

48. Stephen Mokone and J. W. Ryan, *Kalamazoo! The Life and Times of a Soccer Player* (Pretoria: De Jager-Haum, 1980), 34.

49. No record exists of Mokone playing in Serie A. Mokone did make several appearances with Torino's reserves in the De Martino (Reserves) League. After his football career ended, Mokone moved to the United States, where he became an academic. He served nine years in prison for assaulting his American wife. Mokone is the founder and director of the Kalamazoo South African Foundation for Education through Sport.

50. Vasili, *Colouring over the White Line*, 107–11.

51. Peter Raath, *Soccer through the Years 1862–2002: The First Official History of South African Soccer* (Cape Town: Peter Raath, 2002), 13–22.

52. Vasili, *Colouring over the White Line,* 106, 100.

53. Germany witnessed African migration in the 1960s as well. Fortuna Düsseldorf's Ghanaian forward Charles Kumi Gyamfi was probably the first African to play in the Bundesliga (1959–61). Gyamfi's compatriot Ibrahim Sunday later played for Werder Bremen.

54. As Belgium became a launch pad for secondary (or internal) migration within Europe in the 1980s, many Moroccans and Senegalese hoped to earn a move to France, while Nigerians (e.g., Daniel Amokachi, Celestine Babayaro), Ghanaians, Sierra Leonans, Zambians, and others aimed for England.

55. Marc Broere and Roy van der Drift, *Football Africa!* (Cape Town: David Philip, 1997), 99.

56. Paul Darby, "The New Scramble for Africa: African Football Labour Migration to Europe," in *Europe, Sport, World: Shaping Global Societies,* ed. James A. Mangan (London: Frank Cass, 2001), 217–44.

57. Pierre Lanfranchi, Christiane Eisenberg, Tony Mason, and Alfred Wahl, *100 Years of Football: The FIFA Centennial Book* (London: Weidenfeld and Nicolson, 2004), 168.

58. Keita, quoted in J. Copnall, BBC Sport, October 27, 2003, http://news.bbc .co.uk/go/pr/fr/-/sport2/hi/football/africa/3218333.stm (accessed May 14, 2008).

59. The French magazine *France Football* awarded the African Footballer of the Year from 1970 to 1994. CAF has given the award since 1992.

60. Arguably the greatest Algerian player of all time, Madjer subsequently coached the national team and currently works as a football analyst for Al Jazeera satellite television network.

61. For details on Berlusconi, AC Milan, and soccer politics, see Nicola Porro and Pippo Russo, "Berlusconi and Other Matters: The Era of 'Football-Politics,'" *Journal of Modern Italian Studies* 5, no. 3 (2001): 348–70.

62. The information in this paragraph draws heavily from Gary Armstrong, "The Global Footballer and the Local War-Zone: George Weah and Transnational Networks in Liberia, West Africa," in *Globalization and Sport,* ed. Richard Giulianotti and Roland Robertson (London: Wiley-Blackwell, 2007), 122–39.

63. Stefan Szymanski and Andrew S. Zimbalist, *National Pastime: How Americans Play Baseball and the Rest of the World Plays Soccer* (Washington: Brookings Institution Press, 2005), 161.

64. Cf. Tshimanga Bakadiababu, *Le commerce et la traite.*

65. Lanfranchi and Taylor, *Moving with the Ball,* 187–88.

66. Poli, "Migrations and Trade of African Football Players." These numbers are even more remarkable if we consider the implications of the European Commission's 1995 Bosman ruling. By eliminating any barrier to player movement within the European Union, the Bosman case made it more difficult for non-EU players, especially Africans and Latin Americans, to find employment in many EU leagues.

67. Goldblatt, *Ball Is Round*, 768.

68. The main sources for these data are Raffaele Poli, *Les migrations internationales des footballeurs: Trajectoires de joueurs camerounais en Suisse* (Neuchatel: CIES, 2004), 61, and "Africans' Status in the European Football Players' Labour Market," *Soccer and Society* 7, nos. 2–3 (2006): 291. On this topic, see also John Bale, "Three Geographies of African Footballer Migration: Patterns, Problems and Postcoloniality," in Armstrong and Giulianotti, *Football in Africa*, 229–46.

69. Tshimanga Bakadiababu, *Le commerce et la traite*.

70. UN report cited in Bale, "Three Geographies of African Footballer Migration," 240.

71. A major reason for the relatively low number of Africans in Britain is a strict work permit rule that requires players from outside of the European Union to have played in 75 percent of their country's national team matches in the two years immediately preceding the application.

72. Former Ghana coach Petre Gavrila from Romania seems to be the source of the Ghanaian migration to Romania; see Poli, "Africans' Status," 289.

73. Raffaele Poli, "Football Players' Migration in Europe: A Geo-economic Approach to Africans' Mobility," in *The Bountiful Game? Football Identities and Finances*, ed. Jonathan Magee, Alan Bairner, and Alan Tomlinson (Oxford: Meyer and Meyer Sport, 2005), 218.

74. Lanfranchi and Taylor, *Moving with the Ball*, 235.

75. Castles and Miller, *Age of Migration*, 179.

76. Franklin Foer, *How Soccer Explains the World: An Unlikely Theory of Globalization* (New York: HarperCollins, 2004), 141–66. All quotes in this paragraph are from this source (153, 164).

77. M. Gleeson, "The Professionals: Africans in Europe," *African Soccer* (September/October 1995): 28.

78. For more details, see Poli, "Africans' Status," 287–89.

79. Raffaele Poli and Paul Dietschy, "Le football africain entre immobilisme et extraversion," *Politique Africaine* 102 (2006): 173–87.

80. From Darby, "New Scramble for Africa," and Filippo M. Ricci, *African Football Yearbook* (Rome: Filippo Maria Ricci Editore 2000). The Indomitable Lions' twenty-three-man squad in the 2008 African Cup of Nations featured only one player from a Cameroonian club.

81. Poli, "Migrations and Trade of African Football Players," 404; Poli and Dietschy, "Le football africain," 180.

82. Broere and Drift, *Football Africa!* 93–94.

83. Hayatou, quoted in Darby, "African Football Migration to Portugal," 503.

84. James Ferguson, *Global Shadows: Africa in the Neoliberal World Order* (Durham: Duke University Press, 2006), 41.

CHAPTER SIX   The Privatization of Football, 1980s to Recent Times

1. For an overview, see Richard Giulianotti, "Playing an Aerial Game: The New Political Economy of Soccer," in *The Political Economy of Sport*, ed. John

Nauright and Kimberly S. Schimmel (Basingstoke: Palgrave Macmillan, 2005), 19–37.

2. David Goldblatt, *The Ball Is Round: A Global History of Soccer* (New York: Riverhead Books, 2008), 688.

3. Walter LaFeber, *Michael Jordan and the New Global Capitalism* (New York: W. W. Norton, 2002), 70–71.

4. This discussion on African media draws mainly on Louise M. Bourgault, *Mass Media in Sub-Saharan Africa* (Bloomington: Indiana University Press, 1995), chaps. 4–5; and Chris A. Paterson, "Reform or Re-colonisation? The Overhaul of African Television," *Review of African Political Economy* 78 (1998): 571–83.

5. Paterson, "Reform or Re-colonisation?" 575.

6. Data are from September 2008, http://www.multichoice.co.za/multichoice/view/multichoice/en/page235 (accessed May 19, 2009). Note that Multichoice pioneered subscription-based TV in South Africa when it launched M-Net in 1986, a service similar to Canal Plus in France.

7. http://www.sufc.co.za/default.aspx?Id=2136&des=content (accessed May 21, 2009).

8. Gerard Akindes, "Football in Sub-Saharan Africa, New Technologies and Broadcasting Deregulation: Football Development or Electronic Colonialism?" (paper presented at the African Studies Association annual meeting, Chicago, 2008). I am indebted to Gerard Akindes for giving me a copy of his paper.

9. Quoted in ibid., 2.

10. Ibid., 3.

11. Ngugi wa Thiong'o, *Decolonising the Mind: The Politics of Language in African Literature* (Portsmouth, NH: Heinemann; London: James Currey, 1986), 20.

12. Born in Algeria, Darmon introduced the practice of placing corporate logos on team shirts with Nantes FC in 1970. In the 1980s, Darmon's company developed lucrative relationships with the French Football Federation and the National Football League (now Ligue 1). He then capitalized on the privatization of French television by helping his clients sell broadcasting rights to pay-TV station Canal Plus and, later, other satellite channels, thus generating unprecedented revenue streams for French football.

13. Jalala Bouzrara, "Game, Set and Match," *African Soccer,* no. 30 (January 1998): 12.

14. Goldblatt, *Ball Is Round,* 882.

15. CAF also imposed a 5 percent "tax" on prize money to be paid to the eight clubs' national associations, allegedly for "development" purposes. It should also be noted that in 2004 the eight teams eliminated in the Champions League's round of sixteen dropped into the new Confederation Cup, thus giving them a second opportunity to earn valuable prize money.

16. Geoff Hare, *Football in France: A Cultural History* (Oxford: Berg, 2003), 149.

17. Akindes, "Football in Sub-Saharan Africa," 18. The new contract also covered CAF club competitions and youth tournaments. In part due to the global recession, the 2010–16 marketing package, valued at $115 million, had not been sold as of August 2009.

18. Ashwin Desai and Goolam H. Vahed, "World Cup 2010: Africa's Turn or the Turn on Africa?" in *South Africa and the Global Game: Football, Apartheid, and Beyond,* ed. Peter Alegi and Chris Bolsmann (London: Routledge, forthcoming).

19. Radebe, quoted in Osasu Obayiuwana and Anver Versi, "The Economics of Football," *African Business* (June 1998): 10.

20. In this respect, Africa resembles Latin America; see Gideon Rachman, "Beautiful Game, Lousy Business: The Problems of Latin American Football," in *Football in the Americas: Fútbol, Futebol, Soccer,* ed. Rory Miller and Liz Crolley (London: Institute for the Study of the Americas, 2007), 161–73; and J. Luiz Martins do Melo, "Brazilian Football: Technical Success and Economic Failure," in Miller and Crolley, *Football in the Americas,* 193–208.

21. Alan M. Klein, *Sugarball: The American Game, the Dominican Dream* (New Haven: Yale University Press, 1991), 60.

22. Merryman Kunene, "Winning the Cup but Losing the Plot? The Troubled State of South African Soccer," in *State of the Nation: South Africa, 2005–2006,* ed. S. Buhlungu et al. (Cape Town: HSRC Press, 2006), 376.

23. Andreas Mehler, "Football in Africa: Are the 'Democratic' Lions about to Take Over?" http://www.nai.uu.se/publications/news/archives/023mehler/ (accessed May 31, 2009).

24. See Peter Alegi, "Like Cows Driven to a Dip: The 2001 Ellis Park Stadium Disaster, Johannesburg, South Africa," in *Soccer and Disaster: International Perspectives,* ed. Paul Darby, Martin Johnes, and Gavin Mellor (London: Routledge, 2005), 109–23.

25. See Peter Alegi, *Laduma! Soccer, Politics and Society in South Africa* (Scottsville: University of KwaZulu-Natal Press, 2004); and Alegi and Bolsmann, *South Africa and the Global Game.*

26. http://www.enyimbafc.net/sponsors/ (accessed May 20, 2009).

27. Goran Hyden, *African Politics in Comparative Perspective* (Cambridge: Cambridge University Press, 2006), 98.

28. Paul Nugent, *Africa since Independence: A Comparative History* (Basingstoke: Palgrave Macmillan, 2004), 327.

29. This section relies on Paul Darby, Gerard Akindes, and Matthew Kirwin, "Football Academies and the Migration of African Football Labor to Europe," *Journal of Sport and Social Issues* 31, no. 2 (2007): 143–61; and Emmanuel Maradas et al., "Special Report: Football Academies," *African Soccer* 66 (2001): 6–15.

30. As the work of Darby, Akindes, and Kirwin indicates, these categories are somewhat permeable given that academies can change their structure and format over time.

31. Romanian coach Petre Gavrila capitalized on his experience coaching in Africa Ghana's Black Stars by acting as an intermediary in the sale of numerous Ghanaians to Romanian clubs. See Raffaele Poli, "Africans' Status in the European Football Players' Labour Market," *Soccer and Society* 7, nos. 2–3 (2006): 289.

32. Maradas et al., "Special Report," 8.

33. "Kolo Touré on his African Nations adventure," *Worldsoccer.com,* January 17, 2008, http://www.worldsoccer.com/interviews/kolo_toure_on_his_african_ nations_adventure_interview_174537.html (accessed May 22, 2009).

34. Darby, Akindes, and Kirwin, "Football Academies," 150.

35. Only one player from the Feyenoord Fetteh academy ever signed with the parent club in Rotterdam (as of June 2009): Mohammed Abubakari. He now plays in the Greek second division.

36. Maradas et al., "Special Report," 17.

37. Rachman, "Beautiful Game, Lousy Business," 166.

38. Brian Oliver, "Roaring Success," *Observer Sport Monthly,* May 19, 2002.

39. Darby, Akindes, and Kirwin, "Football Academies," 153.

40. Ibid.

41. Ibid., 144.

42. "Special Report," 8.

43. This section is based mainly on these sources: Cynthia F. Pelak, "Women and South African Soccer: A Brief History," in Alegi and Bolsmann, *South Africa and the Global Game,* and "Negotiating Gender/Race/Class Constraints in the New South Africa: A Case Study of Women's Soccer," *International Review for the Sociology of Sport* 40, no. 1 (2005): 53–70; and Martha Saavedra, "Football Feminine— Development of the African Game: Senegal, Nigeria, and South Africa," *Soccer and Society* 4, nos. 2–3 (2003): 225–53, and "Regional Outliers: Female Football in Kenya" (paper presented at the African Studies Association annual meeting, New York, October 2007).

44. Saavedra, "Football Feminine," 225.

45. Wiebe Boer, "Nation-Building Exercise: Sporting Culture and the Rise of Football in Colonial Nigeria" (PhD diss., Yale University, 2003), 410–12.

46. See Jean Williams, *A Beautiful Game: International Perspectives on Women's Football* (Oxford: Berg, 2007).

47. Saavedra, "Football Feminine," 239.

48. Pelak, "Women and South African Soccer." All subsequent quotes in this paragraph are from this source.

49. Saavedra, "Football Feminine," 240.

50. Pelak, "Women and South African Soccer."

51. Ibid.

52. http://www.fifa.com/newscentre/news/newsid=91235.html (accessed May 27, 2009).

53. R. Ammoh, "The Goal Queen," *African Soccer* 63 (January/February 2001): 26–29.

54. Saavedra, "Football Feminine," 232.

55. Quoted in Pelak, "Women and South African Soccer."

56. Sarah Forde, *Playing by Their Rules: Coastal Teenage Girls in Kenya on Life, Love and Football* (Kilifi: Moving the Goalposts, 2008), 185.

57. For more details on MYSA, see Martha Brady and Arjmand Banu Khan, *Letting Girls Play: The Mathare Youth Sports Association's Football Program for Girls*

(New York: Population Council, 2002); and Hans Hognestad and Arvid Tollisen, "Playing against Deprivation: Football and Development in Nairobi, Kenya," in *Football in Africa: Conflict, Conciliation and Community*, ed. Gary Armstrong and Richard Giulianotti (Basingstoke: Palgrave Macmillan, 2004), 210–26.

58. Saavedra, "Regional Outliers," 8.

59. Brady and Khan, *Letting Girls Play*, 19.

60. Ibid., 16.

61. Susann Baller, "Creating the Postcolonial City: Urban Youth Clubs in Senegal," in *Urbanization and African Cultures*, ed. Toyin Falola and Steven J. Salm (Durham: Carolina Academic Press, 2005), 150.

62. Marc Broere and Roy van der Drift, *Football Africa!* (Cape Town: David Philip, 1997), 77.

EPILOGUE   South Africa 2010: The World Cup Comes to Africa

1. On the political and cultural significance of the 1995 Rugby World Cup, see David Ross Black and John Nauright, *Rugby and the South African Nation* (Manchester: Manchester University Press, 1998); and John Carlin, *Playing the Enemy: Nelson Mandela and the Game That Made a Nation* (New York: Penguin, 2008).

2. International sporting events have also served to legitimize authoritarian regimes; see, for example, David Clay Large, *The Nazi Games: The Olympics of 1936* (New York: W. W. Norton, 2007); and Bill L. Smith, "The Argentinian Junta and the Press in the Run-up to the 1978 World Cup," *Soccer and Society* 3, no. 1 (2002): 69–78. For an excellent introduction, see Barrie Houlihan, *Sport and International Politics* (London: Harvester Wheatsheaf, 1994).

3. As early as November 1992, then FIFA president João Havelange had publicly stated that Japan and South Africa were the "most promising candidates for the finals of 2002 and 2006 respectively." See Peter Alegi, "'Feel the Pull in Your Soul': Local Agency and Global Trends in South Africa's 2006 World Cup Bid," *Soccer and Society* 2, no. 3 (2001): 1–21.

4. Quoted in Scarlett Cornelissen, "It's Africa's Turn! The Narratives and Legitimations Surrounding the Moroccan and South African bids for the 2006 and 2010 FIFA finals," *Third World Quarterly* 25, no. 7 (2004): 1303.

5. Letter from Thabo Mbeki to Joseph Blatter (2003), quoted in "South Africa 2010: African Legacy," http://www.sa2010.gov.za/en/node/515 (accessed July 31, 2009).

6. Phillips, quoted in the *Observer Monthly*, June 3, 2007. For a local case study, see Peter Alegi, "The Political Economy of Mega-Stadiums and the Underdevelopment of Grassroots Football in South Africa," *Politikon* 34, no. 3 (2007): 315–31.

7. Monica Degen, "Fighting for the Global Catwalk: Formalizing Public Life in Castlefield (Manchester) and Diluting Public Life in el Raval (Barcelona), *International Journal of Urban and Regional Research* 27, no. 4 (2003): 867–80.

8. Stadium construction is a striking example of this trend, which is not uniquely South African, as the evidence from North America demonstrates; see Ronald

Trumpbour, *The New Cathedrals: Politics and Media in the History of Stadium Construction* (Syracuse: Syracuse University Press, 2007).

9. See, for example, Ashwin Desai and Goolam H. Vahed, "World Cup 2010: Africa's Turn or the Turn on Africa?" in *South Africa and the Global Game,* ed. Peter Alegi and Chris Bolsmann (London: Routledge, forthcoming).

10. Quoted in Alegi, "Political Economy of Mega-Stadiums," 315.

11. *Brisbane Times,* November 30, 2007.

BIBLIOGRAPHY

Agbodeka, Francis. *Achimota in the National Setting: A Unique Educational Experiment in West Africa.* Accra: Afram, 1977.

Ammoh, R. "The Goal Queen." *African Soccer* 63 (January/February 2001): 26–29.

Akindes, Gerard. "Football in Sub-Saharan Africa, New Technologies and Broadcasting Deregulation: Football Development or Electronic Colonialism?" Paper presented at the African Studies Association annual meeting, Chicago, 2008.

Akyeampong, Emmanuel K. "Africans in the Diaspora: The Diaspora and Africa," *African Affairs* 99 (2000), 183–215.

Alegi, Peter. "'Feel the Pull in Your Soul': Local Agency and Global Trends in South Africa's 2006 World Cup Bid." *Soccer and Society* 2, no. 3 (2001): 1–21.

———. "Katanga v Johannesburg: A History of the First Sub-Saharan African Football Championship, 1949–50." *African Historical Review* 31 (1999): 55–74.

———. *Laduma! Soccer, Politics and Society in South Africa.* Scottsville: University of KwaZulu-Natal Press, 2004.

———. "Like Cows Driven to a Dip: The 2001 Ellis Park Stadium Disaster, Johannesburg, South Africa." In *Soccer and Disaster: International Perspectives,* edited by Paul Darby, Martin Johnes, and Gavin Mellor, 109–23. London: Routledge, 2005.

———. "The Political Economy of Mega-Stadiums and the Underdevelopment of Grassroots Football in South Africa." *Politikon* 34, no. 3 (2007): 315–31.

———. "Sport, Race, and Liberation: A Preliminary Study of Albert Luthuli's Sporting Life." In *Sport and Liberation in South Africa: Reflections and Suggestions,* edited by Cornelius Thomas, 66–82. Alice: NAHECS and Sport SA, 2006.

Alegi, Peter, and Chris Bolsmann, eds. *South Africa and the Global Game: Football, Apartheid and Beyond.* London: Routledge, forthcoming 2010.

Alegi, Peter, with Robert Vassen, "Moonlighters Football Club: A History." http://www.overcomingapartheid.msu.edu/sidebar.php?id=15 (April 15, 2009).

Anderson, Benedict. *Imagined Communities: Reflections on the Origin and Spread of Nationalism.* Rev. ed. London: Verso, 1991.

Anderson, David M., and Richard Rathbone, eds. *Africa's Urban Past.* Oxford: James Currey; Portsmouth, NH: Heinemann, 2000.

Anderson-Morshead, A. E. M. *The History of the Universities' Mission to Central Africa, 1859–1909.* London: Office of the Universities' Mission to Central Africa, 1897.

Arbena, Joseph. "Dimensions of International Talent Migration in Latin American Sports." In Maguire and Bale, *Global Sports Arena,* 99–111.

Armstrong, Gary. "The Global Footballer and the Local War-Zone: George Weah and Transnational Networks in Liberia, West Africa." In *Globalization and Sport,* edited by Richard Giulianotti and Roland Robertson, 122–39. London: Wiley-Blackwell, 2007.

———. "The Migration of the Black Panther: An Interview with Eusebio of Mozambique and Portugal." In Armstrong and Giulianotti, *Football in Africa,* 247–68.

Armstrong, Gary, and Richard Giulianotti, eds. *Football in Africa: Conflict, Conciliation and Community.* Basingstoke: Palgrave Macmillan, 2004.

Aye, Efiong U. *Old Calabar through the Centuries.* Calabar: Hope Waddell Press, 1967.

Azikiwe, Nnamdi. *My Odyssey: An Autobiography.* New York: Praeger, 1970.

Baker, Barry G. *A Journal of African Football History, 1883–2000.* Rijmenam: Heart Books, 2001.

Baker, William J. "Political Games: The Meaning of International Sport for Independent Africa." In Baker and Mangan, *Sport in Africa,* 272–94.

Baker, William J., and James A. Mangan, eds. *Sport in Africa: Essays in Social History.* New York: Africana, 1987.

Bale, John. "Three Geographies of African Footballer Migration: Patterns, Problems and Postcoloniality." In Armstrong and Giulianotti, *Football in Africa,* 229–46.

Bale, John, and Joseph Maguire. *The Global Sports Arena: Athletic Talent Migration in an Interdependent World.* London: Frank Cass, 1994.

Bale, John, and Joe Sang. *Kenyan Running: Movement Culture, Geography and Global Change.* London: Frank Cass, 1996.

Ball, Phil. *Morbo: The Story of Spanish Football.* London: WSC Books, 2001.

Baller, Susann. "Creating the Postcolonial City: Urban Youth Clubs in Senegal." In *Urbanization and African Cultures,* edited by Toyin Falola and Steven J. Salm, 139–54. Durham: Carolina Academic Press, 2005.

Barber, Karin. *The Generation of Plays: Yoruba Popular Life in Theater.* Bloomington: Indiana University Press, 2000.

Barreaud, Marc. *Dictionnaire des footballeurs étrangers du championnat professionnel français, 1932–1997.* Paris: L'Harmattan, 1998.

Bediako, Ken. *The National Soccer League of Ghana: The Full Story, 1956–1995.* Accra: Bediako, 1996.

Black, David Ross, and John Nauright. *Rugby and the South African Nation.* Manchester: Manchester University Press, 1998.

Blacking, John. "Games and Sport in Pre-colonial African Societies." In Baker and Mangan, *Sport in Africa,* 3–22.

Boer, Wiebe. "Nation-Building Exercise: Sporting Culture and the Rise of Football in Colonial Nigeria." PhD diss., Yale University, 2003.

———. "A Story of Heroes, of Epics." In Armstrong and Giulianotti, *Football in Africa,* 59–79.

Bolsmann, Chris. "White Football in South Africa: Empire, Apartheid and Change, 1892–1977." In Alegi and Bolsmann, *South Africa and the Global Game.*

Boois, Seth Mataba. *An Illustrated History of the Game of Football in Namibia, 1900–2000.* Windhoek: Namibia Economic Development Services, 2000.

Booth, Douglas. *The Race Game: Sport and Politics in South Africa.* London: Frank Cass, 1998.

Borquaye, Stephen. *The Saga of Accra Hearts of Oak Sporting Club.* Accra: New Times Press, 1968.

Bourgault, Louise M. *Mass Media in Sub-Saharan Africa.* Bloomington: Indiana University Press, 1995.

Bouzrara, Jalala. "Game, Set and Match." *African Soccer,* no. 30 (January 1998): 10–15.

Brady, Martha, and Arjmand Banu Khan. *Letting Girls Play: The Mathare Youth Sports Association's Football Program for Girls.* New York: Population Council, 2002.

Broere, Marc, and Roy van der Drift. *Football Africa!* Cape Town: David Philip, 1997.

Bromberger, Christian. *La partita di calcio: Etnologia di una passione.* Rome: Editori Riuniti, 1999.

Burns, Jimmy. *Barca: A People's Passion.* London: Bloomsbury, 1998.

Carlin, John. *Playing the Enemy: Nelson Mandela and the Game That Made a Nation.* New York: Penguin, 2008.

Castles, Stephen, and Mark J. Miller. *The Age of Migration: International Population Movements in the Modern World.* New York: Guilford Press, 1993.

Chipande, Hikabwa D. "The Introduction and Development of Competitive Football in Zambia, 1930–1969." Master's thesis, Norwegian School of Sports Science, 2009.

Clayton, Anthony. "Sport and African Soldiers: The Military Diffusion of Western Sport throughout Sub-Saharan Africa. In Baker and Mangan, *Sport in Africa,* 114–37.

Clignet, Rémi, and Maureen Stark. "Modernisation and Football in Cameroun." *Journal of Modern African Studies* 12, no. 3 (1974): 409–21.

Coelho, João, and Francisco Pinheiro, *A Paixão do Povo: História do Futebol em Portugal.* Porto: Ed. Afrontamento, 2002.

Conklin, Alice L. *A Mission to Civilize: The Republican Idea of Empire in France and West Africa, 1895–1930.* Stanford: Stanford University Press, 1997.

Connelly, Matthew. *A Diplomatic Revolution: Algeria's Fight for Independence and the Origins of the Post–Cold War Era.* Oxford: Oxford University Press, 2002.

Cooper, Frederick. *Africa since 1940: The Past of the Present.* Cambridge: Cambridge University Press, 2002.

———. *Decolonization and African Society: The Labor Question in French and British Africa.* Cambridge: Cambridge University Press, 1996.

———. "Urban Space, Industrial Time, and Wage Labor in Africa." In *Struggle for the City: Migrant Labor, Capital, and the State in Urban Africa,* edited by Frederick Cooper, 7–50. Beverly Hills: Sage, 1983.

Coquery-Vidrovitch, Catherine. "The Process of Urbanization in Africa (from the Origins to the Beginning of Independence)." *African Studies Review* 34, no. 1 (1991): 1–98.

Cornelissen, Scarlett. "It's Africa's Turn! The Narratives and Legitimations Surrounding the Moroccan and South African Bids for the 2006 and 2010 FIFA Finals." *Third World Quarterly* 25, no. 7 (2004): 1293–1309.

Cronin, Mike. *Sport and Nationalism in Ireland: Gaelic Games, Soccer and Irish Identity since 1884.* Dublin: Four Courts Press, 1999.

Curtin, Philip. *Why People Move: Migration in African History.* Waco, TX: Markham Press Fund, 1995.

Darby, Paul. *Africa, Football, and FIFA: Politics, Colonialism, and Resistance.* London: Frank Cass, 2002.

———. "African Football Migration to Portugal: Colonial and Neo-colonial Resource." *Soccer and Society* 8, no. 4 (2007): 495–509.

———. "The New Scramble for Africa: African Football Labour Migration to Europe." In *Europe, Sport, World: Shaping Global Societies,* edited by James A. Mangan, 217–44. London: Frank Cass, 2001.

———. "Out of Africa: The Exodus of Elite African Football Talent to Europe." *Working USA* 10 (2007): 443–56.

———. "Stanley Rous's 'Own Goal': Football Politics, South Africa and the Contest for the FIFA Presidency in 1974." *Soccer and Society* 9, no. 2 (2008): 259–72.

Darby, Paul, Gerard Akindes, and Matthew Kirwin. "Football Academies and the Migration of African Football Labor to Europe." *Journal of Sport and Social Issues* 31, no. 2 (2007): 143–61.

Degen, Monica. "Fighting for the Global Catwalk: Formalizing Public Life in Castlefield (Manchester) and Diluting Public Life in el Raval (Barcelona). *International Journal of Urban and Regional Research* 27, no. 4 (2003): 867–80.

Desai, Ashwin, and Goolam H. Vahed. "World Cup 2010: Africa's Turn or the Turn on Africa?" In Alegi and Bolsmann, *South Africa and the Global Game.*

Deville-Danthu, Bernadette. *Le sport en noir et blanc: Du sport colonial au sport africain dans les anciens territoires français d'Afrique occidentale, 1920–1965.* Paris: Harmattan, 1997.

Dietschy, Paul, and David-Claude Kemo-Keimbou. *Le football et l'Afrique.* Paris: EPA, 2008.

Dine, Philip. "France, Algeria, and Sport: From Colonisation to Globalisation." *Modern and Contemporary France* 10, no. 4 (2002): 495–505.

Domingos, Nuño. "Football and Colonialism, Domination and Appropriation: The Mozambican Case." *Soccer and Society* 8, no. 4 (2007): 478–94.

Dubois, Laurent. *Soccer Empire: The World Cup and the Future of France.* Berkeley and Los Angeles: University of California Press, forthcoming 2010.

Eckert, Andreas. "Cultural Commuters: African Employees in Late Colonial Tanzania." In *Intermediaries, Interpreters, and Clerks: African Employees in the Making of Colonial Africa,* edited by Benjamin N. Lawrance, Lynn Osborn, and Richard L. Roberts, 248–69. Madison: University of Wisconsin Press, 2006.

Fair, Laura. "Ngoma Reverberations: Swahili Music Culture and the Making of Football Aesthetics in Early Twentieth-Century Zanzibar." In Armstrong and Giulianotti, *Football in Africa,* 103–13.

————. *Pastimes and Politics: Culture, Community, and Identity in Post-abolition Urban Zanzibar, 1890–1945.* Athens: Ohio University Press; London: James Currey, 2001.

Fates, Youssef. "Football in Algeria: Between Violence and Politics." In Armstrong and Giulianotti, *Football in Africa,* 41–58.

————. "Sport en Algérie." In *Geschichte der Leibesübungen,* ed. Horst Überhorst, vol. 6, *Perspektiven des Weltsports.* Berlin: Bartels and Wernitz, 1989.

Ferguson, James. *Global Shadows: Africa in the Neoliberal World Order.* Durham: Duke University Press, 2006.

Foer, Franklin. *How Soccer Explains the World: An Unlikely Theory of Globalization.* New York: HarperCollins, 2004.

Follot, Igor, and Gérard Dreyfus. *Salif Keita: Mes quatre vérités.* Paris: Chiron, 1977.

Forde, Sarah. *Playing by Their Rules: Coastal Teenage Girls in Kenya on Life, Love and Football.* Kilifi: Moving the Goalposts, 2008.

Freund, Bill. *The African City: A History.* Cambridge: Cambridge University Press, 2007.

Fridy, Kevin S., and Victor Brobbey. "Win the Match and Vote for Me: The Politicisation of Ghana's Accra Hearts of Oak and Kumasi Asante Kotoko Football Clubs." *Journal of Modern African Studies* 47, no. 1 (2009): 1–21.

Gaffney, Christopher T. *Temples of the Earthbound Gods: Stadiums in the Cultural Landscapes of Rio de Janeiro and Buenos Aires.* Austin: University of Texas Press, 2008.

Gaye, Daour. *Crises et perspectives du football sénégalais.* Saint-Louis: Xamal, 1999.

Getahun, Solomon. "Introduction: A Short History of Sport in Ethiopia." Unpublished manuscript, 2008.

Gifford, Prosser, and William Roger Louis. *Decolonization and African Independence: The Transfers of Power, 1960–1980.* New Haven: Yale University Press, 1988.

Giulianotti, Richard. "Between Colonialism, Independence and Globalization: Football in Zimbabwe." In Giulianotti and Armstrong, *Football in Africa,* 80–99.

————. *Football: A Sociology of the Global Game.* Cambridge: Polity Press, 1999.

————. "Playing an Aerial Game: The New Political Economy of Soccer." In *The Political Economy of Sport,* edited by John Nauright and Kimberly S. Schimmel, 19–37. Basingstoke: Palgrave Macmillan, 2005.

Goldblatt, David. *The Ball Is Round: A Global History of Soccer.* New York: Riverhead Books, 2008.

Goulstone, John. "The Working-Class Origins of Modern Football." *International Journal of the History of Sport* 17, no. 1 (2000): 135–43.

Grundlingh, Albert, André Odendaal, and S. B. Spies. *Beyond the Tryline: Rugby and South African Society.* Johannesburg: Ravan Press, 1995.

Gunner, Elizabeth, and Mafika Pascal Gwala, eds. *Musho! Zulu Popular Praises.* East Lansing: Michigan State University Press, 1991.

Guttmann, Allen. *Games and Empires: Modern Sports and Cultural Imperialism.* New York: Columbia University Press, 1994.

Hardy, Stephen. "Entrepreneurs, Structures, and the Sportgeist: Old Tensions in a Modern Industry." In *Essays on Sport History and Sport Mythology*, edited by Donald G. Kyle and Gary D. Stark, 45–82. College Station: Texas A & M University Press, 1990.

Hare, Geoff. *Football in France: A Cultural History*. Oxford: Berg, 2003.

Hatton, Timothy J., and Jeffrey G. Williamson. *Global Migration and the World Economy: Two Centuries of Policy and Performance*. Cambridge, MA: MIT Press, 2005.

Hazan, Baruch A. "Sport as an Instrument of Political Expansion: The Soviet Union in Africa." In Baker and Mangan, *Sport in Africa*, 250–71.

Hobsbawm, Eric. *Nations and Nationalism since 1780: Programme, Myth, Reality*. Cambridge: Cambridge University Press, 1990.

Hognestad, Hans, and Arvid Tollisen. "Playing against Deprivation: Football and Development in Nairobi, Kenya." In Armstrong and Giulianotti, *Football in Africa*, 210–226.

Holt, Richard. *Sport and the British: A Modern History*. Oxford: Oxford University Press, 1989.

Houlihan, Barrie. *Sport and International Politics*. London: Harvester Wheatsheaf, 1994.

Hyden, Goran. *African Politics in Comparative Perspective*. Cambridge: Cambridge University Press, 2006.

Iliffe, John. *Honour in African History*. Cambridge: Cambridge University Press, 2005.

Jennings, Andrew. *Foul! The Secret World of FIFA: Bribes, Vote Rigging and Ticket Scandals*. London: HarperCollins, 2006.

Kathrada, Ahmed. *Memoirs*. Cape Town: Zebra Press, 2004.

Katimia, Michael. "The Fight for Recognition." *African Soccer*, no. 35 (June 1998): 52–54.

Keys, Barbara J. *Globalizing Sport: National Rivalry and International Community in the 1930s*. Cambridge: Harvard University Press, 2006.

Kindy, Hyder. *Life and Politics in Mombasa*. Nairobi: East African Publishing House, 1972.

Klein, Alan M. *Sugarball: The American Game, the Dominican Dream*. New Haven: Yale University Press, 1991.

Kunene, Merryman. "Winning the Cup but Losing the Plot? The Troubled State of South African Soccer." In *State of the Nation: South Africa, 2005–2006*, edited by S. Buhlungu et al., 369–91. Cape Town: HSRC Press, 2006.

Kuper, Simon. *Ajax, the Dutch, the War: Football in Europe during the Second World War*. London: Orion, 2003.

LaFeber, Walter. *Michael Jordan and the New Global Capitalism*. New York: W. W. Norton, 2002.

Lanfranchi, Pierre, Christiane Eisenberg, Tony Mason, and Alfred Wahl. *100 Years of Football: The FIFA Centennial Book*. London: Weidenfeld and Nicolson, 2004.

Lanfranchi, Pierre, and Matthew Taylor. *Moving with the Ball: The Migration of Professional Footballers*. Oxford: Berg, 2001.

Lanfranchi, Pierre, and Alfred Wahl. "The Immigrant as Hero: Kopa, Mekloufi and French Football." In *European Heroes: Myth, Identity, Sport,* edited by Richard Holt, J. A. Mangan, and Pierre Lanfranchi, 114–27. London: Frank Cass, 1996.

Large, David Clay. *The Nazi Games: The Olympics of 1936.* New York: W. W. Norton, 2007.

Last, Alex. "Containment and Counter-Attack: A History of Eritrean Football." In Giulianotti and Armstrong, *Football in Africa,* 27–40.

Lema, Bangela. "Sport in Zaire." In *Sport in Asia and Africa: A Comparative Handbook,* edited by Eric A. Wagner, 229–47. Westport, CT: Greenwood Press, 1989.

Leseth, Anne. "The Use of *Juju* in Football: Sport and Witchcraft in Tanzania." In *Entering the Field: New Perspectives on World Football,* edited by Gary Armstrong and Richard Giulianotti, 159–74. Oxford: Berg, 1997.

Lever, Janet. *Soccer Madness: Brazil's Passion for the World's Most Popular Sport.* Prospect Heights, IL: Waveland Press, 1995.

Lindsay, Lisa A. *Working with Gender: Wage Labor and Social Change in Southwestern Nigeria.* Portsmouth, NH: Heinemann, 2003.

Lindsay, Lisa A., and Stephan F. Miescher, eds. *Men and Masculinities in Modern Africa.* Portsmouth, NH: Heinemann, 2003.

Liwena, Ridgeway. *The Zambian Soccer Scene.* Lusaka: LIPPUHO, 2006.

Loy, John W., and Joseph F. McElvogue. "Racial Discrimination in American Sport." *International Review of Sport Sociology* 5 (1970): 5–24.

Ly, Bocar. *Foot-ball, histoire de la Coupe d'A.O.F.* Dakar: Nouvelles Editions Africaines du Sénégal, 1990.

MacClancy, Jeremy. "Nationalism at Play: The Basques of Vizcaya and Athletic Club de Bilbao." In MacClancy, *Sport, Ethnicity and Identity,* 181–99.

———, ed. *Sport, Ethnicity and Identity.* Oxford: Berg, 1996.

Maguire, Joseph. "Race and Position Assignment in English Soccer: A Preliminary Analysis of Ethnicity and Sport in Britain." *Sociology of Sport Journal* 5 (1988): 257–69.

———. "Sport, Racism, and British Society: A Sociological Study of England's Elite Male Afro-Caribbean Soccer and Rugby Union Players." In *Sport, Racism, and Ethnicity,* edited by Grant Jarvie, 94–123. London: Falmer Press, 1991.

Maguire, Joseph, and John Bale. "Introduction: Sports Labour Migration in the Global Arena." In Bale and Maguire, *Global Sports Arena,* 1–21.

Mahjoub, Faouzi. *Le football africain.* Paris: ABC, 1977.

Mangan, James A. *Athleticism in the Victorian and Edwardian Public School: The Emergence and Consolidation of an Educational Ideology.* Cambridge: Cambridge University Press, 1981.

———. "Ethics and Ethnocentricity: Imperial Education in British Tropical Africa." In Baker and Mangan, *Sport in Africa,* 138–71.

———. *The Games Ethic and Imperialism: Aspects of the Diffusion of an Ideal.* New York: Viking, 1986.

————. "Soccer as Moral Training: Missionary Intentions and Imperial Legacies." *Soccer and Society* 2, no. 2 (2001): 41–56.

Manning, Patrick. *Migration in World History.* London: Routledge, 2005.

Maradas, Emmanuel, et al. "Special Report: Football Academies." *African Soccer* 66 (2001): 6–15.

Martin, Phyllis. *Leisure and Society in Colonial Brazzaville.* Cambridge: Cambridge University Press, 1995.

Martins do Melo, J. Luiz. "Brazilian Football: Technical Success and Economic Failure." In Miller and Crolley, *Football in the Americas,* 193–208.

McHenry, Dean E. "The Use of Sports in Policy Implementation: The Case of Tanzania." *Journal of Modern African Studies* 18, no. 2 (1980): 237–56.

Merkel, Udo, and Walter Tokarski, eds. *Racism and Xenophobia in European Football.* Aachen: Meyer and Meyer Verlag, 1996.

Miescher, Stephan F. *Making Men in Ghana.* Bloomington: Indiana University Press, 2005.

Miller, Rory, and Liz Crolley. *Football in the Americas: Fútbol, Futebol, Soccer.* London: Institute for the Study of the Americas, 2007.

Mokone, Stephen, and J. W. Ryan. *Kalamazoo! The Life and Times of a Soccer Player.* Pretoria: De Jager-Haum, 1980.

Moorman, Marissa. *Intonations: A Social History of Music and Nation in Luanda, Angola, from 1945 to Recent Times.* Athens: Ohio University Press, 2008.

Morrell, Robert, ed. *Changing Men in Southern Africa.* Pietermaritzburg: University of Natal Press; London: Zed Press, 2001.

Muka, Théophile. *Évolution du sport au Congo.* Kinshasa: Okapi, 1970.

Mukharji, Projit Bihari. "'Feeble Bengalis' and 'Big Africans': African Players in Bengali Club Football." *Soccer and Society* 9, no. 2 (2008): 273–85.

Murray, Bruce K., and Christopher Edmond Merrett. *Caught Behind: Race and Politics in Springbok Cricket.* Johannesburg: Wits University Press; Scottsville: University of KwaZulu-Natal Press, 2004.

Murray, William James. *The Old Firm in the New Age: Celtic and Rangers since the Souness Revolution.* Edinburgh: Mainstream, 1998.

————. *The Old Firm: Sectarianism, Sport and Society in Scotland.* Edinburgh: John Donald, 1984.

————. *The World's Game: A History of Soccer.* Champaign: University of Illinois Press, 1996.

Ndebele, Njabulo. *South African Literature and Culture.* Manchester: Manchester University Press, 1994.

Ngugi wa Thiong'o. *Decolonising the Mind: The Politics of Language in African Literature.* Portsmouth, NH: Heinemann; London: James Currey, 1986.

Nugent, Paul. *Africa since Independence: A Comparative History.* Basingstoke: Palgrave Macmillan, 2004.

Obayiuwana, Osasu, and Anver Versi. "The Economics of Football." *African Business* (June 1998): 8–10.

Odendaal, André. *The Story of an African Game: Black Cricketers and the Unmasking of One of Cricket's Greatest Myths, South Africa, 1850–2003.* Cape Town: David Philip, 2003.

Ogouyon, Adolphe. "Le football au pays de Vodouns: Le cas du Bénin." *Sociétés et Répresentations* (December 1998): 163–79.

Oliveira, Angelo. *Isto de futebóis.* Maputo: Ndjira, 1998.

Pannenborg, Arnold. "How to Win a Football Match in Cameroon." Leiden: African Studies Centre, 2008.

Paterson, Chris A. "Reform or Re-colonisation? The Overhaul of African Television." *Review of African Political Economy* 78 (1998): 571–83.

Pelak, Cynthia F. "Negotiating Gender/Race/Class Constraints in the New South Africa: A Case Study of Women's Soccer." *International Review for the Sociology of Sport* 40, no. 1 (2005): 53–70.

———. "Women and South African Soccer: A Brief History." In Alegi and Bolsmann, *South Africa and the Global Game.*

Poli, Raffaele. "Africans' Status in the European Football Players' Labour Market." *Soccer and Society* 7, nos. 2–3 (2006): 278–91.

———. "Football Players' Migration in Europe: A Geo-economic Approach to Africans' Mobility." In *The Bountiful Game? Football Identities and Finances,* edited by Jonathan Magee, Alan Bairner, and Alan Tomlinson, 217–32. Oxford: Meyer and Meyer Sport, 2005.

———. "Migrations and Trade of African Football Players: Historic, Geographical and Cultural Aspects." *Afrika Spectrum* 41, no. 3 (2006): 393–414.

———. *Les migrations internationales des footballeurs: Trajectoires de joueurs camerounais en Suisse.* Neuchatel: CIES, 2004.

Poli, Raffaele, and Paul Dietschy. "Le football africain entre immobilisme et extraversion." *Politique Africaine* 102 (2006): 173–87.

Porro, Nicola, and Pippo Russo. "Berlusconi and Other Matters: The Era of 'Football-Politics.'" *Journal of Modern Italian Studies* 5, no. 3 (2001): 348–70.

Posel, Deborah. "Race as Common Sense: Racial Classification in Twentieth-Century South Africa." *African Studies Review* 44, no. 2 (2001): 87–113.

Raath, Peter. *Soccer through the Years 1862–2002: The First Official History of South African Soccer.* Cape Town: Peter Raath, 2002.

Rachman, Gideon. "Beautiful Game, Lousy Business: The Problems of Latin American Football." In Miller and Crolley, *Football in the Americas,* 161–73.

Ranger, Terence. "Pugilism and Pathology: African Boxing and the Black Urban Experience in Southern Rhodesia." In Baker and Mangan, *Sport in Africa,* 196–213.

Ricci, Filippo M. *African Football Yearbook.* Rome: Filippo Maria Ricci Editore, 2000.

Royer, Patrick. "The Spirit of Competition: *Wak* in Burkina Faso." *Africa* 72, no. 3 (2002): 464–83.

Ruedy, John. *Modern Algeria: The Origins and Development of a Nation.* Bloomington: Indiana University Press, 1992.

Saadallah, Rabah, and Djamel Benfars. *La glorieuse équipe du FLN.* Algiers: ENAL; Brussels: GAM, 1985.

Saavedra, Martha. "Football Feminine—Development of the African Game: Senegal, Nigeria, and South Africa." *Soccer and Society* 4, nos. 2–3 (2003): 225–53.

———. "Regional Outliers: Female Football in Kenya." Paper presented at the African Studies Association annual meeting, New York, NY, October 2007.

Sander, Cerstin, and Samuel Munzele Maimbo. "Migrant Labor Remittances in Africa: Reducing Obstacles to Developmental Contributions." Africa Region Working Paper Series No. 64, World Bank, November 2003. Available online at http://www.worldbank.org/afr/wps/wp64.pdf (accessed June 1, 2008).

Sanogo, Bassirou. *La longue marche du football burkinabé.* Ougadougou: Éditions Sidwaya, 1998.

Schatzberg, Michael. "Soccer, Science and Sorcery: Causation and African Football." *Afrika Spectrum* 41, no. 3 (2006): 351–69.

Seddiki, Hocine. *Rachid Mekhloufi: L'imagination au bout de pied.* Algiers: SNED, 1982.

Sharkey, Heather. *Living with Colonialism: Nationalism and Culture in the Anglo-Egyptian Sudan.* Berkeley and Los Angeles: University of California Press, 2003.

Sikainga, Ahmad Alawad. *"City of Steel and Fire": A Social History of Atbara, Sudan's Railway Town, 1906–1984.* Portsmouth, NH: Heinemann, 2002.

Smit, Barbara. *Pitch Invasion: Adidas, Puma and the Making of Modern Sport.* London: Penguin, 2007.

Smith, Bill L. "The Argentinian Junta and the Press in the Run-up to the 1978 World Cup." *Soccer and Society* 3, no. 1 (2002): 69–78.

Sorek, Tamir. *Arab Soccer in a Jewish State.* Cambridge: Cambridge University Press, 2007.

Stanton, Gareth. "Chasing the Ghosts: Narratives of Football and Nation in Morocco." In Armstrong and Giulianotti, *Football in Africa,* 150–66.

Stoddart, Brian. "Sport, Cultural Imperialism, and Colonial Response in the British Empire." *Comparative Studies in Society and History* 30, no. 4 (1988): 649–73.

Stuart, Ossie. "The Lions Stir: Football in African Society." In *Giving the Game Away: Football, Politics and Culture on Five Continents,* edited by Stephen Wagg, 24–51. London: Leicester University Press, 1995.

———. "Players, Workers, and Protestors: Social Change and Soccer in Colonial Zimbabwe." In MacClancy, *Sport, Ethnicity and Identity,* 167–80.

Sugden, John, and Alan Tomlinson. *FIFA and the Contest for World Football: Who Rules the People's Game?* Cambridge: Polity Press, 1998.

Szymanski, Stefan, and Andrew S. Zimbalist. *National Pastime: How Americans Play Baseball and the Rest of the World Plays Soccer.* Washington: Brookings Institution Press, 2005.

Taylor, William H. "Missionary Education in Africa Reconsidered: The Presbyterian Educational Impact in Eastern Nigeria, 1846–1974." *African Affairs* 83, no. 331 (1984): 189–205.

Tignor, Robert L. *Capitalism and Nationalism at the End of Empire: State and Business in Decolonizing Egypt, Nigeria, and Kenya, 1945–1963*. Princeton: Princeton University Press, 1996.

Trumpbour, Ronald. *The New Cathedrals: Politics and Media in the History of Stadium Construction*. Syracuse: Syracuse University Press, 2007.

Tsanga, Soter. *Le football camerounais: Des origines à l'indépendence*. Yaoundé: Centre d'Édition et de Production de Manuels, 1969.

Tshimanga Bakadiababu, Evariste. *Le commerce et la traite des footballeurs africains et sud-américains en Europe*. Paris: Harmattan, 2001.

Tsuruta, Tadasu. "Simba or Yanga? Football and Urbanization in Dar es Salaam." In *Dar es Salaam: Histories from an Emerging African Metropolis*, edited by James R. Brennan, Andrew Burton, and Yusuf Lawi, 198–212. Dar es Salaam: Mkuki na Nyota, 2007.

Valeri, Mauro. *La razza in campo: Per una storia della Rivoluzione Nera nel calcio*. Rome: Edizioni Psicoanalisi Contro, 2005.

Van Onselen, Charles. *Chibaro: African Mine Labor in Southern Rhodesia, 1900–1933*. London: Pluto Press, 1976.

Van Peel, Bénédicte. "Aux débuts du football congolais." In *Itinéraires croisés de la modernité au Congo Belge, 1920–1950*, edited by Jean-Luc Vellut, 141–87. Paris: Karthala, 2001.

Vansina, Jan. *Oral Tradition as History*. Madison: University of Wisconsin Press, 1985.

Vasili, Phil. "Colonialism and Football: The First Nigerian Tour of Britain." *Race and Class* 36, no. 4 (1995): 55–70.

———. *Colouring over the White Line: The History of Black Footballers in Britain*. Edinburgh: Mainstream, 2000.

———. *The First Black Footballer: Arthur Wharton, 1865–1930*. London: Frank Cass, 1998.

Vidacs, Bea. "Football in Cameroon: A Vehicle for the Expansion and Contraction of Identity." In *Football Culture: Local Contests, Global Visions*, edited by Gerry G. T. Finn and Richard Giulianotti, 100–117. London: Frank Cass, 2000.

Waliaula, Solomon. "The Role of Football Cultures in Performing/Constructing Identities to Foster Peace and Stability in the 21st-Century Kenyan Society." Paper presented at the Kenya Oral Literature Association Symposium, 2008.

———. "Wrangling in Kenyan Football: A Symptom of Displaced Identity." Unpublished manuscript.

Waliaula, Solomon, and Basil Okong'o. "The Contemporary Oral Performance: The Case of the Radio Football Commentator." Unpublished manuscript, Moi University, 2009.

Walton, John. "Basque Football Rivalries in the Twentieth Century." In *Fear and Loathing in World Football*, edited by Gary Armstrong and Richard Giulianotti, 119–33. Oxford: Berg, 2001.

Walvin, James. *The People's Game: The History of Football Revisited*. Rev. ed. Edinburgh: Mainstream, 1994.

Wiggins, David Kenneth. "'Great Speed but Little Stamina': The Historical Debate over Black Athletic Superiority." In *Glory Bound: Black Athletes in a White America*, 177–99. Syracuse: Syracuse University Press, 1997.

Williams, Jean. *A Beautiful Game: International Perspectives on Women's Football.* Oxford: Berg, 2007.

Wilson, Jonathan. *Inverting the Pyramid: A History of Football Tactics.* London: Orion, 2008.

Young, Crawford. *The African Colonial State in Comparative Perspective.* New Haven: Yale University Press, 1994.

SERIES EDITORS' NOTE

The field of African history has developed considerably in recent decades, but its discoveries and insights are rarely acknowledged outside the continent. Students and instructors in related areas seek accessible points of entry to an African literature that they often find hard to understand. Even researchers in global topics find it challenging to engage the relevant scholarship on Africa.

In this series we seek to provide access for amateurs, teachers, and students alike. Our titles will offer professional insight into African history but in formats readily integrated into courses in world history, the history of the Americas, diasporic history, and the histories of other world regions. We are aiming to reach advanced secondary school students, college/university undergraduates, and general readers. In modern settings still rife with the residues of centuries of slaving and racial stereotyping, we hope that these descriptions of Africans at work, at home, and engaged in sport and cultural activities will bring out the particular and valuable ways in which Africans have experienced, and expressed, universal human experiences. Too often the media and textbooks still seek to make Africa accessible by resorting to inappropriate modern concepts—"tribes" glossed condescendingly as "ethnicities," or complex African polities reduced to stereotyped "kingdoms" and "empires"—or by the pervasive media coverage of diseases, political disorder, and destitution. Africans, through their histories and cultures, bring great diversity to the human experience and enrich us all, and it is that enrichment this series is intended to offer.

The titles in the series are intended for teaching and for stimulating further inquiry and comparison. Our authors therefore present their topics on accessibly modest scales. They provide references to academic works for specialists from other world regions who want to pursue the literature for Africa on their topics. For teachers and students, these short books will offer a variety of primary source materials relevant to each topic, including images; firsthand accounts, and Web resources. Instructors can both teach basic historical methods to their students and explore the range of unfamiliar sources that Africanists have tapped.

This second volume in the series aims to appeal to fans of the world's most global game, football, or "soccer" as Americans are wont to call it. Peter Alegi's take on African manifestations of, and contributions to, football, appearing here at the moment that the 2010 World Cup is played in the Republic of South Africa, presents an intriguing story of culture, politics, and commercialization that we hope students will find entertaining and instructive about broader patterns of the world's recent history, including globalization itself. For the many specialists—journalists, academics, media producers, business managers—seeking to understand Africans' participation in the sport, Alegi offers insight into the sometimes conflicting priorities of private investment and public support, of play and profit.

The succeeding titles in the series will include John Mugane's *Story of Swahili*, an exploration of the dominant language and culture of eastern Africa. All languages, including the English of this book, are fluid expressions of generational changes and cultural politics. Struggles over Ebonics, slang, and "correct" grammar pervade classrooms in every modern nation. Mugane's story of Swahili provides both a solid linguistic framework and lively insight into a well-known culture of modern Africa.

Charles Ambler's *Mass Media and Popular Culture in Modern Africa* is a further addition to our series Africa in World History. Who knew that Nigeria has become the second-largest producer of video and film in the world, ahead of the United States and behind only India? Film buffs know of Senegalese filmmaker Ousmane Sembène, but do they know that popular visual culture has blossomed in a continent where literacy was limited before the 1960s? Both urban and rural residents in Africa have long been more familiar with films and musical styles than with their political leaders, who dominated the headlines in Europe and the United States. These media were often subtle modes of protest against the authoritarian rule that has otherwise attracted global attention. *Mass Media and Popular Culture in Modern Africa* will be of interest to historians and students of popular culture, media studies, and other fields of sociocultural inquiry.

David Robinson
Okemos, Michigan

Joseph C. Miller
Ivy, Virginia

INDEX

A page number in italic type indicates an illustration on that page. The letter *n* following a page number indicates an endnote on that page. The number following the *n* indicates the note number(s).